Chicago By Gaslight

Chicago by Gaslight

A History of Chicago's Netherworld, 1880–1920

Richard Lindberg

Academy Chicago Publishers

Published by Academy Chicago Publishers
An imprint of Chicago Review Press Incorporated
814 North Franklin Street
Chicago, Illinois 60610
ISBN 978-0-89733-421-1

Cover design: Sarah Downey
Cover art: Tim Mayer

Printed in the United States of America

FOR DENISE

Contents

Photographs and illustrations between pages 110–11

ACKNOWLEDGMENTS

First of all, I want to thank the people at Academy Chicago: Jordan Miller for his support; Anita Miller for her thorough and time-consuming editing, and Sarah Downey for her essential editorial and production contributions.

One of the great pleasures of writing and publishing a book of this nature is the opportunity to share the recollections and tap into the expertise of individuals possessing intimate knowledge of the author's subject matter. I extend my heart-felt thanks to Tom McGee, a died-in-the-wool Chicagoan who helped me penetrate the public and private image of his great-uncle, Mont J. Tennes.

Walter Litt supplied me with fascinating details about his grandfather, the late Ben Hyman.

I wish to cite the valuable assistance of Jerry Gladden and the staff of the Chicago Crime Commission. Also, William J. Helmer; Bob Pruter; the late Bill Reilly and Nate Kaplan, co-founders of the Merry Gangsters Literary Society.

With gratitude and warm affection, I express my appreciation to Ms Dana M Sendzlol, an extraordinary publicist.

Others to whom I am indebted include retired FBI Agent William F. Roemer; Bob Herguth of the Chicago *Sun-Times,* and artist Bob Deckert, of Ft Walton Beach, Florida.

Finally, John J. Flood, Debby Kral and Ruth Apfelbaum, Noel T. Wroblewski, Sol Smith, Ken Labuda, Connie Goddard, Shirley Haas, John Binder, Joe Schiavo, Bruce Miles, and Chuck and Jean Lindberg.

PREFACE

More than a decade ago, I embarked on a fascinating journey into the history of Chicago. The result was a hardcover book called *Chicago Ragtime*. Now, completely revised and rewritten, it has been reborn as *Chicago by Gaslight*, presenting a picture of the city during the period of its most remarkable growth, from the Gilded Age through 1919, when the Old Order yielded to the onrushing forces of the twentieth century. It is a history of a city struggling with political chicanery, reform and social license.

Lincoln Steffens, writing for *McClure's* magazine around the turn of the century, commented that "Political corruption . . . is not a passing symptom of the youth of a people. It is the natural process by which a Democracy is made gradually over into a plutocracy." Chicago alderman Charles Merriam, an early loser in the battle for political reform, was more succinct. "Chicago," he said, at about the same time as Steffens, "is unique. It is the only completely corrupt city in America."

Merriam's observation, obviously born of despair, does not take into account the enormous energy of the city, founded on what was no more than a desolate marsh and a sea of tall prairie grass, heroically rebuilt into a prosperous metropolis from the smoking debris of the great fire of 1871. Robert Casey said, "Chicago is an independent miracle; vigorous, powerful and uninhibited."

Certainly it was vigorously corrupt, but there was also enormous intellectual energy, with writers, poets and publishers, progressive social activists, politicians and lawyers, creative architects and city planners, putting their stamp on the city.

But this book does not emphasize these impressive movers and shakers, although we have detailed the Democratic Convention of 1896. We are dealing to an extent with the netherworld which, until at least the second decade of the present century, often appears to be rather quaint and even endearing, compared to the horrifying criminal viciousness which ensued after Prohibition. We have, of course, the Haymarket tragedy, one serial killer who certainly rivalled Jack the Ripper, assorted murders and attempted murders, and a frightful race war—these things, neither quaint nor endearing, were part of the city's history that should not be forgotten: the Haymarket massacre and the 1919 race war, in particular, were ominous early symptoms of municipal disease that still infects the body politic.

We should thus be careful not to claim moral superiority over past generations, and I have tried not to do that. We should learn from history, and, perhaps from time to time, step back and enjoy it.

—Richard C. Lindberg

I

DERBY DAY, 1885

The social event of the summer season in Chicago in 1885 was the running of the famed American Derby at the Washington Park Race Track, 61st Street and Cottage Grove Avenue. Under a radiant blue sky on June 27, the carriages left the porte-chochères of the stone mansions on Prairie and Michigan avenues, Grand and Drexel boulevards, the homes of the Ryersons, the Catons, the Chauncey Blairs, the Armours. A man's carriage was the measure of his worth when he travelled to Washington Park for the Derby. For weeks, the C.P. Kimball Company had been producing carriages for this day. Twenty-six hand-crafted rigs had been sold to Chicago millionaires in just twenty-one days: double suspension victorias, demi-landaus, tilburys, stanhope phaetons, Tally-ho coaches, langhams, dog carts. The true display of regal ostentation was the promenade down Grand Boulevard and a-cross to Drexel, with its tree-lined parkways and great houses. And while some men chose to ride ahead of their family coaches on their favorite thoroughbreds, everyone wanted an English coachman and an English groom. The demand was so great that some "English" coachmen were actually Americans with fake accents and fake resumes.

The drive south to the racetrack took half an hour at a leisurely pace. A brief noon shower had given way to sunshine, so the carriage tops were lowered and ladies in the conveyances could twirl their parasols as they acknowledged friends they saw along the route. The boulevards were alive with people.

1

A social observer commented in the *Chicago Inter-Ocean*: "Such a gathering of thoroughbred animals, such a meeting of the highest social elements, such a display of fashion, elegance and wealth and beauty had never been seen upon any race course in the country."

Washington Park had been created in the winter of 1882–83 when it was obvious that Chicago Driving Park, on the western fringe of the city, was inadequate. The new racetrack was officially chartered on February 10, 1883, "to promote good fellowship among its members by providing a clubhouse and pleasure grounds for their entertainment where at all times they may meet for social intercourse, and further, to encourage by providing the proper facilities, raising, improving, breeding, training, and exhibiting horses at meetings to be held at stated times each year." Architect Solon Beman's design of the clubhouse was financed by 174 stockholders, where access was limited to the 800 families prominent in Chicago since the days of John Kinzie and Mark Beaubien. These were in the main of English descent—the city's Swedes, Poles, Irish, Jews and Germans were excluded. It was considered a great honor to belong to the Washington Park Clubhouse.

The city's elite belonged to clubs. One of the most prestigious was the Commercial Club, where the sixty members were the captains of trade and industry, who gathered on the last Saturday of each month to discuss an assigned topic over brandy and cigars. These topics, of which members were informed in advance by the club secretary through a courier, ranged from discussion of railroad rates to elegant plans for civic improvement. There were many clubs: the Union League, the Union, the Iroquois, the Calumet, with its imposing 8-by-13 foot portrait of Ulysses Grant which inspired Long John Wentworth, newspaper editor, congressman and twice mayor of Chicago, to donate a 10-by-15 foot painting of himself to hang near it. There was also the Chicago Club, where millionaires gathered to dine and play poker, and where the unwritten motto was said to be, "Dogs, women, Democrats and reporters need not apply."

But the women had their own clubs, which put heavy emphasis

on culture and social reform. There was the Fortnightly Club, founded by Kate Newell Doggett in 1874, where Bertha Palmer and Ellen Henrotin read papers on the obligations of wealth and the social status of women in America and Europe. Mrs Henrotin founded the Friday Club, also concerned with literary pursuits. And, too, there was the Chicago Woman's Club, headquartered in the Art Institute, and open to all interested women, and not just the wealthy activists who were its driving force. The club had 500 members; papers were read on literary topics, but social reform was also on its agenda. Through this club the women put strong pressure on Chicago politicians.

The popular press was not interested in this aspect of the lives of millionaires' wives. "Toilets of unusual elegance," wrote the *Inter-Ocean* reporter on Derby Day, "worn by ladies of position, grace and beauty were seen on every side." It was noted that the ladies wore cool white gowns—at least the gowns looked cool, but they had long tight sleeves which required a button hook to work the numerous buttons running to the elbow, and were worn over layers of muslin-lined skirts and petticoats, under which were hip pads and a bustle, usually made of whalebone. Less affluent women resorted to bundles of newspaper. In the clubhouse, the ladies sipped lemonade and listened to Austin & Rosenbecker's First Regimental Band playing selections from Offenbach operettas. They may well have gossiped about Chicago celebrities like the Leiter girls, daughters of Marshall Field's first partner, who were living in Washington while they looked for titled foreign husbands, a search that was to prove successful for three of them—one, Mary, was to marry Lord Curzon, who became Viceroy of India.

Outside the clubhouse, dark clouds gathered. The tops were hastily raised on carriages near the guardrails. The first drops fell, and then it rained heavily for almost two hours. The track, which had been "fast," degenerated into a muddy quagmire with pools of water. The people in the mud-splashed, topless carriages were soaked, their elegant summer outfits ruined. They were in no mood to buy the programs offered by small boys dashing between the carriages.

3

At three o'clock, the rain stopped and the clouds broke, to cheers from the grandstand. The jockeys, their feet sinking in mud, came out from the stables to inspect the track. The high rollers went back to the odds boards as club secretary John E. Brewster made his way across a makeshift wooden sidewalk to confer with the judges after which Brewster rang the bell to signal the beginning of the races.

The American Derby, the third featured event in the five-race card, and the richest stake in the West, was for three-year-olds, the finest horseflesh in the country. The favorite that day was Ten Stone, owned by Edward Corrigan, a Chicago racing promoter who also ran the West Side grounds. In 1891, Corrigan was to go into direct competition with Washington Park when he founded the Hawthorne Track in the suburb of Cicero.

Just before race time, Ten Stone was scratched. The odds were upset because Isaac Murphy, the "Colored Archer," the most successful jockey in America, was not riding. Murphy had ridden Modesty to win the 1884 Derby. The new favorite was Volante, owned by the Baldwin Stables of California and "Plunger" Walton, a big New York gambler and speculator with an unsavory reputation, rushed to the post to strike a last-minute deal with Corrigan: $500 to the Colored Archer if he agreed to ride, and $1,000 to Corrigan if Volante won. The Archer took ten seconds to decide, and mounted Volante. This upset the odds again, but Walton already had $2,000 on Volante, a magnificent horse wearing black and red with a Maltese cross, the Baldwin colors. Alta Favor and Alf Estell took an early lead, but Volante, urged on by Murphy with whip and spur, forged ahead as they entered the final turn, and won handily. Alta Favor finished second, a full two lengths behind Volante. Plunger Walton was given an $8,000 marker.

That was the high point of the day; people began to leave the park without waiting for the last two races. The crowd, which had been estimated at 20,000—and which was to go as high as 40,000 in future years—dwindled to 2,000 as the broughams and landaus wended their way out of the gates.

It was still too light in the late summer afternoon for the gas lamps to flicker on Michigan Avenue, which was residential then and, north of the Chicago River, was called Pine Street, a very desirable, and expensive, place to live. "Those were leisurely days," Edith Ogden, the wife of Carter Harrison, Jr., recalled in *Strange to Say*, her memoir, "when life seemed easy and there was plenty of time to spare. We had the telephone and the electric light, and to us it seemed that there was nothing more to be dreamed of. But we had much to learn."

There were the "elegant eighties," and the "gay nineties." Since the "roaring twenties," no single adjective has been used to describe a decade.

The final Derby Day at Washington Park was held in June, 1904, just days before Mayor Carter Harrison put an end to trackside betting. The park itself was razed in 1908, because the Washington Park Improvement Association wanted to reclaim the property for commercial development.

Life changed rapidly in Chicago, called by some the most American of cities. As the carriages wended their way home in 1885, the occupants were for the most part unaware that a year later the city was to be shaken by a traumatic event that would blacken the name of Chicago around the world and be permanently inscribed in the history of the labor movement and of American jurisprudence.

II

HAYMARKET

1

On July 21, 1877, a warm Saturday afternoon, an enthusiastic working-class crowd packed Sack's Hall at 20th and Brown streets in Chicago to attend a rally called by the local Working-Men's Party. The air was electric, because some days earlier, on July 16, the Baltimore and Ohio Railroad had cut their workers' wages by ten percent, and this had set off an immediate strike and an eruption of rage that was eventually to paralyze the entire country in a general strike. The main speaker of the evening, who cautioned against violence and advocated change by ballot box, was Albert Parsons, a lean, handsome 29-year-old Southerner, a printer at the *Chicago Times,* who had gained a reputation as a popular labor agitator. Parsons's forbears had come over on the second voyage of the *Mayflower* and some of them had distinguished themselves in the Revolutionary War. Parsons had been born in Montgomery, Alabama, where his father owned a factory. Orphaned at an early age, Albert had been raised by an older brother, an attorney, newspaper publisher and slave owner, in Tyler, Texas. At twelve, Parsons was apprenticed to the proslavery owner of the *Galveston News* and a year later ran off to join the Lone Star Grays, Confederate volunteers. He returned to Galveston, but ran off again to fight for the Confederacy until the end of the war, when he was seventeen.

After the war, Parsons did some farming and earned enough to study at Waco University—now called Baylor—where apparently he began to change his political attitudes, becoming a Radical Republican and speaking out for Negro rights. His brother, too, joined the Radical Republicans. By 1868 Parsons had incurred such hatred from Waco whites that he had to leave the city. He went to work for his brother, who now published the *Houston Telegraph*, as a roving reporter and promotion man and thus met his wife, Lucy, who claimed to be of Mexican and American Indian descent—a claim open to doubt. Her biographer has said she was born a Negro slave. There is also a question about whether Parsons and Lucy were ever legally married. In any case, after he met Lucy, Albert worked in various government positions in Austin, Texas, and then, in late 1873, moved to Chicago, where he joined a typographer's union. It was two years after the Chicago Fire, and the city was being rebuilt. However, it had also been hit by the panic of 1873 which was to continue for six years; thousands upon thousands were out of work, and those who had jobs suffered from cuts in pay. People were starving, the homeless were everywhere and this led to a new militancy in the working poor who rioted, marched and turned to the labor movement in growing numbers, at the same time escalating their rhetoric to threaten revolution against "the ruling classes."

When he arrived in Chicago, Parsons immediately drew a connection between the situation of the new freedmen and the suffering of white workers. In 1876 he joined the two-year-old Social Democratic Working-Men's Party of North America and became a gifted speaker and worker for them, earning the hatred of the establishment as he had in Waco. The *Tribune* attacked him and his party, which was divided because so many of its members were German immigrants who viewed the English speakers with suspicion. The whole Socialist movement was in fact fragmented and eventually, at a convention in Philadelphia in 1876, the International Working-Men's Association, the Social Democrats and labor parties in Illinois and Ohio fused into the Working-Men's Party of the United States. Parsons was the head of the English speakers in Chicago, and the chief orator. He also ran unsuccessfully several times for alderman and for state and county offices on the party ticket. He was, in short, a fountain of energy for the Socialist cause.

The Saturday rally was a success and on Sunday, as the general strike crept nearer, handbills were distributed announcing a mass meeting for Monday night, July 23, in an open space called Market Square, at Madison and Market streets. The response was enormous: workers poured in, in torchlight parades, nearly fifteen thousand of them. Once again Albert Parsons was the main speaker, hailed with shouts from the multitude. Although he praised the Eastern railroad strikers, he repeated his admonitions against violence and urged his audience to use the ballot box to vote for the Working-Men's Party and to organize themselves in unions. The rally eventually disbanded without incident.

By the next afternoon, Tuesday, the entire city was paralyzed by a general strike. Parsons was singled out by the newspapers as the chief rabble-rouser. On Tuesday morning, when he reported for work at the *Times* where he had been employed for three years, Parsons found that he had been fired and, in addition, blacklisted, so that he would not find work as a typesetter. His fellow workers avoided him. From the *Times* building, Parsons went to the *Arbeiter-Zeitung*, which was the party's German-language newspaper. A few hours later two men came in, with pistols under their coats, and told Parsons they had instructions to take him to the office of Mayor Monroe Heath, in city hall. The room was filled with policemen, city officials and various prominent citizens, all clearly upset, and chiefly with Parsons, who was told to sit down opposite Michael Hickey, the chief of police.

Hickey was a twenty-year veteran of the force; he had been accused many times of corruption and intrigues of various kinds. In 1873 he had quit the force in a rage because of charges of dishonesty levelled against him by the *Chicago Post and Mail*. But he was reinstated, and in 1875 Harvey D. Colvin, who had been elected mayor in a reaction against the prohibition-prone administration of *Tribune* publisher Joseph Medill, appointed him chief of police to replace Jacob Rehm, who was forced to resign after it was discovered that he had been part of a whiskey ring that had bilked the government of thousands of dollars. Hickey himself had invested in gambling property controlled by Mike McDonald, the city's gambling king, and was later to be accused of allowing Lake Street vice dens to operate full blast. Twenty-five policemen from the Lake Street station were to refuse to testify before a board of inquiry, and on July 9, 1878, Hickey was to be cast out by a 22-to-11 vote of the city council.

Now Hickey began to lecture and question Parsons in an insulting way, accusing him of coming up from Texas to start a revolution. Parsons attempted to explain that he had nothing to do with the strike and had simply spoken at a meeting, but the people in the room kept interrupting him, demanding that he be locked up, or even lynched. This went on for two hours, after which Hickey walked Parsons to the door and told him he should leave the city at once because his life was in danger; he was being followed everywhere by Hickey's men. He could be assassinated at any time by the "Board of Trade men who would as leave hang [him] to a lamp-post as not." In the light of what happened to Parsons eventually, this was a dreadful prophecy.

Parsons was attacked in the evening paper, the *Times*, for which he had recently worked. Undaunted, he went that night to try to get work at the composing room of the *Tribune*. He was talking to a union friend there, when two thugs came in, seized him and pushed him out the door. They dragged him down five flights of stairs and, waving a gun at his head, threatened to blow his brains out if he ever returned to the *Tribune*. The other employees upstairs were in a considerable state of upset and had to be persuaded to return to work by Joseph Medill.

Parsons left the *Tribune* in time to view a police attack upon workers in Market Square, where about 3,000 people had gathered in response to another call from the Working-Men's Party. The police attacked the crowd with clubs. The *Tribune* editorialized:

> In ordering and compelling the cessation of freight trains on all the railroads, the wedge had been entered for overturning the whole commercial and industrial structure, and the houses if pulled down will fall upon those who have started the work of revolution.

It may not have been a revolution, but a blow at the railroads was a serious act: the railroad by 1877 was the master of interstate commerce. Cities and towns were born or withered away, depending on a railroad baron's decision about which municipality would be granted a connecting line. The railroads created massive wealth, social mobility and progress for some, but they also had a terrible power to corrupt and exploit. The worker who risked life and limb in the railyard had often been the victim of wage cuts, arbitrary reduction of working hours and blacklisting.

On July 25, Wednesday, the *Tribune* headline read, "RED WAR!" The violence in the streets escalated. At the Chicago, Burlington & Quincy roundhouse on 16th Street, a mob of thousands broke in, smashing windows, and destroyed two locomotives and tore up a section of track before a detachment of police from the 12th Street station shot into the crowd, killing three and wounding seven. Two more people were killed and many injured by the police when another mob gathered at 16th and Halsted streets. The newspapers reported rioting and looting of a gun-and-hardware store on Halsted Street. The business community was in a state of panic, demanding that the mayor restore order. The *Chicago Times* called for hand grenades to be thrown against these "guttersnipes and loafers." Vigilante patrols were organized. Army units, including infantry, artillery and cavalry, National Guard and various bands of fighters poured into the city to put down the perceived insurrection.

On July 26, Thursday, the police, without provocation, broke into the Vorwaerts Turner Hall on West 12th Street where members of the Furniture Workers' Union had gathered to negotiate with their employers. The police fired into the assembly, killing one man and injuring many more. This incident was adjudicated and a decision handed down that the police had violated the rights of the people to assemble peacefully. On that same Thursday occurred what has been called "The Battle of the Viaduct," when a mob of about 3,000 fought with stones and railroad spikes against the police, who killed fourteen people and wounded dozens more.

By Friday, the 27th, the strike was over. The city returned to a normal routine, although the hospitals and jails were full and there had been more than twenty-five deaths and two hundred serious injuries—none of these were policemen or other upholders of the status quo. Although the workers did not win more than scattered concessions, they now understood the importance of unified action, and the Working-Men's Party grew enormously in membership and influence, entered political contests and entered on an expanded publishing program. In December of 1877 it changed its name, becoming the Socialistic Labor Party of North America. Chicago was an important center for the party, and Albert Parsons was an important party leader, running for county clerk in 1877, for alderman in 1878 and nominated to run for president of the United States on the Socialistic Labor ticket in 1879, although he was too young to accept this nomination. He also spoke and wrote extensively, his political attitudes gradually becoming more and more radical. He agitated in particular for the eight-hour day.

The party hit a high point in a Saturday night rally on March 22, 1879, at the Exposition Hall on Michigan Avenue, held to commemorate the Revolution of 1848 and the Paris Commune of 1871, both events which struck terror into the hearts of the prosperous classes. The building was crowded to the eaves with more than 30,000 people and thousands more gathered in the street outside. The meeting was so successful that it carried over to the next day, Sunday, when Parsons addressed it. If the theme were not terrifying enough to the Establishment, this fright was increased by the fact that so-called workers' defense groups paraded through the streets during the rally, openly displaying weapons and ammunition.

These groups—the *Lehr-und-Wehr Verein* or Education and Defense Society, the Bohemian Sharpshooters, Irish Labor Guards, *Jaeger Verein*—wore distinctive uniforms, held socialist views, and practiced with rifles and bayonets. They inspired sufficient unease so that in 1879 they were banned by the Illinois legislature, a law that was upheld by the state supreme court. The result was that the groups went underground. One member of the *Lehr-und-Wehr Verein* was August Spies, who was to become part of the Haymarket drama. He was born in Germany in 1855, privately educated, and emigrated to the U.S. In 1872 after his father's death put an end to his education. He settled in Chicago as a small shopkeeper and was radicalized by the strike of 1877, when he joined the *Lehr-und-Wehr Verein* and the Socialistic Labor Party. He was to become increasingly radical, was expelled from the SLP because of his anarchist views in 1880, the same year in which he took over the *Arbeiter-Zeitung*, for which he had been an editor, rescuing it from bankruptcy and building its circulation to 20,000, the highest of Chicago's German-language newspapers.

After the high point of the rally in 1879, the influence of the SLP began to dwindle, as the economy improved, jobs became more plentiful and wages rose. In 1879 Carter Harrison was elected mayor of Chicago. He had been born on a Kentucky plantation in 1825, with colonial family roots, had been educated at Yale and traveled in Europe, settling in Chicago in 1855. He served in Congress before running for mayor, where he was to serve five terms, four of them consecutive two-year terms. No other mayor of that era had the workers' interests more at heart than "Our Carter." He built a machine on patronage and the ethnic vote, allowed the socialists right of assembly and free speech, and made no attempt to enforce blue laws. He was broadminded to the extent that he countenanced gambling, saloons and prostitution. He did not interfere with the gambling dens on Randolph Street, but made Chicago a wide-open town almost in tandem with the gambling czar Mike McDonald. Harrison was popular with the immigrant population, the workers and businessmen. The press disliked him, as did the Protestant clergy who wanted blue laws enforced and the city cleaned up. He was to be assassinated on Saturday, October 28, 1893, by a disappointed office seeker.

In 1881 Albert Parsons and August Spies, along with Michael Schwab, a German immigrant who was the associate editor of the *Arbeiter-Zeitung*, organized a convention in Chicago of revolutionary groups on October 21–23. A new organization was founded: the Revolutionary Socialistic Party. This was the first national U.S. anarchistic association. In 1882 Johann Most, an influential and gifted propagandist and organizer, arrived in the U.S. and traveled across the country, galvanizing socialists with his fiery speeches. He had spent years in European prisons and to the American press he stood for all that was hateful in the socialist-anarchist movement. A year before the Haymarket occurrence, he published a pamphlet, *Revolutionary War Science*, in which he gave detailed instructions on bomb-making and the use of explosives in the class struggle.

The anarchists considered Chicago a headquarters and established a local group called the International Working People's Association. On national holidays like the Fourth of July, Thanksgiving and Christmas—called by the anarchists national capitalistic holidays—the IWPA held large demonstrations in the city, with parades and music, attracting a great deal of attention. The first such demonstration was held on Thanksgiving, 1884.

At that rally, a crowd of three thousand gathered in Market Square in the early winter drizzle to listen to speeches by Parsons, Spies, Samuel Fielden, a self-employed teamster, C.S. Griffin, and Michael Schwab, an *Arbeiter-Zeitung* editor, who spoke in German. Parsons, standing on crates, was the first to address the audience, quoting from the New Testament on the corruption of the wealthy and saying in conclusion that the socialists did not intend to wait for improvements in the lot of the multitude but would do something for themselves and do it in this world. The march then commenced, to the sounds of a martial band playing the "Marseillaise" and other stirring music, and led by standard bearers holding aloft the red flag of revolution and the black flag of anarchism. The procession wended its way past imposing hotels and the clubs of the rich, who watched them from their windows, down the wide boulevards with their impressive mansions, and ended at the offices of the *Arbeiter-Zeitung* and the *Alarm* on Fifth Avenue, where Parsons and Fielden addressed them again.

The following Thanksgiving, to the discomfort of the city fathers, the parade was repeated. The *Tribune* described the marchers as "slick and fatted"—a dubious description. But before that, in April of that year, the opening of the new Board of Trade building on LaSalle Street—a building that had cost nearly two

14

million dollars at a time when there was widespread unemployment—sparked another procession. Parsons announced that the parade would circle the new building, where elaborate dedication ceremonies were being held that evening. The building, which had been in construction for three years, had imported granite staircases, frescoes depicting the development of man from cave dweller onward, rich mahogany panelling and in the "big room" light poured in through huge windows overlooking the "pit" immortalized by Frank Norris. The ceremonies were to be attended by financiers, foreign dignitaries and the pillars of Chicago society. Later in the evening over 400 members of the Board of Trade would pay twenty dollars apiece to partake of a banquet at the Grand Pacific Hotel.

At eight o'clock in the evening the IWPA gathered in Market Square, heard some heated speeches about "the Board of Thieves" and then set off, once more to the sound of music, led by Lucy Parsons and her friend Lizzie Holmes, carrying the red and black flags, and watched by enthusiastic spectators. They marched east on Madison Street to Clark Street and then south to Jackson Boulevard, where the police barred access. The procession detoured to Adams Street and then west to LaSalle, but they were blocked again at Jackson. The Board of Trade Building, glittering with electric lights, was half a block away, and was surrounded by a sea of policemen. The crowd stopped where it was, sang the "Marseillaise" and shouted its defiance to the people in the new building, who could not hear them because they were listening to Frederick Austin's orchestra playing themes from Meyerbeer's *The Prophet*. The crowd remained assembled, listening to speeches heralding the coming of a final confrontation between workers and the establishment. At eleven at night everyone went home in a good mood, but leaving the pillars of the community feeling threatened and insecure.

That summer there was a streetcar strike with serious repercussions. On June 30, the conductors and drivers of the West Division Streetcar Company walked out in sympathy with fifteen members of the Conductors Benevolent and Protective Association, who had been fired for labor agitation. Three weeks earlier

15

they had won, from the company president J. Russell Jones, a raise and a shortening of the sixty-day probation period. When scabs were hired to replace the strikers, problems developed immediately along the Madison Street line.

Drivers standing in the open parts of the cars were attacked with stones. Carter Harrison, riding his horse down Halsted Street, came upon a man tearing up streetcar track with a pickaxe. The mayor dismounted and disarmed the man before a crowd of curious onlookers. Harrison himself was making every attempt to mediate this dispute, but the police were a real obstacle to settlement. A real villain of Chicago history was Captain John Bonfield of the Desplaines Street station, called "Black Jack" because of his brutal reliance on the club. Bonfield had been given a position of responsibility because of influential family connections: his brother Joseph had been a corporation counsel during the mayoral term of Monroe Heath, and his younger brother James had been promoted from bailiff in the criminal court to detective in 1881. When Heath added men to the force, Bonfield had begun his police career at the age of forty-one. Before that he had failed as a grocer and as the owner of a fertilizer company.

Bonfield became notorious during the streetcar strike for trying to settle matters, on July 2, 1885, by attacking everyone in sight, including innocent bystanders, regardless of age or appearance. With the agreement of the city council he instituted a 24-hour emergency curfew: anyone who seemed to be on the street for a suspicious purpose, it was announced, would be clubbed and arrested. At the Western Avenue car barns at Madison Street, angry strikers jeered and threatened the scabs as they arrived for work. Bonfield responded to a distress call from the company and set about subduing the workers. He attacked not only the strikers but men standing on the corner of Madison and Western waiting for an express wagon to take them to their jobs downtown. Although they had nothing to do with the strike, and many of them did not understand enough English to know that a curfew was in force, they were clubbed and taken to the Desplaines Street station where 150 men were locked in the basement, trying to kill time by singing popular songs of the day. They were not allowed visitors.

The next day, July 3, Bonfield repeated this performance, with more deadly results, arresting gas company workers who had been attacked by strikers: the gas company men had been doing their jobs, digging up the street and the strikers had interfered with them. Bonfield had the gas workers thrown into a police wagon and two men who attempted to ask questions were savagely beaten by Bonfield into unconsciousness. One man died a few years later from his injuries and the other became a permanent invalid.

On July 6, the company hired 150 scabs and the strikers responded by throwing a bomb at a streetcar at the intersection of Robey and Van Buren, pulling the driver from the car and beating him. The next day President Jones backed down, agreeing to review the cases of the sixteen fired workers. The brutal strikes ended, but Police Chief Austin Doyle received many outraged complaints about Bonfield's behavior, not just from strikers but from bystanders and local merchants who had been attacked as well. A petition with a thousand signatures was given to the mayor and the city council, demanding that Bonfield be fired.

Carter Harrison called Bonfield on the carpet. In his defense, the captain said, "A club today to make them scatter may save use of a pistol tomorrow." Harrison wanted to fire Bonfield, but his influential connections intervened, and the brutal captain was promoted to inspector and assigned to city hall headquarters.

2

Before 1855, the Chicago police force consisted of a Constable or Chief of the Watch supervising a maximum of nine watchmen in a city of about 80,000. In 1855 the city council created a police department with a Chief of Police, three precincts and about eighty policemen, but no uniforms until, in 1857, Mayor Long John Wentworth issued the men leather badges, canes and a sort of noisemaker called a "creaker." In 1858 a new mayor—John C. Haines—gave them blue coats and caps and replaced the leather badge with a brass one.

The newly formed police department was immediately called into service in 1855 during the Lager Beer Riot, which broke out because of the implementation of a Sunday closing law and an increase in the cost of a saloon license. This reflected growing hostility between immigrants—especially Germans, who loved their beer gardens—and native citizens. The Germans refused to pay the higher license cost and two hundred of them were consequently arrested. The immigrants perceived these actions as discriminatory and the result was a full-blown war between the police, 150 special deputies on the one hand, and an armed mob of about 1,000 enraged people on the other. It is known that one rioter was killed, although there may have been others, and at least one policeman seriously hurt. Arrests were made, but no one was ever tried as a result of the riot. The threat of state prohibition dissolved and did not reappear until 1919.

In 1861, when John Wentworth was elected mayor once more, he removed the blue coats and hats and brass badges, restored the leather badges and capriciously cut the size of the force back to fifty patrolmen under six lieutenants and one captain. Aghast, the state legislature created the Board of Police Commissioners in order to check the mayor's authority over the force. In retaliation Wentworth called the entire force to a meeting at city hall at two o'clock in the morning on March 21, 1861, and told them that he was firing them because the new board intended to fire them anyway. For twenty-four hours the city was at the mercy of thieves and second-story men, but nothing much happened because most criminals did not know that the police force had been dissolved.

The result of this two o'clock purge was a new and superior force, hired by the board the next day. Jacob Rehm was appointed deputy superintendent at an annual salary of $1,500, and fell victim to politics. He resigned twice, retired once, but was called back each time. Finally, after the Whisky Scandal of 1875, he was forced to resign for good.

Chicago's police department has a history of men at the top who had no business being there. During one of Rehm's absences, Mayor Joseph Medill, the fanatically prohibitionist publisher of the *Tribune* , appointed Elmer Washburn who had been warden of the Illinois Penitentiary and who could be relied on to support dry laws. Washburn was well-meaning, but verbose and pompous, completely lacking in tact and political savvy. Charges of neglect of duty were brought against Washburn, but he was cleared on April 28, 1872. Medill punished two of the accusers, E.F. Klokke and Charles Reno, by dropping them from the police board.

Medill's stubborn stand against beer on Sunday caused him to be swept out of office in 1873. The new mayor was Harvey D. Colvin, a former agent for the U.S. Express Company who had run as a liberal independent but who was in actuality a stooge of the notorious gambling czar Mike McDonald. Colvin appointed Michael Hickey superintendent of police. Hickey served for three years and established a pattern of police overreaction to a perceived anarchist threat. He failed to secure reappointment because of his investment in a downtown brothel when reform Mayor Monroe Heath succeeded Colvin. Heath appointed Captain Valorius Seavey, who had commanded a battalion of west side police during the brutal 1877 riot, and whose term as chief was to last only one year. Seavey was a tool of the mayor and the dowtown businessmen who warmly supported Heath's Republican administration.

One incident that pointed to the mayor's links with certain elements of the business community occurred on October 15,

1878, when officers Henry O'Neil and Joseph Mahoney of the Armory police station came up to employees of the Metropolitan Railway Company who were laying sections of track along Lake Street near the Chicago River bridge and threatened them with arrest if they did not immediately stop work. The president of the railway line, David L. Hough, was present. He explained to the policemen that the city council had granted his firm an exclusive franchise along Lake Street, but O'Neil replied that he was acting under orders from Chief Seavey and the mayor and the council's ordinance cut no ice with him. At this point a detachment of club-wielding police drove the workers off the site, and Mr Hough was arrested and taken to jail. The next day the outraged transit official swore out a warrant for Heath, Seavey and O'Neil, charging them with assault and battery.

The three accused posted a $200 bond and the case was settled quietly. Heath and Seavey had acted on behalf of the businessmen and owners of Lake Street property who preferred other traction companies vying for the lucrative downtown franchise.

Seavey died in office on September 8, 1879, and was replaced by Joseph Dixon, who reacted to the anarchist threat by dressing the police in military garb, issuing them muskets and requiring them to march in close order drill. They were taught to operate a cannon purchased by jittery members of the Citizen's Association who feared an impending Red revolution and were determined to stop it at any cost. These plans were dashed when Carter Harrison was elected mayor and appointed William McGarigle, former secretary to Elmer Washburn, as the next superintendent. McGarigle—of whom much more will be said later—is credited with creating the patrol box system, the most important police innovation of the 1880s. The telephone and signal system had been installed in 1880: 375 hexagonal pine boxes supporting lampposts were set up in each police district. Inside the box, which resembled a phone booth, was an alarm box dial, which the caller could use to contact the local police station. On the dial were eleven categories, including thievery, forgery, riot, drunk and disorderly, murder, accidents, fighting, fire and violations of city ordinances. By placing the pointer on one of these categories, a citizen could instantly summon a five man patrol wagon equipped with a stretcher, handcuffs, blankets and clubs. A specially numbered key to each of the boxes was given to 2,144 people who lived in the districts. The key was held in place by a trap lock and could be released only by the officer on the patrol wagon after the call had been answered. Each box cost the city $25. By 1884 this system had resulted in the placing of 857,084 distress calls and a drop in false alarms.

On November 22, 1882, McGarigle was replaced by Austin J. Doyle, a hand-picked favorite of Carter Harrison. Doyle had, like other Irish policemen, risen through patronage—first as a clerk in the recorder's court and then in 1873 as clerk of the criminal court. During his term, 418 men were added to the force because of the growing fear of foreign anarchists and labor unrest: the Citizens' Association bought a Gatling gun and 296 Springfield rifles to protect the city. Doyle's term of office was characterized by both blackmail and frequent clubbings. He was pressured to "retire" on October 15, 1885, following the negative reaction to his handling of the streetcar strike. Carter Harrison arranged a job for him as general superintendent of the Chicago Passenger Railway: Harvey Weeks, the president of the railway, was a Democratic leader and major contributor to Harrison's re-election campaign.

John Bonfield had supporters for the superintendency, but the trade unions and a good many others violently opposed him, and Harrison perceived that with the election a year away and the Irish holding a majority of city offices, it would be politic to appoint someone with a German name. Consequently he appointed Frederick Ebersold, a Bavarian war hero who had fought under Sherman at the battle of Shiloh. "Men of Irish descent now fill a large share of the offices at my command," Harrison announced, "It seems to me that the 160,000 Germans in Chicago should be recognized."

As we have seen, Bonfield, to his chagrin, was given the lesser position of inspector. "I know," Harrison told the press, "that he will be an inspector who inspects and a splendid drill master." Bonfield embarked on an ambitious campaign to drill his men in riot control. A serious power struggle was about to begin in the police hierarchy, involving German and Irish ethnic backgrounds and personal jealousy. During this struggle, the Haymarket bomb exploded.

3

The atmosphere surrounding the Haymarket affair can be somewhat understood when one examines "the war of words" that went on between the socialist newspapers and the mainstream daily press. The rhetoric used by Albert Parsons and August Spies in their newspapers sounded dangerous; it frightened people and alienated the police. For instance, Parsons's *Alarm* on June 27, 1885, gave instructions for the building of a gas pipe bomb "for those who will sooner or later be forced to employ its destructive qualities in defense of their rights . . ."

But comments on the other side were equally—if not more—threatening.

In 1884, Joseph Medill editorialized in the *Tribune* that it might be a good idea to poison meat and other food given to tramps. "This," he said, "produces death within a comparatively short time, is a warning to other tramps to keep out of the neighborhood, puts the Coroner in a good humor, and saves one's chickens and other portable property from constant depredation."

The *Alarm's* response to this appeared on October 4, 1884. It is probable that it was written by Lucy Parsons, an uncompromising radical who, until her death in 1942, was to work closely with anarchists—Emma Goldman among them. "But each of you hungry tramps," the *Alarm* said, " . . . avail yourselves of those little methods of warfare which science has placed in the hands of the poor man, and you will become a power in this or any other land. Learn the use of explosives!" The *Tribune* called Albert Parsons "a blood preaching anarchist fiend."

Indispensable to the background of the Haymarket tragedy was the struggle for the eight-hour day, a struggle which had begun in earnest in 1884 when Samuel Gompers of the Federation of Organized Trades and Labor Unions set a deadline of May 1,

1886, as the date for a general strike if the eight-hour day had not yet been universally adopted. This had clearly not happened, despite the strong support of President Grover Cleveland and other influential politicians. It was one of the demands made by workers at the McCormick Reaper Works on Chicago's southwest side, where young Cyrus Hall McCormick, succeeding his father as head of the company, attempted to build profits by cutting the workers' pay, firing many of them when he introduced new machinery, and setting out to break the union. Catholic immigrant workers were furious when they discovered that McCormick was giving huge endowments to the Presbyterian Theological Seminary at the same time that he was cutting their pay. In April, 1885, the McCormick workers won an agreement that union organizing would not be grounds for dismissal. But despite this, McCormick hired Pinkerton agents to infiltrate the shops and weed out the organizers.

The result was a series of labor clashes in the winter of 1885–86, culminating on February 16 in the lockout of 1,482 employees, many of whom belonged to the Iron Molders' Union No 23. Chief Ebersold placed 350 policemen at McCormick's disposal along the Black Road, which ran from Blue Island Avenue to the Reaper Works and which was covered with charcoal and cinders—hence its name. On March 1, scabs were safely conducted into the plant.

On Saturday, May 1, 1886, Albert Parsons led 30,000 trade unionists in a peaceful march down Michigan Avenue—the first May Day celebration. On Monday, a commitee from the Central Labor Union asked Spies to address the Lumber Shovers' Union, which was striking for the eight-hour day. These men had nothing to do with the McCormick lockout, but a crowd of several thousand of them gathered not far from the McCormick plant to listen to Spies, who delivered a relatively mild speech to some heckling, but a generally favorable response. He concluded his talk at the end of the workday, just as the McCormick scabs began to leave the plant. Some of the lumbermen moved off toward the McCormick gates to join the pickets in harassing the scabs. Spies urged them to restrain themselves, but they ignored him, possibly because many were Polish and Czech immigrants who did not understand what he was saying. The scabs were driven back into the factory under a hailstorm of stones and bottles. Two patrolmen on duty, J.M. Hanes and J.J. Egan, called the Hinman station for assistance. About seventy-five men and five patrol wagons were dispatched.

Captain Simon O'Donnell arrived on the scene from the 12th Street station in a buggy. When he was surrounded by pushing, shoving men, he lashed them freely with his whip and both he and other policemen fired into the crowd, which was throwing stones at them. The result was two strikers killed and many wounded. There were no police casualties.

Spies, unnerved, left the scene of carnage, flagged down a Blue Island streetcar and rushed back to his newspaper office on Wells Street to write what has been called the "revenge circular," because a compositor added the word "Revenge" in bold type without Spies' knowledge, before Spies' opening words, which were "Workingmen to Arms!!!" Spies thought that six workers had been killed, and that is what he wrote: "Your masters sent out their bloodhounds—the police; they killed six of your brothers at McCormicks this afternoon . . ." He ended with an exhortation to "Destroy the hideous monster that seeks to destroy you. To arms, we call you, to arms!" He added an even more strongly phrased exhortation in German at the bottom of the leaflet.

About 1,200 of these circulars were distributed at Working-Men's centers, one of which was Greif's Hall at Clinton and Lake streets, where a group of German anarchists were meeting, apparently to plan drastic action even before they received Spies' circular. After they received it, they decided to hold a protest meeting the next night at the Haymarket, Randolph Street between Desplaines and Halsted, because Market Square might be a bottleneck if the police attacked; it was too small. The Haymarket was an open area on the western fringe of the Loop where farmers and others sold meat, produce and dry goods to the public. Three of the planners of this event were Gottfried Waller, a Swiss cabinetmaker; Adolph Fischer, a printer at *Arbeiter-Zeitung*, and George Engel, a German immigrant who, with his wife, operated a toy store in his house. The state was later to call this planning session the "Monday night conspiracy" for a revolution to begin at the Haymarket, but there is no evidence of that.

The next morning Adolph Fischer ordered 25,000 handbills announcing the Haymarket meeting, as he had been instructed to do the night before. This handbill, which was signed "The Executive Committee," said, after the announcement of the mass meeting at 7:30 that Tuesday night, May 4, "Good speakers will be present to denounce the latest atrocious act of the police, the shooting of our fellow-workmen yesterday afternoon. Workingmen! Arm Yourselves and Appear in Full Force!" When Spies read this last line, he objected because he thought it was too inflammatory, but he himself called for revenge in his *Arbeiter-Zeitung* editorial that afternoon.

Mayor Harrison issued a permit for the Haymarket meeting. He stressed his opinion that the Constitution guaranteed freedom of speech and assembly, and he told Superintendent Ebersold that anything resembling the McCormick fiasco should be prevented at all costs. The mayor said he himself would be there to make sure that everything went well. Captain Bonfield told the press on Monday that there would be no repetition of the 1877 riot, although there might be a few "sanguinary conflicts." But he contradicted himself the next day, saying that there would be "bad work" at the Haymarket. Ebersold sent a large contingent of officers—eighty-four men to be supervised by Bonfield—to the Desplaines Street station, which was half a block from the Haymarket. The Desplaines district covered just one mile of the third precinct, an area normally patrolled by seventy-three men. But for Tuesday night a detachment of one hundred policemen was added, under Captain William Ward. In addition, detectives were assigned to mingle with the crowd at the rally.

Early in the morning on that fateful May 4, an unpleasant incident occurred when an angry crowd gathered outside Sam Rosenfeld's drug store at 18th and Center streets because of a rumor that Rosenfeld was a police agent. Police arrived and dispersed the crowd, which reassembled when the officers left. The result was that the drugstore was looted, and so was the nearby Weiskoph's Saloon. Only after that did the police return.

It has been suggested that Bonfield deliberately allowed this mayhem in order to fan public outrage against the labor movement.

The Haymarket rally was scheduled to begin at 7:30 but when Spies arrived at 8:15, he was surprised to see that it had not yet begun, and that Albert Parsons was not there: Parsons had been set to begin the speech-making, because English speakers always preceded German speakers. Spies had come at 8:15 because he was a German speaker. In addition to all this, there were only two or three thousand people in the Haymarket, which could hold as many as 20,000. Because of this smaller turnout, Spies moved the meeting toward Desplaines Street, adjacent to the alley next to the Crane Brothers factory. Spies learned that Parsons was at a meeting in the *Alarm-Arbeiter-Zeitung* offices; he despatched Balthazar Rau to fetch him and he himself climbed onto a truck wagon and began to address the crowd in English. He said that the meeting had not been called to start a riot, but to talk about the campaign for an eight-hour day and the incidents that had occurred because of it. It was McCormick himself who was the cause of the trouble at his plant, Spies said, and the day would come when men like him would be hanged.

Mayor Harrison, who was in the crowd, heard this speech and did not find it incendiary despite the reference to McCormick; that was the only objectionable thing in it, he thought.

Balthazar Rau contacted Parsons, who was speaking to the American Group at the IWPA. Samuel Fielden was there too, and he and Parsons, along with the other members of the American Group, walked the half mile to the Haymarket, where Spies ended his remarks when he heard that Parsons had arrived.

Parsons gave a speech which was relatively low-key, although it lasted about an hour. He talked about the eight-hour day, the inequalities of the capitalist system and socialism as the only hope of the workers. Although he advised his audience to arm themselves against threats to their inalienable rights, he also reproved those who shouted "Hang him!" when he mentioned Jay Gould's name, saying the movement was "not a conflict between individuals, but for a change of system" and socialism "does not aim at the life of the individual" but is intended "to remove the causes which

26

produce the pauper and the millionaire." If, he said, you killed Jay Gould, a hundred other Jay Goulds would be produced by the system.

Mayor Harrison, in the crowd, listened to the speech and did not find it inflammatory. The crowd, he said, was peaceful. Accordingly, as Parsons was finishing his speech, the mayor went to the Desplaines Street station and told Bonfield that the meeting presented no threat and that he should dismiss his reserves, or at least most of them at other stations. Bonfield told him that he had already dismissed these men, because his detectives had told him the same thing. But he said he wanted to keep the force at Desplaines Street station until the rally ended because he was afraid that some of the crowd might go to the Milwaukee & St Paul freight yards, where the workers were out on strike, and do some damage.

Harrison agreed because he knew about these rumors. He had heard that McCormick's might be attacked that night. He left Bonfield and went back to the Haymarket for a little while before he rode his horse home. It was about ten o'clock.

The wind was rising. Parsons finished his talk, and after introducing Samuel Fielden, who would make the last address, went to sit on another wagon with Lucy, his children, Lizzie Holmes and a few friends. While Fielden was speaking, the wind rose considerably; there was a real threat of rain. People were beginning to leave. Parsons and his entourage, along with Adolph Fischer, went over to Zepf's Hall at Lake and Desplaines streets, where the Furniture Workers were meeting. Fielden prepared to conclude his talk, saying that the workers should do everything they could to wound the law, "kill it, stab it"—everything to "impede its progress."

A couple of Bonfield's detectives in the thinning crowd decided that these were words intended to incite violence. They hurried back to the station and so informed Bonfield, who immediately ordered three divisions commanded by five lieutenants and one sergeant, to fall in on the double quick. The rear detail barely had time to fall into position and the men were almost running when Bonfield ordered them out. A witness, Barton

Simonson, later testified that he saw Bonfield and Captain William Ward at the station earlier in the evening, and that Bonfield said, "The trouble there is that these anarchists get their women and children mixed up with them, and we can't get at them. I would like to get three thousand of them in a crowd without their women and children. I would make short work of them."

Just as Fielden was finishing, the police trotted in, filling the street from curb to curb. Those workers who had been standing south of the alley were forced to the north. The crowd numbered fewer than 300 astonished people. The policemen stopped a few paces from the speakers' wagon, and Captain Ward called out, "I command you in the name of the people of the state of Illinois, immediately and peaceably to disperse!" Fielden, like everyone else there, was astounded. "But we are peaceable," he said. There was a pause. Ward repeated his command, and asked the crowd to assist him. "All right," Fielden said," we will go." He began to step down from the wagon.

Suddenly an object came flying over the heads of the people and exploded with fearful intensity in the midst of the police; the deafening explosion was powerful enough to shatter windows all over the area. Many policemen were severely wounded. After the initial shock, the police began to fire blindly into the crowd, a steady fire for at least two minutes. Bullets whistled through the air and the crowd went into a panic, trying to scramble out of the way, but many people were shot, including Fielden, wounded in the knee, and Spies's brother Henry, in the groin, when he managed to deflect a gun aimed directly at his brother August. The ground was covered with bodies of policemen and civilians. All around the area, for blocks, people were staggering or crawling wounded into drugstores and taverns, crying for help or trying to hide behind whatever shelter they could find. There is no accurate count of civilian deaths and injuries, although there was an estimate that more than fifty people were hurt in one way or another. Four were definitely identified as killed, but other names have brought the possible total to at least ten.

Twenty-five policemen were wounded and seven were killed before Bonfield called a cease-fire. The first victim was 34-year-old

Mathias Degan who died in the Desplaines Street station: a bomb fragment had severed an artery in his leg. Over the next twelve days George Mueller, John Barrett, Timothy Flavin, Michael Sheehan, Thomas Redden and Nils Hansen died, the latter on June 14, the last to die, except for Timothy Sullivan, who died two years later, apparently as a result of a bullet wound received that night. Of these unfortunate men, only Thomas Redden, who, like Mathias Degan, was from the Lake Street station, had been on the force for more than two years.

In all, sixty policemen were injured, most in the leg or hip. The Police Report for 1886 listed "Policemen Suffering Injury as a Result of Bullet Wounds" and it is true that only Mathias Degan died solely from a bomb injury; Mueller, Barrett and Sheehan were killed by bullets, as was Timothy Sullivan, and the others were both shot and injured by the bomb. What seems clear from witness reports is that most of the shooting came from the police— although certainly a small number of anarchists were armed—and that in the furor the police shot their own men.

It must be remembered, however, that it was the throwing of the bomb that triggered the ensuing mayhem. At the same time, the invasion by the police triggered the throwing of the bomb. Bonfield had no reason to order his men to the Haymarket.

An ex-convict named Frank Louis was the first to be arrested in the dragnet that began immediately. It was his misfortune to be struck in the right side of his back when he was returning from a shopping errand. The extracted bullet had been fired from a standard police .38.

In a letter dated June 1, 1886, Bonfield explained his actions to Chief Ebersold.

> At different times between 8:00 and 9:30, officers in plain clothes reported the progress of the meeting and stated that nothing of a very inflammatory nature was said until a man named Fielden or Fielding took the stand. He advised his hearers to "throttle the law." It would be as well for them to die fighting as to starve to death. He further advised them to exterminate the capitalists and to do it that night. Wanting to be clearly within the law, and wishing to leave no room for

doubt as to the propriety of our actions, I did not act on his first reports, but sent the officers back to make further observations.

A few minutes after 10:00 the officers reported that the crowd was getting excited and the speaker growing more incendiary in his language. I then felt to hesitate any longer would be criminal on my part, and then gave the order to fall in, and our force formed on Waldo Place.

Officer Herman Krueger, a former soldier, said later that he had suggested to Bonfield that night that the company deploy and converge upon the "rioters" from the outer edges of the square. Bonfield disagreed, saying the mob would "run like Hell." Later, as the wounds of the broken and bleeding police officers were being treated, Krueger confronted Bonfield and said to him, "Well, this is plain murder! If you were an army officer, you would be cashiered!"

Minutes after the bomb exploded, the dead and wounded were taken to the Desplaines station and the block was cordoned off. At eleven o'clock Bonfield sent a detachment of police to the *Arbeiter-Zeitung* offices at 41 N Wells, but the building was deserted. Parsons had borrowed a five-dollar gold piece from a man named Brown (who was arrested for this crime) and had fled to Elgin, Illinois.

The city was in the grip of anti-Red hysteria.

Chief Ebersold sent immediate word to the governor that the state militia was not needed. Ebersold was eager to prevent public overreaction and, in fact, he and Carter Harrison wanted to play down the entire event. City elections were only months away. By the same token, John Bonfield was strongly interested in damaging Ebersold, and he wanted to emphasize the Haymarket tragedy. Sharing this desire with Bonfield was Michael John Schaak who, second only to Thomas Byrnes of New York, was the most famous 19th-century American policeman. Schaak had been born in Luxemburg in 1843, joined the force as a patrolman in 1869, and within three years had advanced to sergeant. In five years he made over 865 arrests and was said to be familiar with every back alley, gaming house and sporting domain north of the Chicago River. In 1879 he was transferred from the Armory station to Chicago

Avenue and promoted to lieutenant. On two occasions Schaak was shot by Levee hoodlums, but not seriously. He had the good fortune to take part in three of the most prominent police cases of the century: the Kledzic murder case,[1] Haymarket and the Leutgart "sausage vat" murder in the 1890s.

Schaak was the prototype of the overbearing cop, with impressive girth and a handlebar moustache. He was driven by a desire for publicity throughout his 28-year career—during which he had never taken a vacation. But he was eventually to be sullied by scandal.

Schaak pressured Ebersold to let him handle the Haymarket investigation, saying that he had access to informers and was privy to secret evidence. Reluctantly, the chief agreed. The relationship between Schaak and Ebersold was not warm. "I am going to work this case day and night until it is cleared up," Schaak promised the chief on May 7. Schaak gathered his favorite detectives, each of whom was to become notorious in one way or another. They included Charles Rehm (a relative of Jacob Rehm); Michael Whalen (who was to be suspended for complicity in the Dr Cronin murder case of 1889); Jacob Loewenstein (who in 1889 would be suspended with Schaak for fencing stolen goods); Michael Hoffman, John Stift and Herman Schuettler. Of Schuettler, an historian was later to write: "Clubs, bricks and stones were common weapons of offense, and Schuettler was as adept with them as he was with his knuckles. He was arrested for fighting with a truck teamster at age seventeen." He began a rapid climb in the department in 1883 when he helped secure the first poisoning conviction in Cook County. Wealth, power, influence and a term as police chief awaited Schuettler in the next thirty years.

The first socialist was arrested on May 4: an unnamed man who was in possession of four revolvers when he attempted to escape. He was booked for murder. Bonfield believed that the Haymarket bomb had resulted from an armed conspiracy among members of the *Lehr-und-Wehr Verein*. Chris Komens of 231 20th Street, a member of this group, was arrested and found to be in possession of dynamite and rifles. Bonfield instituted a veritable reign of terror in the city over the next eight weeks.

On May 5, August Spies, Samuel Fielden and Michael Schwab were arrested at the *Arbeiter-Zeitung* offices. Spies's brother Christian, who had happened to drop in to the offices, was also arrested. Oscar Neebe, a labor organizer and part owner of a yeast firm, stopped in at the *Arbeiter-Zeitung* to ask about the Haymarket incident and was arrested there, along with Adolph Fischer and the entire printing staff. Arrests came thick and fast in the city. Not only anarchists were rounded up, but radicals of any stripe and even anyone who had anything to do with labor reform. Many people who had nothing at all to do with Haymarket were taken from their homes without proper warrants and refused bail; the jail cells were crowded even with women and children. Homes were searched, furniture broken, residents handled roughly.

George Bartels and Frank Schmidt were arrested at 71 W Lake street by George Hubbard, for possession of socialist literature. When a friend, Charles Franks, came to visit Bartels and Schmidt at the Central station, he was asked by an officer if he would participate in a socialist parade. When Franks said that he would, he was arrested too.

Oscar Neebe was interrogated at central police headquarters and released; he obtained permission from Mayor Harrison to resume publication of the *Arbeiter-Zeitung*. On May 27 he was arrested by Officer Whalen of Schaak's detail and named in the indictment that came down that same day.

Schaak was active throughout the month of May, planting detectives in labor meetings and meeting mysterious women in the middle of the night—or so he claimed. Someone set his house on fire. Schaak's reputation was enhanced on May 14 when Herman Schuettler, after a fierce struggle, brought in 22-year-old Louis Lingg, who had emigrated from Germany ten months before to avoid the military draft. Lingg was the youngest and most radical of the men arrested after Haymarket. William Seliger, a carpenter, had provided Lingg with a job and a small house at 442 N Sedgwick Street. Seliger and Lingg had manufactured bombs in their spare time.

Schaak and Bonfield had joined forces, splitting the department into two feuding cliques. "Are you the chief or am I?"

Ebersold asked Schaak on May 11. Schaak accused Ebersold of being friendly with Clark Street drunks and of allowing reporters to spend a lot of time with the incarcerated anarchists. State's Attorney Julius Grinnell attacked Ebersold for taking a vacation in California at this tense time. "What do you want me to do?" Ebersold asked. "Throw my train tickets in the lake?" In May of 1889 Schaak was to produce a book called *Anarchy and Anarchists* in which he painted what was probably an exaggerated picture of the department under Ebersold:

> The department was rent and paralyzed with the feuds and jealousies between the chiefs and subordinates. This too was at a time when the people of Chicago were in a condition of mind bordering on panic. It is charity to say no more. He [Ebersold] had neither a proper conception of his duties nor the ability to perform them.

Ebersold responded that "Schaak wanted to keep the pot boiling, keep himself prominent before the public. Well, I sat down on that . . . and of course Schaak didn't like it." He said further that he had begun to think that there wasn't much to all this anarchist business, although in his report to the city council in 1886 he described the "extensive preparations which these people had made and planned for the destruction of life and property."

A bizarre episode, of which Schaak took advantage to blacken Ebersold's reputation, involved the arrest of Michael Schwab's 23-year-old brother-in-law, Rudolph Schnaubelt, a machinist by occupation, who had emigrated to the U.S. from Vienna in 1884. He was extremely active in the IWPA and, at six foot two and 200 pounds, had a reputation for militant revolutionary fervor. When Schnaubelt learned on May 5 that Michael Schwab had been arrested, he went at once to see Sigmund Zeisler, an attorney for the Central Labor Union, and made some rather incriminating remarks about the police, among them a statement that the bombing had "served them right." On May 7 Schnaubelt was arrested; he said that he had been on the speaker's wagon on May 4, but that he had left the meeting shortly before the bomb was thrown. Other people who had been there said they saw him leave about twenty minutes before the police arrived. The police apparently saw no reason to hold Schnaubelt, and released him. He did not wait around to be arrested again, but fled that night to Canada, where he eventually took ship to England. In May, 1887, he took passage for Buenos Aires, and dropped from sight.

Schnaubelt's flight made him the prime bomber suspect. Schaak, in *Anarchists and Anarchy*, put the blame for Schnaubelt's escape squarely on Chief Ebersold, who, he said, had ordered Schnaubelt released and had in fact told the police to "lay off." There is no evidence for this, but in the emotional atmosphere of the time, it had a devastating effect on Ebersold's reputation.

During the month of May, 1886, thirty-one indictments were presented, 200 people were arrested, the police raided ten labor meeting halls and seventeen saloons, were supporting forty-five families in return for their testimony and had coerced several others into presenting false testimony. On May 27 the grand jury indicted ten men as accessories to the murder of Officer Mathias J. Degan, for murder by pistol shots; for general conspiracy to murder and for unlawful assembly. These were Parsons, Spies, Fielden, Louis Lingg, Michael Schwab, Adolph Fischer, George Engel, Oscar Neebe, Rudolph Schnaubelt and William Seliger, who turned state's witness and escaped prosecution.[2] Schnaubelt, as we have seen, had fled the country.

Albert Parsons, too, had disappeared immediately after that night. He was sought everywhere; a $5,000 reward was offered for information leading to his arrest. The press was virulent; he was called a beast and a "miscegenationist": the *Chicago Times* called him a fiend and a coward, and took pains to explain that he was "the husband of a negress."[3] Parsons had gone to Geneva where his friend Lizzie Holmes had a house, then to Elgin and from there to Waukesha, Wisconsin, where he found refuge with another socialist.

A legal defense committee was set up for the accused men: contributions poured in from all over the country and the organizers succeeded in persuading William Perkins Black, 44, a prominent corporate attorney who had been a captain in the Civil War and had won the Congressional Medal of Honor, to head the defense team. Black in turn persuaded William A. Foster, a recent arrival from Davenport, Iowa, to join him. The other two lawyers were from the Chicago Labor Union: Sigmund Zeisler and Moses Salomon.

The judge in the case was Joseph E. Gary, who had been elected to the Superior Court in 1863 and had a reputation for independence and fairness. The prosecutor was Julius S. Grinnell, whose reputation was also good, but who had political ambitions.

The trial began on June 21. Against the strong opposition of William Foster, but with equally strong encouragement from William Black, Albert Parsons came back from Wisconsin and surrendered to the court on the morning of the trial. It was an action that was to cost Parsons his life. The judge was clearly biased against the defendants: he began to rule against them from the beginning, refusing to delay the trial to defuse popular sentiment, or to grant separate trials for four of the defendants to obviate the possibility that evidence against one would be taken as evidence against all. It took twenty-one days to choose a jury, because everyone interviewed had a strong prejudice against the defense. Nevertheless, Judge Gary did not exclude these hostile jurors—some of whom even had police connections. Throughout the trial the judge made disparaging remarks about the defendants.

Grinnell, who also used inflammatory language, attempted to establish a link between all the defendants to prove a general conspiracy, although he believed that Rudolph Schnaubelt had actually thrown the bomb. George Engel, the toy store owner, had been at home with his wife when the bomb was thrown, but he had been at the Monday night meeting. The state contended that he had been in constant contact with Louis Lingg and planned to bring the bombs to the Haymarket from Neff's Hall on Clybourn Street. Adolph Fischer had been at the meeting and had printed the fatal announcement, inserting the line, "Workingmen Arm Yourselves and Appear in Full Force!" Although Michael Schwab had left the Haymarket at eight o'clock, he had helped Spies edit the handbills earlier in the day. The cases against Albert Parsons,

35

August Spies and Samuel Fielden are well known, but the case against Oscar Neebe hinged on the fact that he owned two dollars' worth of stock in the *Arbeiter-Zeitung*, that he was with the others in the *Arbeiter* office when it was raided, and that he continued to publish inflammatory tracts after the bombing.

The case against the anarchists was a general indictment of the movement. The march on the Board of Trade Building, which was surely irrelevant, was introduced as evidence of a general plan to overthrow the existing order. Unreliable witnesses were paraded before the court and, despite discrediting cross-examinations, their testimony was accepted as truth. Lieutenant Martin Quinn of the Chicago Avenue station testified that he heard Samuel Fielden tell the crowd, "Do your duty and I'll do mine," just before he pulled out a pistol and fired at the police from atop the wagon. Quinn said he heard this statement from fifty feet away; Louis Haas said he heard it from fifteen feet away. Their statements were contradicted by Captain William Ward, who said that he was close enough to Fielden to touch him and that he didn't remember his making any comments like that.

The state's most important witness was Harry Gilmer, a former deputy marshal and employee of the West Park Commission, who testified that he had stopped at the Haymarket gathering on his way home from a meeting at the Palmer House with the governor of Iowa. Gilmer said that he had been standing under the lamppost near Crane's Alley and he had seen Spies light the match to the bomb before handing it to Schnaubelt. Sixteen other witnesses swore that the bomb had been thrown from a location south of the alley. Gilmer said that he had seen Adolph Fischer at the meeting, but it was conclusively proven that Fischer was at Zepf's Hall the whole evening. Gilmer's character was impugned: Deputy Sheriff John Garrick said that Gilmer had once been his tenant but that he had evicted him because of "bad character." John Brixley had known Gilmer since 1880; he said he could not be believed under oath.

Carter Harrison appeared for the defense. He recounted his movements that night and said he had believed there was no threat to the public safety and had called for the police reserves to be sent home. His testimony cost him the 1886 election.

Judge Gary, whose behavior during the trial shocked even his colleagues, instructed the jury that the defendants could be found guilty if the evidence demonstrated that they had conspired to overthrow the law by force and if Officer Degan had been killed as a result of the conspiracy. On August 20, the jury retired. It took them only three hours to find the defendants guilty, with the exception of Neebe. An hour later they found Neebe guilty too. He was sentenced to fifteen years in prison; the seven men received the death penalty. Date of execution was set for December 3, 1886. Neebe requested the death penalty: it was better, he said, to be executed than to die by inches. His request was not granted.

The press was delighted with the sentences: the *New York Times* called for "death for the cowardly savages." The public and indeed many in the labor movement agreed: these men had to die because of their political beliefs.

Now attempts were made to save the men from the gallows. William A. Foster left the case and was replaced by Leonard D. Swett, who had been a legal associate of Abraham Lincoln. Swett and Black appealed unsuccessfully to the Illinois Supreme Court, and then Swett and General Ben Butler took the case to the U.S. Supreme Court, which refused to intervene. The last hope lay with Richard Oglesby, the governor of Illinois.

As time went by, some of the virulence toward the condemned men began to ebb. There was a considerable outcry against the trial and the verdicts from such respected men as the novelist William Dean Howells, the journalist Henry Demarest Lloyd and the economist Henry George. Lyman J. Gage, a prominent Chicago banker, led the call for executive clemency from Oglesby, for which Gage was attacked by Marshall Field, Cyrus McCormick, George M. Pullman and Philip D. Armour—the bastions of Chicago economic power. Despite this, Oglesby commuted the sentences of Fielden and Schwab to life imprisonment: he may have been influenced by the letters piling up on his desk, not only from Chicagoans, not only from Americans, but from such famous British intellectuals as William Morris, George Bernard Shaw, Edward Carpenter, Frederick Engels, Oscar Wilde, Annie Besant and Olive Schreiner. Oglesby heard also from the French Chamber of Deputies and the Municipal Council of Paris and from concerned people in Australia. Oglesby would have commuted Parsons's sentence as well, but he, like Engel, Fischer and Lingg, refused to sue for clemency, because they maintained their innocence. Spies did ask for clemency, but withdrew his request.

While the governor was considering the pleas, several bombs were discovered in Louis Lingg's cell. Their size made them useful only for killing their user, but the public once more went wild, surmising that the anarchists intended to destroy the prison and everyone in it. It was feared that this incident would ruin the possibility of commutation, and it led to a question about Lingg's sanity. This was not the only strange event that occurred during the men's incarceration. Another was the marriage of Spies to Rosnina Clarke Van Zandt, the attractive 24-year-old daughter of a wealthy pharmaceuticals manufacturer who lived at Huron and Rush streets. She attended the trial every day, elegantly dressed. She became infatuated with Spies, visited him in prison and began to help him write his autobiography. Her family supported her in her conviction that Spies was innocent.

In December of 1886, Canute Matson became the new sheriff of Cook County. He cut off Miss Van Zandt's visits, and she and Spies decided to marry. This caused a public outcry; even the defense lawyers were upset because they thought this action would jeopardize the appeal. The sheriff would not allow a jail wedding, but proxy marriages were legal in Illinois: on January 29, 1887, Henry Spies stood in for his brother in the ceremony. Captain Schaak called the wedding "the product of a deranged mind" and a mob attacked the Van Zandt home.

Spies hung a photo of his wife in his cell; she kept an engraving of him on her mantelpiece. Matson refused to allow the couple to meet in the jail, ignoring a February 17, 1887, letter from Nina's father, which spoke of "the distress and anguish" of his child and begged Matson "to let her in today or tomorrow." Spies himself wrote Matson on February 23, saying that his wife was ill and that if she was permitted to enter the jail, she would wear a veil so that the reporters would not recognize her. This letter too was ignored.[4]

On the day that Oglesby rendered his decision, November 10, early in the morning, Louis Lingg put a dynamite cartridge in his mouth and lit it. He lingered six hours before he died, at 2:50 in the afternoon. At 5:20 the same afternoon, Oglesby commuted the sentences of Fielden and Schwab to life imprisonment. He said he could not commute the sentences of Parsons, Spies, Engel and Fischer, because they had not requested commutation. The reaction to the governor's action was relatively muted: the *Tribune*, possibly because Oglesby was a Republican, commented only that he was "a humane and sympathetic man, and averse to the shedding of blood" and had shown himself "more than once" to be "the warm friend of the working class."

November 11, 1887, was the day of the execution. There was tremendous fear that there would be a Red revolution, and that an attempt would be made to rescue the condemned men. Three hundred armed policemen were deployed around the old county jail at Dearborn and Illinois streets. The streets were cordoned off with heavy rope, behind which stood policemen with rifles. Ebersold dispatched two detectives to infiltrate the crowd outside the jail and positioned two companies of sharpshooters on the roof and at the windows. Regiments of militia were guarding city hall with cannon and Gatling guns; a watch was kept on the homes of the judge, jury and prosecutor; factories were closed and the city trembled with fear and anticipation.

There was in fact a plot to attempt a rescue, but it was defused by the condemned men themselves, who believed that their martyrdom would in the end serve a better purpose. So nothing happened. The mood was sombre. Two people in the crowd were arrested: one, described as a "genius crank," apparently because he was wearing glasses, was taken in for carrying a concealed pistol. But most of the people who gathered outside the jail were simply curious onlookers.

The police turned away the Van Zandt carriage when Nina arrived to say goodbye to her husband. Lucy Parsons, who had been told she could see her husband, arrived with her children and was shunted from street corner to street corner in search of permission. Finally she and the children were taken to the Chicago Avenue station where they were locked in separate basement cells, strip-searched and held until the execution was over.

In the courtyard between the jail and the courthouse, Spies, Engel, Parsons and Fischer were executed before 200 witnesses, including a representative of the German Government. Before the trap was sprung, Parsons said, from under his hood, "Will I be allowed to speak, oh men of America? Let the voice of the people be heard! Oh—" he was cut off. Spies issued a prophetic warning: "The day will come when our silence will be more powerful than the voices you strangle today!"

When it was over, Schaak remarked to Ebersold, "The law is vindicated. The anarchists will understand they cannot do as they please in this country." Inspector Bonfield wept, leading the *Tribune* to comment, "It had taken nearly two years to see the disciples of anarchy get their desserts, but he saw it at last, and felt that the brave men who went down that night had been avenged."

Several hours afterward, reporters interviewed Sheriff Matson in his office. He saw no reason to be jubilant, he said; he had merely upheld the law. Someone asked him whether he had taken "any significant meaning from the last words of the dead men."

"No, I do not. With the strained public sentiment, I did not deem it expedient to have the men make long speeches at that time."

On the bulletin board of the Palmer House, a notice was posted: "Trap fell. Spies Parsons Fischer and Engel expiate their crimes and the law vindicated."

The funeral was the largest the city had ever seen; more than 20,000 people travelled ten miles west of the city by special train to Waldheim Cemetery, where there was dedicated, in June, 1893, a monument, designed by Albert Weinert, to the men known as the Chicago Martyrs. Spies's last words were engraved on the base. Eight thousand people attended the ceremony. William Haywood, who was to found the Industrial Workers of the World, and Joe Hill, the legendary labor organizer, announced that on their deaths, their ashes would be scattered on the graves of the Haymarket men.

Not only the socialists and labor organizers were upset by the executions. A strong demand arose for a pardon for the surviving defendants. When John Peter Altgeld became governor in 1892, he was presented with a petition signed by sixty thousand people—many of them his colleagues from his days as a lawyer and a judge. The governor, a Democrat who had a reputation as a liberal, but who had not involved himself in any way with the case, began to study it. Ironically, it was Judge Gary himself, upset by the growing agitation against his trial, who helped to push Altgeld toward a decision, by publishing in the *Century* magazine for April, 1893, a bitter and often inaccurate article defending the verdict and attacking not only Black but Black's wife Hortensia, who had written a letter to the *Chicago Daily News* in defense of the accused.

On June 26, 1893, Governor Altgeld pardoned Fielden, Schwab and Neebe, and condemned Judge Gary for conducting the trial "with malicious ferocity," for favoring the prosecution and for attempting by "insinuating remarks" to prejudice the jury, which in any case had been chosen by faulty methods. The evidence, Altgeld said, had not proven guilt; he particularly excoriated the judge for the article in the *Century*, the ferocity of which, the governor said, was "without a parallel in all history... even Jeffries of England contented himself with hanging his victims and did not stoop to berate them after death."

Altgeld was strongly attacked for the pardon, and for his criticism of the judge; even those who had supported clemency complained about this "personal" attack. "I denounced not Gary the man, but Garyism," the governor replied. William Perkins Black, too, was criticized for his role in the Haymarket trial and its aftermath. His thriving law practice fell off and his income dropped by two-thirds. Eventually, however, his reputation revived. Altgeld, excoriated across the country, was posthumously vindicated. His pardon of the anarchists guaranteed him a place in history.

Schaak and Bonfield were toasted as heroes at the time. Chicago industrialists expressed their gratitude by contributing $31,371.50 to the Policeman's Benevolent Association and $31,371.93 to the heirs of the slain officers. The railroads, which had borne the brunt of the labor agitation, combined to donate $10,759. Cyrus Hall McCormick, the man most responsible for the troubles on the Black Road, donated $250.

Despite the tragedy of Haymarket, which had created martyrs in the men who had been executed, Bonfield and Schaak continued to pursue the anarchists, infiltrating meetings and even tampering with mail. Indeed, the statistics on arrests suggest that it was suspected socialists and petty criminals or vagrants who bore the brunt of police interest, while real scourges of society like Mike McDonald went their way unmolested. There were 1,036 policemen on the city payroll in 1886, a 100 percent increase in manpower over 1881. And there were 1,700 more arrests in 1886 than in 1878, but these were offenses like loitering on street corners, vagrancy, thievery and failing to hitch a horse.

In 1886 Carter Harrison was replaced by John Roche, who had been a Lake Street machinery merchant; on February 14, 1888, Ebersold was succeeded by George Hubbard of the central station; it was a position Schaak had wanted, but did not get. The *Daily News* commented that "Ebersold is charged with being partial in giving soft snaps to certain favorites, and extending advantages to his own nationality, German." Hubbard allowed Bonfield a free hand to harass and intimidate members of the trade union movement. Lucy Parsons was arrested for distributing a pamphlet which her husband had completed in prison and which was sold by the Knights of Labor for ten cents a copy.

In January, 1889, the *Chicago Times* published a series of bold exposés of the police department. Bonfield was accused of allowing gambling along Halsted, State and West Madison streets—raids were engineered on occasion but only "suckers and irresponsible darkies" were brought in, the paper said—and using his position to play politics. He had tried to stop William Buckley, once a captain in the first precinct, from winning a seat in the

Illinois General Assembly by intimidating saloonkeepers into supporting Buckley's opponent, "Ike" Abrahams, a bondsman and lawyer for "low-life" clients. Bonfield had an old grudge against Buckley, and had tried to deny him his pension.

The *Times* asserted that Bonfield and William Ward ran a secret protective racket: gamblers and brothelkeepers had to pay up or be raided. The Louisiana Lottery operated directly across the street from the central station in open defiance of the law. A former Chicago policeman and well-known pool hustler, John Brennan, had opened a saloon, frequented by officers, next door to the Desplaines Street station; Brennan shook down the call girls in the lockup and shared his profits with several policemen who were silent partners in the enterprise.

Bonfield had accepted a gold police star from the madam of a notorious Clinton Street brothel, in return for protection. When the *Times* city editor discovered that Bonfield was strutting about the station showing off his star, Bonfield went to him to plead for mercy, saying that his father was sick and could not survive a public scandal.

The *Times* editors were not afraid to step on red-baiting toes, as they proved with this editorial of January 6, 1889:

> If an inoffensive citizen was arrested without cause and the outrage was denounced, Bonfield's cry of anarchist would be heard. Again the *Times* does not, and will not shut its eyes to official attempts to hoodwink the public. If a judge on the bench or a police officer at his desk lays the plans for an alleged dynamite plot, engages the men to work it, takes measures that will insure notoriety and on the strength of exposure, jeopardize the liberty and perhaps the lives of the innocent for his own glorification, the *Times* will expose the diabolical work.

Bonfield reacted to these charges in a characteristic way: on the morning of January 5, *Times* editors James West and Joseph Dunlop were arrested for criminal libel. The arrest had been timed so that Dunlop could not meet the bondsman and was incarcerated in a basement cell at the Harrison Street lockup that was a cesspool even by the standards of the day. The mayor interceded and Dunlop was released, although Schaak attempted unsuccessfully to arrest him again as he was leaving the building.

Schaak had problems of his own. His Haymarket partner, Jake Loewenstein, had been shot by his wife, Mabel, who announced that her house had been a warehouse for goods confiscated from prisoners by her husband and Bonfield. Louis Lingg, she said, had left his fiancée a gold watch, a brooch, a shawl and a vase, which Schaak had appropriated. In addition, prisoners had been routinely brought to the Loewenstein house to have confessions "sweated" out of them, and witnesses were pressured there into giving false testimony.

The *Times* was sued, but the suits were thrown out. On February 7, 1889, Schaak, Bonfield and Loewenstein were suspended from the police force, pending an investigation. Bonfield attempted to run his own detective agency, but failed at it and drifted into permanent obscurity.

On Memorial Day, 1889, a monument was dedicated to the memory of the policemen who died at Haymarket Square that night. The money was raised by a group of businessmen headed by Richard T. Crane and the *Chicago Tribune*; the monument was designed by Frank Batchelder of St Paul, Minnesota. Its central image, sculpted by John Gelert, is a policeman with upraised hand, meant to be William Ward, although the model was a policeman named Thomas Birmingham, who had served at the Desplaines street station on the fatal night.[5]

Both Bonfield and Schaak died in 1898: Schaak on May 18 from pneumonia, and Bonfield on October 19 from Bright's Disease. Police raids on Greif's Hall near Lake and Clinton continued into 1892. That year the *Chicago Herald* accused the police of carrying on these raids so that the Citizens' Association would continue to supply them with funds to fight the anarchists.

Frederick Ebersold died on January 21, 1900. He had been collecting the largest pension ever given to a retired policeman, but this apparently did not prevent him from isolating himself in his Chicago home and going into a decline: the cause of death was listed as starvation.

Little is left of the original Haymarket area. Zepf's Hall still stands at Lake and Desplaines streets, a grey, neglected building with a boarded-up front. The site of the Desplaines station is now a parking lot: the ancient lock-up was razed in 1950 and the last police detail for the district was transferred to Monroe Street. The cobblestone alley is still there, but the building from which the bomb was apparently thrown, is gone. The old square is not marked in any way.

The incident at the Haymarket rocked not only the city of Chicago, but the Western world, to its foundations. The labor movement was split—with many prominent radicals justifying the bomb-throwing—and the conceptions of the fairness both of the American judicial system and the population itself underwent a negative change. It was a cataclysmic experience.

III

The Boodlers and the Great Escape

1

It was William McGarigle who helped to put the word *boodle* ("n. 1. a bribe or other illicit payment. 2. loot or booty.") in the dictionary. He set a new standard for Cook County corruption, but it is questionable whether he could have done it without Mike McDonald.

Michael Cassius McDonald arrived in Chicago in 1855, a snappy roguish gambler, fond of the drink. He had done his part for the Union during the war, working as a recruiter, collecting commissions from the Government for every man he signed up. When they deserted and re-enlisted, McDonald split the second commission with them. After the war he learned his trade from Colonel Jack Haverly, the first man to make gambling a full-time occupation. In Chicago, McDonald established his reputation among the sportsmen in the Loop poolrooms and then drifted into Democratic circles; he organized the campaign of Harvey Doolittle Colvin, Chicago's post-fire mayor, who won in 1873 and gave the gamblers an open town.

With gamblers Harry Lawrence and Morris Martin, whom he eventually bought out, McDonald opened The Store, a four-story building at Clark and Monroe streets, with gambling on the first two floors and lodging on the second two. It became a mecca not only for gamblers, but for con men of all sorts.

McDonald never used ropers to bring in customers: they cost too much and he was able to hire the right people to make sure that only suckers were steered in. Up and down Randolph Street, the boys called him "Sure Thing Mike." The dealers, Billy Tyler, George Noyes, Charley Winters, Cliff Donaghue and Frank Gallin, were bad boys all. By the time of Carter Harrison's first election in 1879, McDonald was receiving tribute from other Loop gamblers. He regularly took twenty-five percent of Jeff Hankins's profit at 134 S Clark for "protection." It was understood that without Mike's divvy, there would be raids.

In 1879, Carter Harrison appointed William McGarigle superintendent of police. McGarigle was only twenty-nine, and had had a meteoric rise through the police department since he had come to Chicago from Milwaukee in 1868. His family was middle-class—his father was a postal clerk and general contractor—and he had been educated at one of the better German schools in Milwaukee. He joined the Chicago police force as a patrolman on Webster Street in 1871. Quick-witted and intelligent, he ingratiated himself quickly with Jake Rehm and Elmer Washburn. Rehm promoted him to the detective bureau in 1873 and Washburn made him his private secretary.

As police chief, McGarigle was innovative. He systematized arrest reports, created a workable bookkeeping system and hired the first female police officers. But his personal integrity was another matter. He made the most of his position, going on a "fact-finding mission" to Europe in May of 1881 and taking time out to visit Ireland and kiss the blarney stone. It was widely understood that it was Mike McDonald who was behind Carter Harrison's appointment of McGarigle as police chief.

In addition to his gambling activities, McDonald was a professional bondsman, who supplied tickets out of jail to sixty-six offenders in the lower court and twenty-one under appeal. Political favors in the ethnic wards translated into votes on election day, and buying and selling justice was a big favor. McDonald became a silent partner in the Chicago Democratic machine. With his friend McGarigle installed as sheriff, McDonald could be sure that forfeitures on bonds would not be pressed against him. The sheriff could also help the bondsman by driving the offender out of town, after he had already deposited his money with him.

McGarigle's connection with McDonald did not go unnoticed. The press charged that McGarigle was protecting McDonald's operations and giving police secrets to the gamblers. McGarigle stoutly denied this. "So far as anyone giving away secrets of the department to any gambler is concerned, no matter who the man might be, he would not remain a minute on the police force after I found out," he said.

In 1882, the Cook County Republican party mounted a serious campaign for prohibition. This alarmed McDonald, who saw it as a first step toward a general crackdown on all his enterprises. In order to choke off the Republicans, McDonald talked McGarigle into running for Cook County sheriff. It had already been a bad publicity year for McDonald: on March 7 he had been indicted for keeping a gaming house—along with "Mockingbird" Whalen, "Kid" Leonard, Johnny Dowling, Jeff Hankins, Jim Conlisk, James C. Gore, owner of Chapin & Gore's Restaurant, and Potter Palmer himself. Palmer was charged with maintaining a gambling den next to the Lawler & Smith establishment at 178 N State Street.

Joseph Gary, who was to preside over the notorious Haymarket trial, was the judge. McDonald denied any knowledge of gaming on his premises, despite the fact that he said he did lend money to gamblers from time to time. He was released because of insufficient evidence, although a city detective testified that he had seen thirty people playing roulette or faro in The Store. This was not the first time McDonald was arrested and released.

McDonald's reputation was understandably bad and there was an outcry when the press learned that McGarigle, who was perceived as his man, was running for sheriff. The *Tribune* commented:

> If the Bourbons get control of the county as well as the city offices, McDonald's bread will be buttered on both sides. The

safer the business of buying and selling justice is, the more largely will he go into it. If he can get his creatures in the County Board, and so direct the drawing of juries, he will be able to not only furnish bail-bonds on "short notice and easy terms," but to guarantee an acquittal on any charges at "greatly reduced rates."

Mayor Harrison warned McGarigle that he would probably lose, and that if he did, he could not be reappointed police chief. McGarigle chose to ignore this advice and was easily nominated by a unanimous vote of the Democratic state convention. Despite Harrison's doubts, it was generally believed that McGarigle's chances were excellent.

McDonald advised McGarigle at the outset to disavow any personal connection with him and to attack the gamblers forcefully. But McDonald showed up at the candidate's rallies. In the 16th ward, he strode into the hall with McGarigle trailing behind him. The band played "Hail the Conquering Hero" while McDonald stood at the rostrum. "Gentlemen," he said, "I didn't get up here to make a speech, but to treat you to some beer." McGarigle helped pass out the beer while McDonald distributed victory cigars. The meeting was well attended. McDonald had mailed out form letters signed by the party brokers—Harvey Weeks, John Mattocks and John McAvoy—to urge contributions.

Carter Harrison, despite his apparent qualms, stumped the German and Irish wards on McDonald's behalf and on his own, telling them that the Republicans would take away their drinking privileges. "I think the best plan is, since you are going to let men drink, to let them have the good stuff," Harrison said. "Kentucky, where I was raised, is a great state for making whiskey. Up to the time I was twenty-five years old, I never saw a man who had the delirium tremens. I knew a good many men who drank too much and a good many of them were not often sober. But they were not poisoning themselves, for good old bourbon did not give them the delirium tremens. A fellow would drink, go to bed, sweat it off, get up in the morning, do his work, and yet he was a tolerable good sort of a fellow after all."

when they were out, the deputy got so drunk that he passed out in his seat and McGarigle drove the buggy back to the jail. When Ed McDonald's only son was killed in a freak accident, playing on a fire escape at the county hospital, both McDonald and McGarigle were given time off not only to attend the funeral, which of course was *pro forma*, but to tend to their affairs. They were both sentenced to three years in prison.

While McGarigle languished with McDonald in cell 79 of the county jail, the second stage of the trial, known as the "omnibus" phase, took place. Indictments were returned against Commissioners Adam Ochs, Michael Leyden, Chris Giels, Richard McLaughery, Christian Casselman, Dan Wren, Michael Wasserman, Harry Varnell, John Van Pelt, Richard Oliver, James "Buck" McCarthy, Charles Lynn and the chairman of the County Board, George Klehm. For Leyden, Wren and Van Pelt, it was a second indictment.

The presiding judge in this trial was Egbert Jamieson. The commissioners were arrogant and, with the exception of Van Pelt, corpulent. They were a collection of unsavory hacks, most of whom had businesses which could profit from their county connection. McLaughery was a farmer from the town of Palos, Leyden was a butcher and Wasserman owned a restaurant. Varnell had a racetrack with Ed McDonald. Giels spoke with a heavy German accent and his testimony was irrational and confused. Grinnell sought to demonstrate that a larger conspiracy had existed among the commissioners, and that McGarigle had been appointed "collector" of commissions in that secret meeting in the courthouse janitor's room. Again a series of contractors paraded across the witness stand; they all had immunity in exchange for their testimony, but they were disgraced in the community. They made it clear that boodling had gone on in the county for at least six years. James W. Kee, for instance, a milk distributor, told of charging the county 12 1/2 cents a gallon and paying an annual fee, which rose from $1,000 in 1881 to $2,500 in 1886, directly to Fred Bipper, the meat man, who collected from some contractors.

3

Meanwhile, McGarigle was hoping an appeals court would grant him a new trial. His chances were slim. The Republican mayor, John A. Roche, had timed a crackdown on gambling to coincide with the boodle case. The gamblers' income had dried up and with it any funds that could be channeled toward the defense. McGarigle turned to Grinnell, who was looking for testimony that would implicate Mike McDonald. McGarigle met with Grinnell twice, once at the Union League Club and once at Sheriff Matson's house. Neither of these meetings was productive, and McGarigle asked for another. This was set for Friday, July 22, but Grinnell cancelled because he was tired. The meeting was changed to the following morning at ten, but Grinnell cancelled again. Sheriff Matson, who had accompanied McGarigle to the two abortive meetings, and who had taken every step to insure his prisoner's comfort—meals were catered into McGarigle's cell every afternoon from the elegant Revere House at Hubbard and Clark—felt he had to make up to McGarigle for the disappointment and agreed to let him go to his home in the Lakeview district later in the day.

That afternoon McGarigle received a visit from indicted commissioners Harry Varnell and Buck McCarthy, who were joined by defense attorneys Alexander Sullivan, William Forest and Luther Laflin Mills. The conference lasted two hours. When they left, McGarigle was visited by Dr Leonard St John, 33, a Canadian on the county hospital staff who lived at 539 W Monroe Street. McGarigle had saved him from an embarrassing malpractice suit.

Earlier that afternoon, at three o'clock, St John had gone to the docks to chat with John Irving, the captain of the Canadian schooner *Edward Blake*, which St John owned with his brother Fred. The schooner had just arrived from Michigan with a load of salt for the Philip Armour Company. It was loading grain at the Pacific Elevator at Archer and Ashland avenues before continuing on to Kingston, Ontario. After conferring with St John, Captain Irving told his first mate to make sure that the *Edward Blake* was moored at the north pier near Rush Street, with a tugboat, at eleven o'clock that night.

St John spent an hour with McGarigle at the jail. McGarigle asked the jailer to telephone Sheriff Matson and ask him what time he was coming to pick him up. At 5:30 they learned that Matson was coming at 8:30 that night.

Matson stopped to buy a basket of fruit and he and McGarigle arrived at the McGarigle house at 832 W Grace Street in Lakeview, near the corner of what is now Broadway, but was then called Evanston Avenue. Edward Doepp, a druggist, and a hospital electrician named Oakes were waiting on the front porch of the spacious two-story building which McGarigle had bought at the time that the first boodle indictments came down. Doepp had received a mysterious telephone call a short time before, instrucing him to get out to Lakeview as soon as possible and to bring hospital clerk Edward Dougherty with him because McGarigle had some accounts to settle. Dougherty was not available, so Doepp brought Oakes. When they arrived shortly before McGarigle and Matson, Anna McGarigle seemed surprised to see them. She said her husband was coming home to take his usual Saturday-night bath.

McGarigle arrived, embraced his wife and children, and everyone went into one of the two parlors, adorned with oil paintings and an upright piano. There was a bedroom, a bathroom and a library also on the first floor. Everyone shared Sheriff Matson's basket of fruit; McGarigle went out to the barn with his son George to look at a horse that had been scratched by a nail. Matson's coachman Jacob Spiegel left the sheriff's rig to follow McGarigle out to the barn, for which Spiegel was later arrested as an accomplice. Matson remained chatting with Doepp in the front parlor.

McGarigle came back and went to take his bath. His wife Anna laid out a set of clean underwear for him and then went into the bedroom for a nap.

After half an hour, Matson remarked, "This is getting monotonous," and sent McGarigle's eleven-year-old daughter Bessie to find out what was delaying her father. When she did not return, Matson went to the bedroom and knocked, rousing Anna

McGarigle, who looked into the bathroom and informed the sheriff, with a look of surprise, that her husband was gone. Matson glanced out the open bathroom window: it was only an eight-foot drop to the ground. The house and grounds were searched: a buggy, carriage and phaeton stood in the coach house. Matson rushed to the Webster Avenue police station and within the hour a score of policemen and Mooney-Boland detectives were combing the entire north side. Anna McGarigle suggested her husband might have gone to see his friend E.J. Lehmann, who lived several doors away. But Lehmann was out of town.

What had happened was that around nine o'clock, as McGarigle was arriving home with Matson, Dr St John was completing a house call. McGarigle waited in the bathroom until he saw a red lantern signalling from a carriage in the road. He jumped through the window, retrieved his suitcase from the barn and leaped into the carriage, which sped away. A Clark Street barkeep later told the police that he saw a carriage speeding along, a lathered bay horse being lashed by the driver.

The *Edward Blake* had arrived at the north pier at eight o'clock. Captain Irving was waiting for McGarigle in a cigar store at Illinois and Rush streets. McGarigle was dropped off a block or so away and walked to the store, where he shook hands with Irving, presented him with a pass signed by St John, and the two men proceeded to the boat. Paul Swanson, a Swedish sailor, remembered that the man whom Irving introduced as "Mr Williams" seemed to avoid the light and made a hasty retreat below. The tugboat *Flossie Thielcke*, from the Dunham Line, steered the *Edward Blake* into Lake Michigan.

In Chicago, Inspector Bonfield, who had received his first assignment from McGarigle but had had a falling-out with him, carried out a house-to-saloon dragnet at three in the morning. And the next day, while McGarigle stood on the deck of the *Edward Blake* in a beige Prince Albert suit and a plug hat, crowds of the curious gathered outside the house on Grace Street. The police were offering a $2,500 reward for information about the fugitive. Anna McGarigle and her children worked their way with difficulty to their carriage through a mass of reporters. She did not know where her husband was, she said, although nobody believed her. A reporter asked whether McGarigle would be back in a few days.

"You bet he won't!" his nine-year-old son Eddie said.

His mother smiled and climbed into her carriage. The question was debated: Was he still in Chicago? Was he in Canada? Mexico? Someone suggested that he might have been kidnapped.

The *Edward Blake* moved northward toward Mackinac. The Chicago authorities contacted a revenue cutter off the Milwaukee shoreline and requested that the *Edward Blake* be stopped and searched, but the cutter refused to intervene. The schooner passed through the Straits of Mackinac in a fierce northern gale, went by St Ignace and into Lake Huron. The *George Marsh*, an American schooner loaded with cedar, came too close to the *Edward Blake* in the storm and McGarigle's ship crashed into the starboard quarter of the *George Marsh*. In the confusion, McGarigle leapt on board the *George Marsh*, even though he mistakenly thought it was a police boat hunting him. McGarigle begged the captain, John Freer, to put him ashore and the sympathetic captain agreed.

A yawl was dropped from the side of the *George Marsh* and McGarigle entered it, to be rowed ashore by a sailor. At this point a tugboat, the *Orient*, came steaming up: it had been chartered by a *Record-Herald* reporter who wanted to interview McGarigle. A chase ensued, and McGarigle leapt out of the yawl at Green Island Shoals, as the *Orient* pulled back from the shallow water.

McGarigle ran up the beach, dodged between some railroad cars and headed for the nearest town while a dozen people on the shore cheered; they were used to seeing American fugitives come ashore. For some reason, McGarigle went into a store in Narnia to buy a hat. Word had certainly spread, for the clerk asked him whether he was McGarigle. He left in haste.

That night he slept in a livery stable, and the next day he was cornered by the persistent *Herald* reporter. McGarigle traded an hour interview for one night's room and board at the Western Hotel. He told the reporter that he believed he would have come down with typhoid fever if he had stayed in the jail. It was imperative for him to get out, he said. The reporter waited one day to file his story.

The *Edward Blake* went on to Port Colborne, Ontario, where it was met by Fred St John, Charles Chapin of the *Chicago Tribune* and, later, Captain Freer of the *George Marsh*, who said he dropped McGarigle off at a desolate beach near Point Edward. McGarigle's trunk was unloaded from the *Edward Blake*. "Where did that come from?" Captain Irving said. He said he didn't know anything about his passenger.

In Chicago, McGarigle's many friends celebrated in the bar at the Sherman House and other places, while gloom spread among the Republicans. In 1842 the United States and Canada had signed the Ashburton Treaty, agreeing that forgery and fraud were not extraditable offenses. Cook County officials asked Secretary of State Thomas F. Bayard to take up the matter with the Canadian Government, since it appeared that Canadian citizens had knowingly assisted a fugitive. But the Cleveland Administration was not prepared to break a treaty in order to apprehend a minor Democratic official.

Grinnell did not give up. He tried to have McGarigle arrested on an old libel charge stemming from his time as police superintendent. Detectives attempted to track McGarigle, but it was difficult: he drifted from St Catherine's to Toronto, to Niagara Falls, to Sarnia and finally to Banff in the British Northwest Territory. While he was moving westward, a conductor for the Detroit & Milwaukee Railroad found a bottle which had washed ashore at Grand Haven, Michigan. It was wrapped securely in oil cloth and in it was a handwritten note signed W.J. McGarigle. It was addressed "To my friends in Chicago" and said, "A few more hours and I will be safe through the straits and in Canada. Sheriff Matson, please accept my thanks for the bath, but I have concluded it in British waters. Oh, Ed, I wish you were here with me. Goodbye till we meet."

Banff was Canada's first national park, opened in 1895 after the Canadian Pacific Railroad linked the Northwest Territory to the big cities of the East. McGarigle took up residence in the Sanitarium Hotel under the shadow of Sulphur Mountain. He shared his room with the Rev Charles Williams of the Banff Methodist Church. McGarigle soon involved himself in community affairs, joining the church choir and directing plays for the church theatre company. He started a livery business and invested in the hotel. When he wasn't shooting bear or fishing for speckled trout, McGarigle took the time to canvass on behalf of a friend running for the legislature. Thanks probably to some Chicago electioneering techniques, the friend won. The grateful townspeople wanted to elect McGarigle chief of the fire department, but he settled for a banquet instead.

In January of 1889, a *Tribune* reporter interviewed McGarigle in Banff. They went on a midnight sleigh ride through the forest, for a swim in zero weather in a sulphur pool and had a sumptuous venison dinner with some of McGarigle's friends. When the dishes were cleared, each guest rose and sang a favorite song. McGarigle's was "America the Beautiful," after which he wept.

The Canadian detectives eventually abandoned the search when Grinnell's funds dried up. Dr St John and Captain Irving were indicted in Cook County, but since they were Canadian citizens, their cases were dismissed.

4

In Chicago, the "omnibus" case continued. George Klehm, chairman of the County Board, entered into a secret agreement with Grinnell to tell what he knew in return for immunity. He had been forced into boodling, he said, against his will. Each night the two men met secretly in Lakefront Park and Klehm told Grinnell details of political corruption and intrigue, including the jury-packing scheme in which juror George C. Tait was handpicked by the boodlers. As the trial went on, Klehm signalled Grinnell about the truth of witnesses' statements, tugging at his earlobe or curling his index finger, without looking directly at the prosecutor.

At 8:50 p.m. on August 5, 1887, the great boodle trial came to an end, with the jury voting eleven to one for conviction. Leyden, Van Pelt, Varnell, Wasserman, Ochs and McLaughery received two-year sentences; Lynn, Oliver, Casselman, Giels, McCarthy and Klehm were fined $1,000 apiece. Klehm received no accolades for having turned state's evidence. The *Tribune* called him "the meanest pecksniff of them all." Oyster Joe Mackin, secretary of the Democratic Central Committee, who had earned his sobriquet by inventing the free lunch with a glass of beer, commented from his cell in Joliet that a real man of honor would rather go to the pen than squeal on his pals. Buck McCarthy was not delighted at having gotten off with a fine. He snapped at a reporter who congratulated him, "What in hell do you mean? I shouldn't have been fined a goll-darned cent. I say it's an outrage!" He paid his fine and was later elected alderman. In 1896 he was a delegate to the Republican convention where, during a caucus, another delegate punched him in the eye.

Chris Giels went with Grinnell to the clerk's office to find out what he owed, including court costs. He remarked that he had settled up once before, borrowing the money to pay a substitute when he was drafted into the army.

On the whole, there were handshakes all around and back slaps for the jurors. The exception was John Van Pelt, who seemed put out, commenting to an onlooker, "I can live through two years, and when I get back here I will live long enough to get even with the sons-of-bitches who worked so hard to put me in the hole." He lived until 1902, but there is no record of his having acted against any principals in the trial.

Seven of the commissioners resigned their offices on August 8, 1887, but the other six refused to resign. "This thing of administering the affairs of a great county from the jail cannot be tolerated," Judge Jamieson said; "Prisoners in the county jail cannot and will not legislate for the county." The boodlers did no legislation from jail; they spent a lot of time ordering from the Revere House: their morning newspapers, cigars, and for breakfast, nutmeg melon, mutton chops, porterhouse steak, wine, cheese and cheesecake.

Ed McDonald's motion for a new trial was denied in the appellate court, but his appeal was approved by the supreme court. After eighteen months in jail, Ed was back on the street.

After two years, McGarigle tired of exile in Banff and contacted Joel Longnecker who had replaced Julius Grinnell, now a judge, as state's attorney. He offered to return to Chicago and enter a guilty plea if his sentence would be reduced to a $1,000 fine, the maximum allowable under Illinois law. The two men met in London, Ontario, and returned to Chicago on the morning of May 30, 1889. From the Grand Trunk depot, they drove straight to Judge Shepard's courtroom, interrupting a trial in session.

McGarigle's temples were greying; he was nattily turned out in a dark grey tweed suit. One of the jurors bolted from his seat to shake McGarigle's hand and had to be restrained by a bailiff. In addition to Longnecker, McGarigle's partner E.J. Lehmann was present, as well as his lawyer Francis Adams, who addressed the judge, saying that McGarigle had been in Canada, could not be extradited and could have remained there. "He wanted to come back," Adams said, "and if a new trial is granted upon the conditions that we have talked about, he will plead guilty and submit to a fine."

Judge Shepard said he was inclined to accept the State's Attorney's recommendations. Longnecker withdrew the motion for a new trial, and in the judge's chambers, the order was signed. McGarigle walked out into Clark Street a free man. He took a carriage to his Lakeview home and had a joyful reunion with his family, after which he talked to the reporters who beseiged the house. "I have always loved Chicago," he said; "I could not live long away from it. Chicago is the only place on earth—the only city in which life is worth living. Can you wonder then that I have suffered so much for being compelled to leave it?" Asked whether he intended to return to politics, he responded that he had good friends in the city who would not hesitate to trust him with all the property they owned.

But McGarigle was finished with public life. Like other politicos before and after him, he bought a Clark Street saloon, which he called the Round Bar. He died on April 19, 1917, obscure but contented.

Mike McDonald was too clever and too powerful to be caught in the boodle trap. What apparently destroyed him was his domestic life. His first wife, the mother of his three children, Guy, Cassius and Harold, was Mary Noonan, an impulsive woman who shot and killed a policeman when he invaded her rooms on the third floor of The Store during a raid in 1878. McDonald got Mary off, and, possibly to avoid further similar incidents, built an imposing mansion for his family on Ashland Avenue. Mary was still restless, though, and ran off with a traveling entertainer named Billy Arlington. McDonald followed the couple to San Francisco and Mary, perhaps intimidated by her husband's threats, had a change of heart and returned home. McDonald built a private chapel for her at Ashland Avenue, and arranged for a Belgian priest, Father Moissant, to become her confessor. In 1889 Mary ran off to Paris with Father Moissant.

Mike nursed a broken heart, but recovered when he met a burlesque dancer named Dora Feldman Barkley, who was about twenty years his junior. He was so much taken with her that he paid her retired baseball-player husband, Sam Barkley, $30,000 to agree to a divorce. Sam was reportedly distraught over losing Dora, but managed to invest the money in a Clark Street saloon, the Old Rag Shop, a few doors down from McGarigle's Round Bar. In 1898 McDonald divorced Mary Noonan, converted to Judaism, and married Dora, establishing her in a new mansion on Drexel Boulevard at 45th Street. The marriage lasted nine years, although very early on, Dora fell in love with Webster Guerin, a youth still in high school, who lived at 655 W Harrison Street. Their liaison lasted through the marriage, although Webster had a roving eye. Dora supplied him with money and set him up as a commercial artist. When on February 21, 1907, she discovered that he had been dallying with another, Dora went to his office in Suite 107 of the Omaha Building at Van Buren and LaSalle, and shot him dead.

McDonald was crushed at her duplicity and his heart, some say, was broken for the second and last time. He took to his bed, lingering until early August. Mary Noonan, who had returned from Paris to run a boardinghouse in Chicago, was at his bedside, along with his brother Ed. McDonald had supported Mary financially even after the divorce. Dora was not present in the room because she was confined in the Laura S. Buck Sanitarium at 5642 W Washington Boulevard, since her lawyers were claiming temporary insanity.

McDonald proclaimed Mary his true wife. But in his will disposing of his two-million-dollar estate, Mary was left nothing. The executors were instructed to pay for Dora's defense and to give both her and the three sons a daily allowance to live on. The bulk of the money went to charity. He died on August 9, 1907, at the age of sixty-six.

Dora pleaded temporary insanity and was acquitted.

Within eighteen months, Dora and the children petitioned the court in vain for relief from the will. There was in fact not enough money for them to erect a proper monument at McDonald's grave. On January 30, 1909, Dora, Guy, Cassius and Harold McDonald placed a signed announcement in the personal column of an afternoon newspaper:

> The undersigned requested the executors to erect a monument to the memory of Michael C. McDonald and wish it understood by his friends that through no fault of their own it has not been done.

On that sad note ended the Great Boodle Scandal. It was not without consequences. It demonstrated above everything the clear need for civil service reform. All the corrupt commissioners had been appointed with no real aptitude for their job and most had obvious conflicts of interest; they were controlled by Mike McDonald. The festering situation had finally erupted. It was certainly one of the factors contributing to the passage of the first major civil service law in 1895—another nail in the coffin of the Gilded Age.

IV

1896: The Summer of Silver and Gold

1

In May of 1896, Sarah Bernhardt came to Chicago to star for four splendid days in *Izeyl* at the Columbia Theatre and to recreate her greatest roles: *Gismonda*, *Phédre* and *Camille*. Bernhardt had not been in Chicago since 1876; she expressed wonder at the changes she perceived—the new Masonic Temple, Public Library and Art Institute—and disappointment that most of the Columbian Exposition buildings were gone. She occupied a private suite at the Auditorium Hotel; the rest of her cast had to find cheaper accommodations because the tour promoters refused to pay for their keep.

The theatre was packed, although May marked the beginning of the summer season when prosperous Midwesterners departed for Green Lake, Wisconsin; Hot Springs, Arkansas; Colorado Springs and the elegant Grand Hotel at Mackinac Island in Michigan, where yachts from Chicago filled the harbor, and the audience for entertainment in the casino often included Vice-President Adlai Stevenson. For those who liked sport, there was golf and bicycling, both new on the American scene. When betting was outlawed at Washington Park, a golf course was constructed there, tended by a horse-pulled mowing machine and one hundred sheep.

Cycling was a sport with more mass appeal. It was in 1894, when the coaster brake was added to John Kemp Starley's design of the safety bicycle with two wheels of equal size, that cycling became a craze. Before that, in the 1870s, only a few courageous souls could be seen maneuvering their shaky six-foot "front-wheelers" over the rough Chicago streets, where the slightest rut could cause a serious overturn. In 1896 a bike cost $100, but one could frequently be bought with twenty dollars down, three references and a one-dollar weekly payment. At first, the best machines were built by Pope Manufacturing and A.G. Spaulding companies. But in 1895, when Ignaz Schwinn and meat packer Adolph Arnold opened their factory at Lake and Peoria streets, Chicago became a cycling capital: there were 6,000 workers, 600 dealers and forty-eight cycling clubs with 10,000 members. The first bicycle bank robbery was reported on May 14, 1896, at Buffalo, Illinois, a small town ten miles from Springfield. Two men rode up, dismounted and leaned their machines against a hitching post. They walked into the bank, demanded $10,000 from the tellers, mounted their bikes and rode away, never to be seen again.

But it was not only bank robbers who profited from the bicycle. Women could share the sport with men, wear new comfortable fashions like bloomers, and achieve a measure of independence. Families rode to spend Sunday in the park carrying in hammocks suspended from handlebars. Real estate agents, butchers, messengers and anyone who needed to be mobile used the bicycle to transact business.[6]

2

On a less happy note, May of 1896 was the month in which the serial killer Herman Webster Mudgett, who used the alias H.H. Holmes, was hanged at the Moyamensing Prison in Philadelphia. He was accompanied to the gallows by two priests, a lawyer and Alexander Richardson, the assistant superintendent of the prison. He died denying guilt, and was left hanging for a full half hour because the officials wanted to be sure that he was really dead.

Holmes, or Mudgett, should certainly rank above classic murderers like Dr Crippen and Ted Bundy—to say nothing of Jack the Ripper. In fact, legend has had it that on the gallows,

Holmes began to confess that he was Jack the Ripper. But much is not known about the man and much that is known is open to question because the journalistic practices of Holmes's day were frequently impressionistic rather than accurate. We know that Holmes was born into a respectable family in Gilmanton, New Hampshire, but the date is variously given as 1858 and 1860. It seems to be agreed that in 1878 he married Clara Lovering. It is believed that he then taught school in Clinton County, New York, and in 1882 went back to school himself in Burlington, Vermont, transferring a year later to study medicine at the University of Michigan in Ann Arbor. He apparently took his wife, Clara, with him to Ann Arbor and it has been said that she worked as a seamstress to finance his education; it is also said that he paid his tuition by using a corpse, stolen from the school dissecting room, to swindle an insurance company.

Holmes's primary interest in medical school was in techniques of dissection and embalming. Despite his fascination with these subjects, he abandoned his studies, and apparently also his wife, in 1884, sending Clara back to Gilmanton, with or without an infant son who may or may not have existed. One reporter wrote that Holmes confessed that he had killed and dissected this infant, but since Clara never mentioned this, we can probably discount it. It was certainly something that would have caught her attention.

In 1886 Holmes appeared in Chicago, working in a drugstore in Englewood on the south side, owned by Mrs E.S. Holden, a widow. In 1887 Mrs Holden disappeared. Holmes took over the drugstore, saying that he had bought it from the widow who had, in his words, "gone West" without leaving a forwarding address.

In 1887 he filed for a divorce from Clara, but was unsuccessful; the case dragged on until 1891, when it was dismissed because he did not appear in court. This did not prevent him from marrying, on January 28, 1887, Myrtle Belknap, whose father John was a prosperous Wilmette merchant. This marriage definitely produced offspring, a daughter, but it was hardly a success in any other way. Myrtle remained in Wilmette, while Holmes was operating the drugstore in Englewood and doing various other things in other places so that he was rarely at home. As if that were not bad enough, John Belknap discovered that Holmes had tried to cheat him out of some property by forging his name to deeds. It has been said that Belknap also realized, in retrospect after the forgery discovery, that Holmes had tried to kill him by giving him poison in a prescription. Holmes always maintained that he had earned a medical degree at Michigan, speaking later of a "diploma" which had brought him "a good theoretical knowledge of medicine, but no practical knowledge of life and/or business." It is not clear whether Belknap reported the forgery and the attempted murder, if any, to the police—it seems unlikely that he did—but Myrtle severed the relationship in 1889.

Holmes may have been too busy to care about this. He was still operating Mrs Holden's drugstore, where he had expanded his business to include jewelry, probably stolen, and he went at one point to Terre Haute, Indiana, where he was involved in an insurance swindle with a watery-eyed sot named Benjamin Pitezel, an ideal accomplice, a man who would do anything for a pint of gin. Pitezel went to jail as a result of this felony, but Holmes remained untouched. He was busy making plans for what was to be known as his castle, an immense house which he intended to erect across the street from the drugstore, on a vacant lot at 701 W 63rd street.

In 1890 he became a partner in the ABC Copier Company in the Monon Block on South Dearborn street. The copier had been invented by Frederick George Nind, who had originally been in partnership with Thomas B. Bryan, but Bryan had sold his interest to Holmes. Nind returned one day from a business trip to be told by Wharton Plummer, Holmes's lawyer, that the business was failing, but that the good news was that a group in Pittsburgh had agreed to assume the debts and to pay $25,000 in addition. Nind signed away his share and later testified that "the scheme placed Plummer, who was really representing Holmes, in full possession of the business. I agreed to the arrangement and as a matter of fact did not receive a cent."

Holmes did run the business into the ground after Nind left, supposedly cheating out-of-state clients who contracted to have blueprints reproduced. He found time too to sell worthless patent medicines, setting up the Silver Ash Institute, which had a sure-fire cure for alcoholism. Worthless patents were a specialty of Holmes's. While he was building his castle, he notified the local gas company that he had invented a process that would convert ordinary tap water into natural gas. He showed the company representative a contraption that looked like a washtub on stilts with a gas meter and an amazing array of pipes, pulleys and wires protruding from all sides of it. When Holmes turned the thing on, water churned through it, and there was a distinct smell of gas.

The company man was convinced by this demonstration, and Holmes was offered $25,000 for his patent. He did not collect, because when workers came to remove the invention several weeks later, it was discovered that Holmes had tapped into a natural gas main under the house. It was reported later by the press that Holmes managed to sell his gas-making device to an unsuspecting Canadian businessman for $2,000. There was also a report that Holmes had found water under his house as well; he bottled this, calling it pure artesian well water and sold it to the citizens of Englewood.

The drugstore, unlike many of Holmes's enterprises, was a going concern. In 1890 Holmes hired Ned Connor of Davenport, Iowa, as a watchmaker and jeweler, at a salary of twelve dollars a week. Connor, his wife Julia and his little daughter Pearl moved into an apartment above the store. Julia was ambitious and difficult, it was said; she threw jealous tantrums if Ned seemed to be too attentive to female customers. Holmes sensed an affinity with her and fired his bookkeeper to hire her. Then he transferred the title of the drugstore to Connor as a protection against creditors. He suggested to Connor that he, Holmes, take out an insurance policy on the lives of Julia and Pearl, but Connor balked at this. Julia had several times threatened suicide and Ned had no desire to provide her with encouragement, although he certainly did not enjoy living with her.

She was deeply impressed with Holmes and harassed her husband in nightly tirades, crying, "Why can't you be more like Dr Holmes? What kind of man did I marry?" Whether Connor suspected that Julia had become Holmes's mistress or whether he simply tired of her tantrums, he left her and went to work for a jeweler downtown.

Julia moved with her daughter into one of Holmes's buildings at 7403 N Honore Street. With Connor gone, Holmes took out the policy on their lives. There is no question that Julia knowingly assisted Holmes in his shady dealings with insurance companies and private speculators. When Holmes incorporated his jewelry business on August 15, 1890, Julia was listed as director, along with her friend Kate Durkee and Holmes's insurance agent C.W. Arnold.

Holmes mortgaged the drugstore because he needed the money for his castle.

Much has been written about the Englewood Castle. The *Tribune* for November 25, 1894, described it as well as anyone has:

> In America's wide domain there is not a house like unto that one, and there probably will never be. Its chimney sticks out where chimneys never stuck out before. Its staircases do not end anywhere in particular. It has winding passages that bring the rash intruder back to where he started from, and altogether it's a very mysterious building.

The castle, which overshadowed every other building on the block, was three stories high, apart from the stone basement, and measured 162 feet long by fifty feet wide. It was brick, with wooden bay windows—covered, oddly, with sheet iron—and ornamental parapets above them. There were over sixty rooms in the building, thirty-five on the second floor alone, and fifty-one doors cut into walls in every imaginable place. Holmes acted as his own architect and supervised various construction crews, which were hired and fired as if at whim. More probably, he did not want anyone to comprehend the plans for the place. There were trapdoors, hidden staircases, secret passages, rooms without windows but with chutes leading to the basement cut into the walls, and a staircase which, far from ending nowhere in particular, as the

Tribune said, opened on a thirty-foot drop over the alley behind the house.

When the castle was completed in the spring of 1891, Holmes said that he planned to rent rooms to visitors to the Columbian Exposition. The police could later find no evidence that Holmes had done away with any of these tourists, although some of them had found their way to the castle. What he did do was advertise for stenographers, and some of these unfortunate women met a dreadful fate at his hands.

He rented out stores on the ground floor. These lessees seem to have remained physically unscathed, but two of them at least had an unnerving experience at Holmes's hands. C.H. Gove and Delos Matteson undertook to pay Holmes $300 a month for a small store facing 63rd Street. The men were short of cash, so Holmes accepted a mortgage on their furniture, $200 toward the first month's rent and promissory notes for a half-month's rent for the balance of the year. After they spent $100 of their own money on repairs to the shop, Holmes served a five-day notice on them because the notes they had signed had been *judgment* and not promissory notes. They were evicted and Holmes kept their money and their furniture.

There was another furniture story. Holmes furnished his castle with the finest furnishings from the Tobey Company and the French-Potter Crockery firm, both of which accepted written guarantees signed by H.S. Campbell, whom Holmes said was his financial backer. There was no H.S. Campbell; Holmes's lawyer, Wharton Plummer, signed that name on the guarantees. There was of course no payment. The story goes that the companies sent agents to repossess the merchandise, but found the place empty. Holmes had moved all the furniture into a spare room, bricked it up and covered the partition with wallpaper. Someone tipped off the companies, whose people broke down the wall and recovered their property. They did not press charges.

In 1893, Minnie Williams, a twenty-one-year-old blonde woman who aspired to be an elocutionist, met Holmes at a gathering following one of her recitals. Holmes told her his name was Harry

Gordon, and that he was a wealthy inventor. Minnie Williams was the heir to some prime real estate in Fort Worth, Texas, worth $60,000, and a $15,000 farm, both owned by her uncle, C.W. Black of Jackson, Mississippi, who had raised Minnie and her sister Nannie after their father was killed in a train crash.

Holmes became engaged to Minnie and persuaded Nannie to leave her job as a teacher at the Midlothian Academy in Texas to come to Chicago for the wedding. This did not sit well with Julia Connor who, as we have seen, had a jealous and contentious disposition. Both she and her daughter Pearl disappeared. When Ned Connor inquired about them, Holmes told him that they had gone to Michigan. Later in his confession Holmes said that Julia had died from a bungled abortion he performed on her, and that he had poisoned Pearl.

In April of 1893, the Fort Worth property was deeded to Benton T. Lyman, a name used by Ben Pitezel. The deed, filed in the Fort Worth county clerk's office, was notarized by Holmes. In October, Minnie's brother Baldwin Williams was killed in a mining accident in Leadville, Colorado, an "accident" which Holmes had supposedly arranged. Minnie assigned Baldwin's $1,050 life-insurance benefit to Holmes at the castle address. When the insurance company asked questions, Holmes and Minnie set out for Denver to get the matter settled. Nannie had been murdered in June of 1893. Holmes said later that Minnie had hit her sister over the head with a chair in a fit of jealous rage and that he had protected Minnie by dropping Nannie's body into Lake Michigan in the dead of night. Some people in Englewood believed this.

Holmes and Minnie were accompanied to Colorado by another young woman, Georgianna Yoke, who had left Franklin, Indiana, with a tarnished reputation, to work in the Siegel-Cooper department store. When she applied for a job at the castle, Holmes told her he was Henry Howard, the nephew of Henry Mansfield Howard of Denver and that Minnie was his cousin. On January 17, 1894, Holmes married Georgianna Yoke at the Vendome Hotel in Denver, with Minnie as witness. Possibly Minnie thought that Georgianna's inheritance of $3,000 was the motivation for the marriage and that the unfortunate girl would join Nannie and Baldwin as a contributor to Holmes's well-being. In any case the honeymoon party traveled to Fort Worth, where Holmes claimed Minnie's property, and engineered a horse swindle, which was later to help lead to his downfall. He bought carloads of horses with bogus notes which he signed with the alias O.C. Pratt. The horses were sent to St Louis and sold.

Since Minnie had now served her purposes, Holmes returned with her to Illinois and disposed of her, either incinerating her in a stove or dissolving her body in acid.

Another victim was a young woman named Emmeline Cigrand, who was hired as a stenographer. She had worked with alcoholics at the Keeley Institute in Dwight, Illinois, at the same time that Ben Pitezel was drying out there, and therefore her experience made her a good employee for Holmes's bogus Silver Ash Institute. Emmeline apparently expressed a desire to return to her home in Anderson, Indiana; she was engaged to marry a man named Robert Phelps. Neither Phelps nor Miss Cigrand were seen anywhere after Phelps dropped in to see her at the castle. Holmes wrote to her parents that she had run off to marry Phelps. He even had wedding announcements printed, but without any address. He later confessed to the murder of both young people, including a description of the torture of Phelps in a "stretching" experiment.

Another young person who was tortured and murdered was Emily Van Tassel of 641 Robey Street. She was only seventeen years old, and worked in a candy store on the first floor of the castle. Holmes did his stretching experiments on her too.

In July of 1894, Holmes was arrested for selling mortgaged properties; the complaint was filed by the Merrill Drug Company. Holmes was bailed out by Georgianna Yoke, but while he was in jail waiting for her, he struck up a conversation with Marion Hedgepath, who was serving a twenty-five-year sentence for train robbery. Holmes had a plan to cheat the Fidelity Mutual Insurance Company of Philadelphia out of $10,000 by taking out a policy on Ben Pitezel. Holmes promised Hedgepath a $500 commission in return for the name of a lawyer who could be trusted.

Hedgepath suggested he talk to Colonel Jeptha Howe, the brother of Hedgepath's public defender. Howe found the scheme both brilliant and foolproof.

Pitezel rented a store at 1316 Callowhill street in Philadelphia, and hung out a shingle: "Patents Bought and Sold. B.F. Perry." A policy was taken out on his life. Pitezel and his wife Carrie were told that the plan called for Pitezel to drink a potion that would render him unconscious; a doctor would be called to examine him. Holmes would doctor Pitezel's face so that it would look as though he had been severely burned. When the doctor left to call an ambulance, a corpse would be substituted for Pitezel and the insurance company would be notified that the insured man had died of burns.

The arranged "accident" took place on the evening of September 4, 1894, when neighbors heard a loud explosion. The next morning a carpenter named Eugene Smith went to see "B.F. Perry" about a patent. The door was locked, and Smith became suspicious and summoned a policeman. Together they broke into the store and found a severely burned dead man lying face down next to a broken bottle of benzine, a pipe and several matches. The death was considered an accident, and the body was held in the morgue for eleven days when, no one claiming it, it was committed to potter's field, after which Jeptha Howe filed an insurance claim, explaining, with Carrie Pitezel's support, that B.F. Perry was really Ben Pitezel.

Carrie Pitezel thought that Ben was hiding in New York; she had no idea that he had actually been the corpse in the shop. The insurance company paid the claim and the funds were distributed to everyone except Marion Hedgepath. This oversight, which was typical of Holmes's instinct to cheat people, cost Holmes dear. Hedgepath brooded over this wrong for a while and then told Major Lawrence Harrigan of the St Louis police department about the plot. Harrigan notified W.E. Gary, a Fidelity Mutual claims investigator who, in turn, hired the Pinkerton Agency which put detective Frank P. Geyer on the case. Geyer immediately began an investigation.

Holmes meanwhile was on the road with Georgianna Yoke and Carrie Pitezel and her three children, Howard, Nellie and Alice. They were seen in Cincinnati and then on October 1 in Indianapolis. Carrie Pitezel was sent off to the East. Holmes apparently murdered Howard Pitezel in an isolated farmhouse in Irvington, Indiana. From Indiana Holmes went to Detroit, where the little girls wrote poignant letters to their mother. By this time, it appears that Holmes knew about Geyer's investigation. He crossed the border into Canada, and rented a frame house in Toronto at 16 St Vincent Street. There, telling the children he was playing a game of hide-and-seek, he locked them in a large trunk, ran a gas pipe into the trunk, and asphyxiated them. He borrowed a shovel from a neighbor, saying that he wanted to bury a sack of potatoes, and buried the trunk in the basement floor.

In Philadelphia, Benjamin Pitezel's body was exhumed and identified.

Holmes and Yoke went to Boston; from there Holmes made a side-trip to Tilton, New Hampshire, to visit his wife Clara. He told her he had been seriously injured in a railway accident on the Lehigh Valley Road, had lain for weeks in a hospital on the point of death, and with total amnesia. He had been nursed back to health by a Good Samaritan named Georgianna Yoke, and had married her because he had forgotten about Clara. Now his memory had returned, and he wanted to reconcile with Clara and to come back to her the following April. Clara, who later said that his eyes had hypnotic power, expressed sympathy for all his troubles and agreed to the reconciliation. Before he left New Hampshire, Holmes borrowed $300 from his brother, Arthur Mudgett.

Holmes returned to Boston and on November 17 he was arrested for the horse swindle he had carried out in Fort Worth. He did not relish the idea of being extradited to Texas where horse-stealing could lead to a lynching, so he confessed to the insurance fraud. On the train back to Philadelphia, Holmes offered his guard $500 if he would agree to be hypnotized. The guard refused.

Carrie Pitezel and Colonel Howe were arrested.

Detective Geyer made it a personal crusade to sift through all the lies Holmes was telling and had told, to find clues to the whereabouts of the Williams girls and the Pitezel children. Holmes's story was that Minnie Williams had taken the children with her to London, where she planned to open a massage parlor. Geyer traveled across the Midwest, interviewing people in Cincinnati, Minneapolis, Detroit and Chicago. On June 3, 1895, Holmes pleaded guilty to a charge of fraud. A month later, the search of the castle began. The whole thing evolved into a nightmare.

The guest rooms of the castle were on the third floor. There were sliding walls, and in the south front room, a sort of vault, large enough for one person standing up. It was said that a noxious acid, usually benzine and oil, was spread on the floor or placed in a bowl inside the vault. When the doors were closed, the acid would absorb the oxygen and the victim would slowly choke to death. There were also apertures in the walls for a gas pipe to be fitted through. Police found a single footprint on the door, probably from a woman's shoe, which indicated that someone had tried to kick her way out. But this was hopeless, because the walls and doors were made of iron. Bodies were taken to the basement through a secret passage or perhaps down a chute. Here they were dissected, placed in a vat of quicklime or burned in the kiln.

On July 15, Detective Geyer found the decomposed bodies of Alice and Nellie Pitezel in a trunk in the cellar of the house on St Vincent Street in Toronto. Howard Pitezel's remains were not found until August 27.

Crews from the city construction department began excavation of the cellar on July 20. The floor was damp and uneven and the smell of gas hung low in the air. The men tore away the masonry on the alley wall, discovering a large tank that emitted noxious fumes. One of the laborers struck a match, and the tank exploded, burying them in piles of rubbish, but fortunately no one was seriously hurt. The tank, cedar and zinc-lined, was fourteen feet long.

Six feet below the surface of the cellar floor, they came upon the bones of a child. Inside a stove they found Minnie Williams's watch, some buttons from her dress and several charred tintypes. Under the stairwell leading to the basement, a policeman found a ball of woman's hair wrapped in a cloth.

Ned Connor was brought to the castle. As the police led him through the dank basement, he stopped suddenly and pointed to an oil-stained garment hanging from a hook. He said it belonged to his wife Julia. Connor himself, who, like Georgianna Yoke and Carrie Pitezel, miraculously survived encounters with Holmes, remarried and was able to lead a normal life, despite the loss of his child Pearl.

On August 19, the Englewood Castle went up in flames. Three explosions rocked the neighborhood shortly after midnight and minutes later the fire started. Within half an hour the roof had caved in. A gallon can of gasoline was found in the rubble. Various theories were put forward about the motivations for what was undoubtedly arson: the police thought it was the work of safecrackers; others thought that associates of Holmes may have feared that a police search of the upper floors would reveal their connection with him. Robert L. Corbitt, a neighbor, published a book about his search of the castle; he said he had found letters postmarked London and theorized that Minnie may well have been living there. Possibly the fire was the work of outraged citizenry. But whatever the reason, that was the end of the Englewood Castle.

The trial began in Philadelphia on October 28, 1895, before Judge Michael Arnold. Among the witnesses was Georgianna Yoke, who testified that she had married Holmes on January 17, 1894, and that she had believed he was divorced. Holmes evinced some emotion while she was on the stand; it appeared that he was fond of her.

The jury retired on November 2. For some reason, they deliberated for a few hours before they returned a unanimous guilty verdict. On November 30, Holmes received the death sentence.

The dreadful revelations connected with this case naturally caused a tremendous public response. Holmes himself provided a confession, and recanted the next day—the confession was a horrifying litany of torture and murder. He credited himself, if it can be put that way, with the murder of one man of whom no trace was found. This was a "Mr Warner," whose first name has never been given, who was apparently the inventor of a glass-bending process. Holmes had opened an office as the registered agent of the Warner Glass Bending Company and had sought outside investors in the patent. Holmes said that he had disposed of Mr Warner:

> It was so arranged that in less than a minute after turning on a jet of crude oil atomized with steam, the entire kiln would be filled with a colorless flame, so intensely hot, iron would be melted therein. It was also this kiln that I induced Mr Warner to go with me, under pretense of wishing certain minute explanations of the process, and then stepping outside, as he believed to get some tools. I closed the door and turned both the oil and steam to their full extent. In a short time not even the bones of my victim remained.

All in all, Holmes confessed to the murders of twenty-eight people. Of these, ten were certainly murdered by Holmes. Julia Connor, he said, died of a bungled abortion, and Benjamin Pitezel was burned to death. Holmes said he poisoned Pearl Connor, Emily Van Tassel and Minnie Williams. He said he suffocated Emmeline Cigrand, Nannie Williams and the Pitezel children, Howard, Nellie and Alice.

But it should be noted that some people claimed as victims by Holmes were found by the police to be alive and well. There is a question about another claimed victim, Robert Phelps, the fiancé of Emmeline Cigrand. Phelps may never have existed. Holmes said he tortured and suffocated him. Then there was the mysterious Mr Warner, who was allegedly burned alive, and Minnie's brother Baldwin, who was killed in Leadville, Colorado, supposedly on Holmes's instructions.

There were others in Holmes's confession. He said he had also poisoned a Dr Robert Leacock of New Baltimore, Michigan, an Anna Betts and a Gertrude Connor; that he had suffocated a castle maid named Lizzie; a castle tenant named Sarah Cook from Hamilton, Ontario and her unborn child; a Mary Harracamp, also from Hamilton, and an Omaha woman named Kate who, like Lizzie, had no last name. Then there were three men who were allegedly killed by blows to the head: Charles Cole, a castle tenant; a Dr Russell—no first name—and a Mr Rodgers of Morgantown, Pennsylvania, who received his blow to the head during a fishing trip. A Robert Latimer, whom Holmes said had attempted to blackmail him, had been imprisoned in the castle and starved to death.

Finally, there were three people whose names Holmes said he did not know. One was a tenant in the castle and one was a banker from Wisconsin. Both of these had been killed by chloroform. The last was killed at 74th and Honore streets. The press feasted on all these gruesome details. People undoubtedly realized in retrospect that they had had narrow escapes in encounters with the fiend of 63rd Street. One of these was Jonathan Belknap, the great-uncle of Myrtle Belknap whom Holmes had "married" in Wilmette. It will be remembered that Holmes had forged the signature of Myrtle's father John to some deeds and that John later realized that Holmes had tried to poison him. When the frightful details came out, Jonathan Belknap said that he had spent a night in the castle in 1891 and that he now realized that Holmes had probably tried to kill him too. To avoid prosecution, Holmes had told Belknap that he would make restitution in a few days and asked the older man to come for dinner and spend the night. Belknap said that he agreed and that after dinner, Holmes led him through a labyrinth of dark passages and winding stairways to a windowless room on the third floor. "Good night, Mr Belknap," Holmes allegedly said, and went out, closing the only door to the room behind him. Belknap said he was apprehensive and could not sleep. He kept the gaslight on, and locked the door. After a few hours, the light flickered and went out, but gas was still coming through the jet.

Fortunately Belknap was still awake and relit the gas with a match, but he wondered why the light had gone out, since the room was airless; it had no window and no sudden gust of wind could have extinguished it.

About an hour later, he heard someone in the hall; he opened the door and found Patrick Quinlan, the janitor, standing there. Quinlan mumbled something and walked away.

Belknap said that he had now concluded that the gas jet in his room was controlled from a pipe at the end of the hall, and that Holmes or Quinlan had opened the pipe sometime during the night, and blown air into it to extinguish the flame in Belknap's room. Quinlan, he decided, had come into the hall to enter his room and remove his body.

The reader may make of this story what he will.

Two Catholic priests visited Holmes in his cell before the execution. He accepted communion and asked their blessing, but refused to repent. "I wish to state here," he was quoted as saying, "so that there can be no chance of misunderstanding hereafter, that I am not guilty of taking the lives of the Pitezel children or their father Benjamin F. Pitezel, of whose death I was convicted, and for which I am to hang today."

There were those who swore that before the noose choked off his words, Holmes cried out, "I am Jack—." This is another hypothesis to add to Jack the Ripper lore, but it seems doubtful that even Holmes could have been so busy in London in a decidedly non–jet age, and and even more doubtful, if that is possible, that he would have engaged in any activity that did not bring him in a few dollars. On the other hand, he was clearly a sadist.

The community was traumatized by him. Another legend associated with the execution says that a lightning bolt ripped from the sky at the second that the rope snapped Holmes's neck. And was it, people asked, only a coincidence that the jury foreman, Linford Biles, was electrocuted by a live wire on his roof several weeks after the hanging? Or that Emmeline Cigrand's father died in a gas explosion? Or that a fire in the Fidelity Mutual Insurance offices nearly ruined the company? And what about William A. Shoemaker, Holmes's lawyer, who was later disbarred? And the Catholic priest who gave Holmes communion in his cell was found robbed and murdered in his churchyard.

It was thought that guided by some unearthly power, Holmes's terrible capacity to pervert and destroy extended beyond the grave. Patrick Quinlan, the faithful janitor and manservant who constructed a number of the tunnels and secret passageways inside the evil castle, ingested strychnine and died at his home in Portland, Michigan, on March 6, 1914. From his deathbed Quinlan told his friends and neighbors that he could no longer sleep at night and wished for death.

3

At the end of July, on the brink of a killer heat wave, Nellie English and her brother Joseph went for a walk down Van Buren Street. Nellie was a twenty-year-old operator at the Chicago Telephone Company; Joseph tended bar at Houlihan's on Root street. At Clark and Van Buren streets, in front of George Baker's drugstore, the couple encountered William Hawkins, who had been a fiancé of Nellie's in Galesburg, her hometown. Words were exchanged and as Hawkins turned to leave, Joseph English drew a 32-calibre pistol and shot him twice, in the face and the hip. As Hawkins slumped to the sidewalk, English handed the gun to his sister, who pumped two more shots into her fallen swain. A bystander wrested the pistol from her and she and her brother were escorted to the Harrison Street lockup. Hawkins was taken first into the drugstore, and then to St Luke's Hospital, where he explained to the press that Nellie was no better than she should be, and so he had broken off their engagement.

In the lockup, Nellie and Joseph said that Hawkins was a cad who had forced Nellie to leave home because of her damaged reputation. For some reason the police brought the English couple to Hawkins's bedside, where Hawkins's brother Frank attempted to attack English, and several nurses rushed to protect Hawkins. Brother and sister were taken back to Harrison Street.

On August 3, Nellie and Joseph were released on $10,000 bond. Hawkins eventually recovered. "I know now," Nellie observed, referring to the late serial killer, "that Holmes was a better man than Hawkins."

August 3 saw the beginning of a week-long heat wave: the wooden tenements, the brick office buildings, the streets, the stables, were infernos. On August 5, twenty-nine cases of heat prostration were reported. It must be remembered that people remained fully clothed: women in petticoats and skirts that covered the ankle, men in long-sleeved shirts and suits. Sixty horses collapsed on August 3; normally only ten to twenty horses died on the city's streets in the summer. The Union Rendering Company, which had a contract for horse carcass removal, was swamped with calls; there were twelve-hour delays in their arrival. The city offered ten dollars a horse to anyone who would remove them from the streets, where they were causing traffic jams.

The delays in horse removal created an impossible situation at the county hospital, where a horse carcass rotted in the sun just below the patients' windows. City temperatures reached ninety-eight that day, but the windows at the hospital had to be kept closed because of the awful stench.

There were the usual share of horse accidents too. At the corner of Madison and Dearborn one afternoon, a dray, owned by the A.C. McClurg Company and driven by Albert Thorsen, negotiated through the traffic. A Madison streetcar passed alongside the wagon. It was at that moment that Thorsen noticed that a four-foot manhole in the cobblestone street was missing its cover. Thorsen foolishly tried to squeeze the wagon between the open manhole and the streetcar. He might have made it, but the grip car jarred the wagon and shoved the horse.

Thorsen shouted in alarm. Ed Jansen, a city employee working inside the manhole, heard the commotion and prudently moved back along the tunnel. The horse tried to leap across the hole: his forelegs cleared it, but his rear did not; it fell in. The terrified animal, half in and half out, tried desperately to extricate himself: his hind hooves beat a lively rhythm on some underground pipes containing Chicago Telephone Company wire.

A crowd formed and everyone offered a solution. The police pushed the bystanders back, but they regrouped around the trapped horse, blocking the streetcars. An iron pipe, fourteen feet long and three inches wide, was passed under the horse's shoulders.

Twenty-five men tried to pull him out, but the pipe bent into a U, and the animal could not be budged. Finally Hook and Ladder Truck No 6 arrived. The firemen strapped a twelve foot piece of timber to their ladder to prevent it from snapping in half. After a couple of tries in which a great many men assisted, the horse was lifted from the manhole, dazed and scratched, but otherwise well. Half a block away Ed Jansen emerged from another manhole with the help of fellow workers.

Tenement dwellers were most affected by that terrible summer weather. Their rickety shacks absorbed the heat, and they were forced to seek relief in the streets. On August 9, twenty-two people died of heat prostration. One man, driven mad by the heat, slashed his throat with a razor. In the Jewish district on the west side, people passed the nights in the gutters, lying on wooden paving blocks. Exhausted mothers watched over their young from tenement doorways. From Canal Street west to Halsted, the sidewalks were a sea of sweating misery. Family bedding was spread out amid the garbage. In some cases the family dog stood guard over sleeping children.

On Barber Street, east of Clinton, a mother set up a bed for her infant, using her body as a shield against the drunks who stumbled out from the local tavern. Children made temporary beds for themselves on top of peanut vendor pushcarts, while their parents quarrelled with their neighbors in ten different languages over scarce sidewalk space.

That was Chicago's nasty side. The slums were filled with sickness, starvation and crime. Women's long skirts dragged across the ground, picking up dirt and germs, transmitting them to their young. Infant mortality was high. The saloon around the corner provided a quick escape from the worries of the day. There was little organized civic welfare. Five days a week, dedicated women from neighborhood missions walked through the slums, visiting the sick and indigent, providing food, a sympathetic ear, and whatever advice they could give. On Saturday these Good Samaritans did their paperwork, and on Sunday they went to church. They themselves were frail and undernourished; their lunch was tea and a roll served on a rough board covered with newspaper in a neighborhood bakery. It was often difficult for them to communicate with the parents of large families, huddled in cellars, who spoke no English. On Sebor Street, where newly arrived Italian immigrants lived, a missionary visited a widow who supported her five children in her dingy hovel by washing rags. The visitor inspected the hands of the youngest child and expressed the hope that his hands would be clean when he came to church on Sunday.

In 1888 Jane Addams founded her famous settlement house, fashioned after Toynbee Hall, which she had visited in England. She and her band of conscientious, educated women—Ellen Gates Starr, Julia Lathrop, Louise Bowen—took over the mansion of Charles Hull at 335 S Halsted Street, a slum neighborhood that had once been suburban, and created Hull House, a center where the needy could come for help, both physical and emotional.

There was entertainment for the poor, of course. There were Fourth of July picnics at Lincoln Park, excursions to Sharp Shooter's Park, which was later called Riverview and which offered rides and games, and roasted peanuts could be bought for a penny on the street.

Prominent Chicago merchants and their wives, and professional people, offered philanthropic support to the missions and Hull House. Lyman Gage, who had tried to help the Haymarket prisoners, organized a social welfare group; Potter Palmer's wife Bertha and her friends devoted time to alleviating the plight of millinery workers and seamstresses. Some of Chicago's more fortunate citizens were certainly aware that a progressive attitude toward labor and the poor amounted to enlightened self-interest. But on the eve of the Democratic Convention of 1896 the poor still slept in the gutters.

4

The Democratic Convention came to Chicago in July of 1896. It was to go down in history because of the "Cross of Gold" speech delivered by William Jennings Bryan of Nebraska, who was then thirty-six years old, the son of a prominent trial lawyer in Salem, Illinois, and a graduate of the Chicago Union College of Law. Bryan had served two terms in the U.S. House of Representatives and had run unsuccessfully for the Senate in 1894. He was a handsome figure, over six feet tall, and his oratorical style and booming voice were striking and spellbinding. He was called the "silver-tongued orator," a phrase with a double meaning, because Bryan had staked out a crucial position for free coinage of silver.

In 1896 the country was suffering from a deep depression, especially in the agrarian South and West. After the Civil War, the congressional Republicans had decreed that mortgages had to be paid in gold; this had created a financial burden for farmers who had bought their property with paper money and many of them now faced foreclosure. There was thus a strong agrarian animus against gold. Advocates of silver—mostly Democrats and Populists, with a minority of Republicans—wanted free coinage of silver to increase the money supply, which they believed would increase economic activity and raise farm prices. This was an emotional social issue rather than an economic one. The silver camp saw the "gold bugs" as creatures of the big Northern cities: evil bankers, trusts and railroads. On the side of silver was the rural image of Jefferson.

Thus, in July of 1896, the Democrats came to the sweltering city with lines drawn between silver and gold and with silver in the majority. The two-term Democratic president, Grover Cleveland, had come down firmly on the side of gold, so there was almost no chance that he would be renominated, although at that time there was no law against a third term. Cleveland's policies had done nothing to alleviate the economic depression; he was not popular. It was to be an open convention: there were at least four favored candidates for the nomination. The Republicans had held their convention in St Louis in mid-June, and nominated

William McKinley of Ohio, who had actually gone on record favoring silver, but who had come out for the gold standard under pressure. He did pledge to work for international free coinage of silver, but this was not enough for the silver Republican minority, led by Senator Henry Teller of Colorado, who reluctantly abandoned his party and went over to what was called the Democracy; twenty-one Republican delegates bolted with him.

In the first week of July, as the Democrats gathered, Bryan was polling last in a field of roughly seven candidates, although there were newspapers who praised him. The favorites, all pro-silver, were Richard Parks Bland of Missouri, Governor Horace Boies of Iowa, and Governor Claude Matthews of Indiana.

Representative Bland, known as "Silver Dick" because of his long association with the Free Silver movement, was one of the authors of the Bland-Allison Act of 1878, which authorized the Secretary of the Treasury to buy a monthly minimum of two million dollars, and a maximum of four million dollars, worth of silver. Among the dark horses were Joseph Blackburn of Kentucky, John Daniel of Virginia, Vice President Adlai Stevenson of Illinois, Stephen White of California, the foul-mouthed Senator Ben "Pitchfork" Tillman of South Carolina, and of course Bryan himself.

The gold bugs were led by William C. Whitney, 43, a New England financier and lawyer, who had served as Secretary of the Navy. He arrived with a contingent of millionaires in a special New York Central train. The gold candidates were Senators William Vilas of Wisconsin, George Gray of Delaware, David Bennett Hill of New York and Governor William Russell of Massachusetts.

One hundred laborers worked for a week to get the Coliseum ready. The building, in its second location at 63rd and Stony Island Avenue, was the largest permanent exhibition hall in the world, covering five-and-a-half acres. The convention area could seat 20,000 people. A fan-shaped space was set up for the 906 delegates; it was 125 feet wide and eighty feet deep, divided into five sections. Behind the delegate seats were rows of seats for spectators and then galleries extending to the eaves. The speaker's stand and platform was on the east side of the hall, where there were also seats for the National Committee and special guests. The sergeant-at-arms sat in front of the speaker and on both sides of the stand were tiers of seats for reporters. Behind the platform a telegraph room had been set up, with chairs and tables.

At the major hotels there were huge portraits of Bland. In the Palmer House, a large portrait of Governor Boies, whose candidacy Bryan had supported in the past, hung at the south end of the rotunda. The Whitney gold bugs had the choicest rooms and they set up their headquarters in the spacious clubroom.

The day before the convention opened, the Potter Palmers gave a tea party at their mansion at 100 N Lake Shore Drive. Mrs Palmer wore a nile green chiffon dress with white silk embroidery. The guests—who included Republican senators Blackburn, Vilas, Gray and Daniel, and Republicans Cyrus McCormick and Joseph Medill—strolled about the garden, admiring the American Beauty roses and the view of Lake Michigan. Bryan was not invited.

On the morning of July 7, great crowds surged about the entrance to the Coliseum. The district was dry, so hawkers sold cold tea, lemonade and milk, as well as fans. Despite the ban on alcohol, a saloon opened behind a building across the street, for the convenience of the conventioneers. The proprietor stood on the pavement, announcing, "Saloon in the rear, sir!" Two policemen stood guard there. When challenged by irritated temperance advocates, the officers, apparently in earshot of the press, responded that this was Chicago and there was no law to keep a man from "barking for trade for his saloon" and that they did not intend to exceed their duties; they had been told to watch for crooks and not to bother their heads about saloons.

At 12:48 the National Committee chairman, William P. Harrity of Pennsylvania, banged down his oak gavel, which had once been part of the Fort Dearborn blockhouse. At the same time an electric gong sounded, to signal the opening of the convention. The hall was hung with huge portraits of former Democratic presidents—Jefferson, Andrew Jackson, James Buchanan—and flags and other patriotic symbols.

The first struggle of the day was the need to name a temporary chairman of the convention. This was an important post, because the temporary chairman would also be the keynote speaker, and this speech could in fact decide the nominee, if it were strong enough. There was a good deal of tension in the hall because, although the silver men were definitely in the majority, the Democrats had a rule that the nominee had to be chosen by a two-thirds majority. This of course made it more difficult for a candidate to win the nomination; the advantage it presented to less well-known aspirants was that it could cause a great many ballots and the delegates then might tire and throw the nomination to a dark horse. There was also the possiblity, which made the two-thirds rule attractive to the gold men, that the exhausted delegates might go for a compromise candidate. The convention could, by a simple majority, overthrow the two-thirds rule and make the nomination easier for the most popular man. But they were reluctant to do that, because the rule had been in effect since Andrew Jackson's day. It was not, in fact, voted out until 1936.

The National Committee, which was controlled by the gold bugs, recommended that Senator David Bennett Hill be named temporary chairman. The committee thought Hill might be acceptable because he was a bimetallist and therefore open to compromise. In addition, he had strongly opposed the policies of Grover Cleveland, whom the silver men detested. But Hill was too conservative for the silver people, of whom Governor John Peter Altgeld, the head of the Illinois delegation, was one. Altgeld was a power at the convention, despite the fact that he had been pilloried by the press because of his pardon of the three Haymarket prisoners. The Populists admired him.

The silver men wanted a strong orator for temporary chairman, and Bryan was the logical choice. But Bryan did not want the chairmanship because he did not want to make the keynote speech. He wanted to speak later, preferably after everyone else, closer to the actual balloting. Since Bryan had taken himself out of the running for this post, the silver men nominated Senator John W. Daniel of Virgina, who was considered a superb speaker. The silver forces went into raptures over Daniel's name and he was handily elected, but not, ominously, by a two-thirds majority.

In any case, the acoustics in the hall did not favor any orator who did not have an extremely powerful voice. The speech Daniel made was not what his supporters had hoped for, and so both he and Hill, because of his defeat, lost support.

The next big struggle for Bryan was the decision the Credentials Committee had to make between competing silver and gold delegations. Nebraska had a gold delegation which Bryan had tried to challenge before the pro-gold National Committee. Since the chairman of the Credentials Committee was a friend of Bryan's, the committee seated the silver delegation and ousted the gold. In addition, the committee gave extra silver votes to the territories and replaced four Michigan gold bugs with silver men. These manipulations ensured a two-thirds silver majority for the convention.

Bryan had to fight off another election, that of permanent chairman of the convention. The Committee on Permanent Organization wanted Bryan, but he talked frantically against himself and finally persuaded them not to choose him. He knew that as a presiding officer he would have to shout over the noise of the crowd, calling for order, and would inevitably injure his voice.

Bryan had no organization behind him. His headquarters was in two rooms in the rundown Clifton House. But he had some influential friends. He was elected to the Resolutions Committee which drafted the platform planks. Bryan drafted the crucial money plank demanding the "free and unlimited coinage of silver" at sixteen to one, and the equality of the silver dollar with gold as full legal tender. The plank demanded also that paper money be issued only by the Government and not by banks. For the rest, the Democratic platform called for arbitration of labor disputes—a reaction against Cleveland's interference in the Pullman strike—opposed a third term for the president, supported the Monroe Doctrine and advocated the admission into the Union of the silver territories of Arizona, New Mexico and Oklahoma. It also opposed immigrant labor and the railroad trusts.

Bryan was asked by Senator James K. Jones of Arkansas, the head of the Credentials Committee, to organize the debate on the platform. Bryan was delighted: he knew that the debate would be lively, in part because of the platform's repudiation of Grover Cleveland, the only Democrat to win the presidency since the Civil War. The gold men had presented a strong minority dissent. Senator Jones himself had a sore throat and could not speak and although he was a Bland supporter, he felt that Bryan deserved an opportunity to speak at the convention because of his longstanding loyalty to the silver cause.

Bryan and Senator David Bennett Hill, the minority leader of the Resolutions Committee, agreed that each side would speak for one hour and fifteen minutes. Hill, Senator Vilas and ex-Governor Russell would speak for the minority. The only silver man who had volunteered to speak was Pitchfork Tillman. That satisfied Bryan, who had no desire to share the limelight, and who knew that Tillman was rash and unpredictable.

Tillman wanted to talk for fifty minutes, and to make the closing address. Bryan knew the lasting impression the closing address would make. He pulled strings on the committee with Jones and Hill to get the closing speech for himself.

The news that Bryan would close the debate increased a modest groundswell for him that had begun with his earlier successes in driving out the Nebraska gold delegation and drafting the money plank. The *Tribune* commented, "The Nebraska stable has entered a dark horse in William Jennings Bryan, who is of sound wind and believed able to go the distance." North Carolina pledged to Bryan, and other delegations began to show support for him, including several Southern states. Bryan's confidence grew.

The night before the debate, a group came to the Clifton House to ask Bryan to throw his support to Senator Henry Teller, the silver Republican who had bolted to the Democrats. Bryan's response implied that he himself had a good chance for the nomination, causing the incredulous legislators to make an effort to stifle their amusement. That same evening, as he sat at dinner in a restaurant on Dearborn Street with his wife and a friend, Bryan watched the Bland marching bands and the pushing and shoving streams of delegates, some for Boies, and remarked,

"These people don't know it, but they will be cheering for me just this way by this time tomorrow night. I will make the greatest speech of my life tomorrow in reply to Senator Hill." He concluded, "I am the only man who can be nominated. I am what they call 'the logic of the situation.'"

The press did not agree. Bland was predicted to be the winner by the third ballot at the latest. Bryan's name was not even listed in most considerations of likely candidates.

On the morning of July 9, Senator Jones read the platform to the assemblage and when they heard the money planks, the delegates went wild with enthusiasm. The first speaker was Tillman of South Carolina; his was an angry sectionalist stance. He attacked the Eastern financial interests, accusing them of exploiting the South and the West. His talk of "secession" succeeded in enraging the Northerners in his audience and they began to shout and hiss at him—a tactic that only made him more belligerent. His speech was clearly a failure.

Hill gave a sensible argument for gold and against the silver position. He defended the president and attacked the Populists, whom he accused of dominating what should have been a Democratic convention. It was a good speech, but the convention wanted more red meat, something they could get their teeth into.

Senator Vilas, too, attacked free coinage, but the crowd was tiring of these arguments, which they did not want anyway. They began to shout him down. Undeterred, he talked on and strayed into some of the time allotted to Governor Russell of Massachussetts, who protested to Jones. Bryan, seizing the moment to get more time for himself, suggested that time on both sides be extended by ten minutes. Russell and Hill were happy to agree.

Russell was young and attractive, but a sick man, who would not live past forty. He defended Cleveland, saying, "The minority also feels that the report of the majority is defective in failing to make any recognition of the honesty, economy, courage and fidelity of the present Democratic Administration." The crowd respected Russell's own courage in making the speech despite the weakness of his voice and listened to him politely.

The silver people were upset; they had not had a convincing advocate. Now they pinned their hopes on Bryan, and he did not disappoint them.

In the gallery Edgar Lee Masters saw Bryan leap up from his chair and seem to glide toward the podium. The crowd went berserk, climbing on chairs, pounding the floor with whatever was handy when their voices gave out. Bryan had no problem projecting his own voice to the farthest corners of the huge amphitheatre, where others had had great difficulty in making themselves heard. He began:

> Mr Chairman and gentlemen of the convention, I would be presumptous indeed to present myself against the distinguished gentlemen to whom you have listened, if this were a mere measuring of hostilities; but this is not a contest between persons. The humblest citizen in all the land, when clad in the armor of a righteous cause, is stronger than all the hosts of error. I come to speak to you in defense of a cause as holy as the cause of liberty—the cause of humanity.

He did not attack the East, trying to avoid a narrow sectionalism; he could not achieve a two-thirds majority by alienating the Northern delegates. But he spoke against the "encroachments of organized wealth" and said that Easterners had too narrow an idea of who was engaged in business—it was not just members of the Board of Trade, but farmers, merchants, even coal miners. He spoke in favor of the income tax and the right of government alone to print and coin money. But for him silver was the predominant issue; he traced the successes of the silver movement over the past year and said that no reform was possible until the money system was reformed.

He drew a dichotomy between city and countryside. Farms, he said, were the backbone of the cities. You could destroy cities, and they would rise again. But if you destroyed the farms, the cities could not exist. The cities, he said, were in favor of the gold standard. He made a point that has a familiar ring one hundred years later: there were, he said, two theories of government. In one, it was believed that "if you legislate to make the well-to-do prosperous, their prosperity will leak through on those below," but the other, the Democratic theory, held that "if you legislate to make the masses prosperous, their prosperity will find its way up through every class that rests on them."

All these points resonated extremely well with the convention; they were met with roars of approval. At last Bryan moved into his stunning finale:

> If they dare to come out in the open field and defend the gold standard as a good thing, we will fight them to the uttermost. Having behind us the producing masses of this nation . . . we will answer their demands for a gold standard by saying to them "You shall not press down upon the brow of labor this crown of thorns; you shall not crucify mankind on a cross of gold."

He stood as though crucified, with his arms outstretched, took one step backward, and left the podium. There was a dead silence, and then as he moved to the floor the delegates went berserk, waving, screaming, parading, fighting to reach him. He had captured them.

It was not a new speech for him; he had delivered some of it when he was a congressman. This included the "cross of gold" image. His definition of the businessman was the only new part of the speech. And there were those who saw a certain emptiness in these silver phrases. While the enraptured Democrats hoisted Bryan to their shoulders and carried him around the hall, Altgeld turned to Clarence Darrow and said, "I have been thinking over Bryan's speech. What did he say, anyhow?"

But Altgeld was a Bland man. Many people wanted to begin the balloting on the spot, but Bryan refused, saying that if his boom could not last overnight, it wouldn't last until November. In reality he wanted time to work on the Bland and Boies men, who would certainly be assaulted by impassioned nominating speeches from their supporters. Altgeld believed the Bryan boom would die quickly.

All the next day delegates were buttonholed and pressured from all sides. Nominations began at 8:30 at night; there were

25,000 in the hall. Senator George G. Vest nominated Bland. When Judge Henry T. Lewis of Maine rose, it was assumed that he would second Bland's nomination. However, he nominated Bryan instead. The other nominations followed: Boies, Governor Robert F. Pattison of Pennsylvania, Governor Claude Matthews of Indiana, Joseph Blackburn of Kentucky and John McLean, the millionaire publisher of the *Cincinnati Enquirer.*

At about one in the morning, the convention adjourned until ten the following morning. Altgeld predicted that the South was going to Bryan, but that Bland would take the West and win the nomination. But there were rumors that Altgeld might not be able to hold his Illinois delegation.

On the first ballot the next day, Bland led with 233 votes—not a strong showing. Bryan had 103, Pattison 95 and Boies 86. New York and New Jersey refused to vote, reflecting the estrangement of the gold men from the proceedings. On the second ballot, Bland went to 281, Bryan 195, Pattison 100 and Boies dropped below 50. There were 162 abstentions. Fear was rising that there could be a deadlock.

On the third ballot, Bland received 291 votes, and Bryan 217. Signs of upset began to emanate from the Illinois delegation. On the fourth ballot, delegations, beginning with Alabama, began to switch to Bryan. There was tremendous turmoil in the hall, including fist fights as delegates struggled to seize standards from each other. Bryan took the lead with 280 votes over Bland's 241; Pattison went to 96 and Boies got only 33 votes. The abstentions remained steady at 162.

A decision was made that the two-thirds rule should apply only to those who voted and should not include abstaining delegates, or the entire convention. This made it much more possible for Bryan to be nominated.

Emotions in the hall were at fever pitch. On the fifth ballot, Altgeld, who had stayed with Bland until his delegation rebelled, announced all 48 Illinois votes for Bryan. This caused a landslide. Bland withdrew, and Bryan was nominated unanimously.

He gave his first speech of the campaign that night from the Monroe Street balcony of the Clifton House, bathed in electric

100

light. An aide draped an American flag around the candidate's massive shoulders. Someone in the crowd called to him, "Must we keep off the grass when you are president?" This question came from a man who had been part of General Jacob Sexler Coxey's army of unemployed men who, under the Populist banner, had marched on Washington in 1894, seeking a public works program to alleviate their plight. General Coxey had been arrested for walking on the Capitol lawn.

"There will be no sign up to keep off the grass when I am president," Bryan said, to the delight of the crowd in the street. The Bland marching band turned out in full force for Bryan, for which he expressed his gratitude to them. He extended his hand toward them. "Now," he said, "you have all shaken hands with me. A great deal of sentiment will be developed in this campaign. We are going to have songs as well as speeches."

The next step was the election of a vice-presidential candidate. None of the main defeated candidates would accept that nomination, a sign that they did not believe Bryan to be a strong candidate. Since Bryan had no money, the party wanted a millionaire in the second spot. A favorite was John R. McLean, the Cincinnati publisher, a strong silver man. But Bryan rejected him, saying he was "immoral" and stood for "privilege." The next choice then was Arthur Sewall of Maine, owner of a merchant fleet and with many business interests, including the Maine Central Railroad. He, although privileged, was more acceptable to Bryan, who wanted an Easterner on the ticket to help bind up some sectional wounds. Despite Bryan's endorsement, Sewell did not win nomination until the fifth ballot.

William McKinley, at home in Canton, Ohio, where he was to remain for most of the campaign, told reporters he had no comment on Bryan's nomination. Grover Cleveland followed suit, although it was his own party's ticket. He was on a fishing trip, but an aide announced that the President had nothing to say. William Whitney publicly repudiated the ticket.

Bryan's last stop in Chicago was Alfred Brisbois's photography studio at 125 S State Street. Since the windows had to be kept closed to protect the camera focus, the candidate had to sit stiffly for over an hour in the stifling heat. "Can't you bring on a few windmills?" he asked, as he mopped his face with a red bandanna. He wore a black alpaca coat adorned by a "16 to 1" button.

He was offered a private Pullman car for his return to Nebraska. His friend the reporter Willis Abbot, who was there when the invitation arrived from the railroad, told him not to accept the offer. "You are the Great Commoner," Abbot said, "the people's candidate, and it would not do to accept favors from the great railroad corporations." Bryan agreed with this, and thereafter he was always known as the Great Commoner. In 1901 he was to found a weekly newspaper in Lincoln called *The Commoner.*

Bryan became the candidate of two other parties, the Populists and the National Silver Party, both of which convened in St Louis. The Silver Party readily nominated the Democratic ticket. The Populists, however, balked at accepting Sewall and instead nominated Thomas Watson of Florida for the vice-presidential slot. Thus Bryan was put in the uncomfortable position of running a sort of dual campaign with two vice-presidential candidates.[7] The Populists were laboring under the delusion that Sewall would step down in favor of Watson. This Populist nomination brought votes to Bryan, but it also tarred him with a radical brush, especially in the East. The New York press predicted revolution if Bryan won; the *New York Times* called the Populists "freaky Coxeyites" and Bryan "irresponsible, unregulated, ignorant, prejudiced, pathetically honest" and a "crank." Bryan was also called "the Prince of Anarchy" and a "Popocrat." John Hay, who had been assistant private secretary to President Lincoln and was to serve McKinley as Secretary of State, called Bryan "a half-baked, glib little briefless, jackleg lawyer." The campaign against him was vicious. Mark Hanna, the Ohio politician who was managing McKinley's campaign, sent out teams of speakers to go into campaign stops just before Bryan, to mimic him and parody his speeches so that often audiences found his words and mannerisms laughable.

In early September, the gold Democrats had their own convention in Indianapolis and nominated John M. Palmer of Illinois and Simon B. Buchner of Kentucky, who had been a Confederate general, on what they called the National Democratic ticket. This splinter Democratic group worked hard against Bryan, and many gold Democrats made a pretense of supporting the National Democrats, but in actuality worked for McKinley. In the East, newspapers, clergymen and academics joined together to attack Bryan. He was contemptuously referred to as "the Boy Orator of the Platte." Some conservatives even hinted that if Bryan won, they would not accept his election, but would rebel. Altgeld was especially used against him, because of the unfair but persistent perception of the Illinois governor as a wild-eyed anarchist.

Undeterred, Bryan put on the most inclusive presidential campaign ever conducted up to that time, covering over 18,000 miles and giving more than 3,000 speeches. When election day came, he was home in Omaha, surrounded by Western Union operators and reporters. McKinley, who had stayed at home on his front porch, won the election. But Bryan's showing was far from ignominious. It is true that McKinley won the electoral college overwhelmingly: 271 votes to Bryan's 176. But McKinley took only 50.88 percent of the popular vote, while Bryan's total was 46.77 percent. Bryan in fact garnered one million more votes than Cleveland had when he won in 1892. Two million more people cast votes in 1896. But Bryan's total popular vote was larger than that of any previously elected president.

He did best in the Mountain States and the South. He had not campaigned heavily in the Northeast, and he did badly in New England and the Middle Atlantic states. He fared less badly, but not too well, in the Middle West, and on the Pacific coast he carried only the state of Washington.

It was immediately obvious that there had been a tremendous amount of election fraud. Even some Republican journalists believed that fraud was so widespread, especially in Illinois, Ohio—where Mark Hanna was boss—Indiana and California, that Bryan was defeated by it. The National Democratic ticket caused much confusion. Many voters did not know which Democratic party they were voting for. This was especially obvious in Minnesota. Palmer did not get a tremendous number of votes, but his presence on the ticket threw several rural states to McKinley. And then there was the fact that Bryan was no match for the money behind McKinley.

Bryan accepted his defeat philosophically, and it was agreed, even by many of his enemies, that his performance had been magnificent. He was now the central figure in the Democratic party, and was nominated again in 1900, when he lost once more to McKinley. In 1904 he lost the nomination to Alton B. Parker, who disavowed the silver plank in the platform fashioned by Bryan, and who lost to Theodore Roosevelt. In 1908 the Democrats nominated Bryan a third time. He was defeated by William Howard Taft.

His career was far from over, however. In 1912 he supported Woodrow Wilson, who rewarded him by making him Secretary of State, a post he held until 1915, when he resigned because he was strongly anti-war and disagreed with Wilson's belligerent tone toward the Germans over the sinking of the *Lusitania*. Nevertheless he supported Wilson again in 1916 and backed him when war was declared. He remained a power in the party until 1924 when he supported William Gibbs McAdoo, Wilson's son-in-law, over Al Smith for the nomination. By that time his day was over. He threw himself heart and soul into the fundamentalist fight against the teaching of the theory of evolution, and when he appeared for the prosecution in the Scopes trial in Tennessee in 1925 against his old supporter Clarence Darrow, it was obvious that he was no longer the man he had been. He died five days after the trial ended.

It could be said of William Jennings Bryan that he was vindicated by history, except of course in the case of fundamentalism and of Prohibition, which he supported in 1920 and which, when enacted, proved to be a disaster for the country. But other things for which he stood—the income tax, the popular election of senators, woman suffrage, public information about newspaper ownership—all these things were eventually enacted and proved his farsightedness, strong intelligence and faith in democracy. He was always sincere and never a demagogue. It was in many ways a fateful summer of 1896 in Chicago.

V

A New Century, 1901

On Monday night, December 31, 1900, the city was blanketed with snow. Silk- and paper-shaded electric lamps lit the windows of the Michigan Avenue mansions; candles glowed in the tenement windows of the poor, to welcome in the new century. On top of the Montgomery Ward building was the Midwest's brightest beacon, the Statue of Progress, reaching toward the prairie and farmlands.

At State and Madison streets, revelers shouted, drank gin from bottles, and fired revolvers into the air. The blast of tugboat horns could be heard in the distance. The restaurants were crowded, as were the saloons. Mayor Carter Harrison—the second Carter Harrison, his father having been assassinated in 1893—had publicly vowed to uphold the midnight saloon-closing law, but privately he had instructed Chief of Police Joseph Kipley to wink at the law that night.

At the Coliseum, the American Red Cross was sponsoring a midnight service in honor of the nations who had been signatories to the Geneva Convention of 1864. The audience included representatives of those nations, the clergy and prominent Chicagoans. William Penn Nixon read messages from President McKinley, William Jennings Bryan and Clara Barton. At a few minutes before midnight, as the congregation was singing "Old One Hundred," an old man with a flowing white beard, in tattered clothing, suddenly appeared at the podium, shouting, "Hear me, brothers and sisters, I am the savior!" He was Friedrich Trostel, a German umbrellamaker. He succeeded in reading several Bible passages before he was tackled by the sergeant-at-arms.

The congregation sang "Praise God from Whom All Blessing Flow," while Trostel was bundled off to a waiting police wagon.

As twelve o'clock struck, the lights dimmed in the Tiffany chandeliers of the grand ballroom on the top floor of the Potter Palmer mansion on Lake Shore Drive. A trumpeter, standing against the red velvet curtains, heralded the arrival of the new century, while electric bulbs, mounted on the carved wall, spelled out "1901." The Palmers were hosting their annual New Years Ball, this year in honor of Mrs Palmer's friend Mrs Griswold Gray of New York. Earlier, Mrs Palmer, respendent in black velvet, diamonds and pearls, had supervised a light supper for twenty-five young socialites. The other 150 guests—including Robert Todd Lincoln, Richard Crane and Frank Lowden, a future governor of Illinois—had arrived after nine o'clock.

Potter Palmer had married Bertha Honore in 1871 when he was 44 and she was 21. Then came the disastrous Chicago fire. He rebuilt the Palmer House, which had been destroyed, making it one of the choice hotels in the city and helped to redevelop the downtown area, promoting State Street into the leading shopping center. Palmer believed that the days of Prairie and Michigan avenues, as the locations for the city's most elegant mansions, were numbered. He cast his eye northward and east, toward the lake shore. The Newberrys, the Ogdens and the Arnolds lived in that area, but east of them was marshland. Palmer began to buy up parcels of land there from the city at reasonable prices. He brought in machinery to dry up the marshes, and put in a beach. The city then put in Lake Shore Drive, which ran from Pearson Street to North Avenue: this was to be the Gold Coast. Palmer mapped out a plot on the east half of a block bounded by Schiller and Bank streets and commissioned the architects Henry Ives Cobb and Charles S. Frost to design what was to become known as Palmer's Castle. Work on it began in 1882.

Palmer owned enough of this Gold Coast property to be able to decide who his neighbors would be. In 1885, when the castle was completed, the Palmers were joined in the area by families who had moved from Prairie Avenue: the Herman Kohlsaats, George Meekers, Franklin McVeaghs, Hampstead Washburns. Mrs Palmer was unquestionably the queen of Chicago society and where she led, others followed.

The mansion had cost Palmer one million dollars. In 1893 he spent another $41,000 expanding and improving the butler's pantry, the dairy room and the picture gallery on the top floor next to the grand ballroom. Despite this lavish spending, Palmer had a reputation as a sharp man with a dollar: he kept a close eye on his workers, making sure that they did not cheat him by collecting pay for hours they did not work.

Red sandstone steps led up to the limestone-and-granite turreted castle which had been decorated by a virtual army of Italian artisans. The octagonal entrance hall had no doubt been inspired by the great halls of medieval castles: it was three stories high, hung with Gobelin tapestries and graced with a gigantic fireplace surmounted by the Honore family coat of arms. The oak floor was layered with Oriental rugs and tiger skins. Stained glass windows illuminated the landings on the wide staircase.

On the second floor was the white-and-gold Louis XVI drawing room; the tile floor was set with Mrs Palmer's signature pink roses. Also on this floor were the dining room, panelled in mahogany, where fifty guests could be easily seated, the library and the billiard room, each with its own great marble-and-oak fireplace, with carved walls, tapestries or murals and Venetian mosaics. There was also Mrs Palmer's bedroom, with carved ceilings and blue taffeta bedcurtains, and her small sitting room, where she conducted her considerable charitable business. In her spacious bathroom, mother-of-pearl roses were set into the china wash basin.

On this New Years Eve the Palmer ballroom was hung with white silk entwined with evergreen boughs. The guests danced to music provided, as on most elegant social occasions in Chicago, by Johnny Hand's orchestra, and admired the party favors that had been imported from Paris. At one-thirty in the morning, a light supper was served in a parlor filled, as many of the rooms were, with American Beauty roses. Then it was time for the coachmen to pull their carriages up the driveway to the porte-cochère. The next day the guests would be involved with the traditional New Years Day receptions.

They were undoubtedly optimistic about the future; most people were. As early as 1897, the *Tribune* had asked civic planners what they thought Chicago would be like in 1990. One respondent said that "such a vulgar thing as a horse will never be seen upon the downtown streets of the city." Louis Enricht, Cook County surveyor, believed that there would be a "free and sovereign state of Chicago," covering 1,600 square miles—all of Cook, DuPage and the "northern townships" of Will County—and with a population of ten million. In the south, the city would extend into Indiana as far as Valparaiso and "if the state of Indiana will cede that valuable parcel of territory, then indeed will Chicago be the queen of the world." This estimate was based on the growth rate of the city since the fire, and on the influence of the railroads.

Architect James J. Egan foresaw "superstructures, some as high as sixty stories" which would be made possible by electric-powered elevators. Wooden tenements would be a thing of the past and coal heat would be outmoded. He foresaw a massive enclosed stadium seating 125,000. (Soldier Field did indeed come into being, although it was not an enclosed stadium but an open one.) Yale professor Henry Davis foresaw the disarming of all nations because no new weapons could be invented. Astronomer Garrett Serviss talked about space travel in 1990. "The air ship of the 20th Century may find one of its useful applications in carrying the astronomer and his instruments a little closer to the stars."

The *Tribune* observed, in concluding this survey, that "to attempt to picture in fancy all that Chicago will be a century from now would be beyond the power of the 19th century mind."

Not every journalist took a sanguine view of what could lie ahead. On Christmas eve, 1900, Richard LeGallienne wrote a somber editorial for the Hearst newspapers:

One may easily predict two events which are certain to happen
and which, by judging the outcome of such events in the past,
are to act as formative influences. I refer to the great war of
which we can already see the opening moves, and the death
struggle between capital and labor which will be fought out in
America, and which will be for the 20th Century what the
French Revolution was for the 18th and 19th.

On that New Years Eve, as the landaus and broughams left
the Palmer mansion and clip-clopped through the deserted
streets of the near north side, the last of the celebrants from State
and Madison streets climbed aboard streetcars. Earlier in the
evening Detective P.F. McLaughlin, a veteran of the Haymarket
troubles, was making his rounds when he was stopped by a
pedestrian waiting for a streetcar near Randolph and LaSalle
streets, who pointed to the entrance of a nearby railway tunnel.
"I saw somebody come out of there in a big hurry," the pedestrian
said. "You'd better check."

McLaughlin went down to investigate. Under an arch between
some columns, resting against the concrete, he found a metal
object. It was a three-and-a-half-inch pipe bomb, similar to some
that had been thrown during labor disturbances. It would have
been detonated by the next Lincoln Avenue car that passed by
and the force of the Chicago River running directly overhead
would have caused the tunnel to collapse and kill all the passengers.

The next day the bomb was exploded on a secluded portion
of the lakefront. It was said that the force of the explosion was felt
in buildings half a mile away.

Detective McLaughlin prevented a major disaster that would
have been remembered for a hundred years and could well have
caused an anti-labor reaction similar to the Haymarket trauma.
He was the first hero of the new era who seemed to get the "age
of miracles" off to the right start.

Derby Day at Washington Park, c. 1890. Society bestowed its solemn nod of approval upon the Sport of Kings, which on other days of the year was looked upon as a deplorable vice. *Courtesy Chicago Historical Society, William T. Barnum photo.*

Early Police Cars. *Courtesy Kenan Heise.*

Uproar after the explosion of the bomb at Haymarket Square. Chicago, May 4, 1886. *Courtesy Chicago Historical Society, copyright by Paul Morand.*

John Bonfield
Inspector of Police

William H. Ward
Ex-Capt. Third Precinct

HERMANN SCHUETTLER.   MICHAEL HOFFMANN.   MICHAEL WHALEN.

CHAS. REHM.   JOHN STIFT.   JACOB LOEWENSTEIN.

Chicago Police Detective squad hand-picked by Michael Schaak to arrest "anarchists."

The dead and dying were stretched upon the floor of the Desplaines Street station.

Frederick Ebersold
General Superintendent of Police

The Haymarket Monument

William McGarigle, General Superintendent of Police. Appointed December 30, 1880. *Courtesy Chicago Historical Society.*

William McGarigle's Home at 832 Grace Street. *Illustration by Bob Deckert.*

VOL. VII, No. 9.　　　　CHICAGO, SATURDAY, FEBRUARY 26, 1887.　　　Terms: { Ten Cents per Copy. / $4.00 per Year, in Advance.

"The raid on the vermin." The illustrator of this issue of the *Graphic* portrays the rats' nest of corruption being cleaned out. *Courtesy Chicago Historical Society.*

Cook County Hospital, c. 1885. The vermin-infested Ward 18 stood atop the County Morgue.

The most evil building in Chicago during the not-so-gay nineties was the Holmes Castle. Before Holmes's crimes were discovered, the building at 63rd and Wallace disguised unspeakable perversion and horror. *Illustration by Bob Deckert.*

Herman Webster Mudgett, a.k.a., H.H. Holmes. *Illustration by Bob Deckert.*

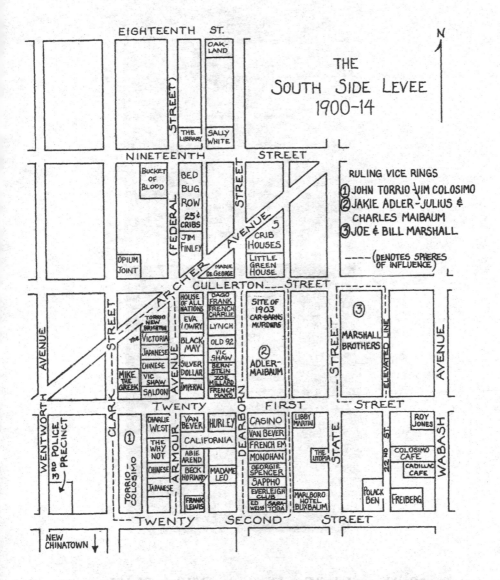

The Why Not, Bucket of Blood, House of all Nations, Bed Bug Row and the Old 92 were but a few of the bordellos that comprised the old Levee. *Illustration by Bob Deckert.*

"Bathhouse John" Coughlin (top) and "Hinky Dink" Kenna (bottom), Lords of the Levee. *Courtesy Chicago Crime Commission.*

Chicago Coliseum, 1904. *(above–Courtesy of Chicago Historical Society, Charles R. Clark photo)* The bustling street scene stands in contrast to the quiet desolation of South Wabash in 1984 *(below–photo by Bob Deckert)*, when only the outer façade of the building remained.

Freiberg's Dance Hall, 1911. Ike Bloom's place was the command post of the Levee, but he disguised its true purposes by advertising it as a dance academy. *Courtesty Chicago Historical Society.*

Hinky Dink Kenna (arrow) and the Rough Riders of the late 1890s. *Courtesy Kenan Heise.*

Mont Tennes family portrait. Left to right: son Horace, Mont, wife Ida, eldest son Ray, daughter Dorothy, Mont Jr. *Courtesy Thomas McGee.*

Big Jim O'Leary's Halsted Street gambling fortress. *Illustration by Bob Deckert.*

The Illinois National Guard stands watch over homes damaged by rioters. Chicago, 1919. *Courtesy Chicago Historical Society.*

VI

Low Life In the Levee

1

The First Ward—one of thirty-five city wards—encompassed the heart of the city, reaching north to the Chicago River, south to 29th Street, east to Lake Michigan and west to Canal Street. In the north end of the ward was the Loop district with its city hall, office buildings, department stores, hotels, restaurants and theatres. There too were the notorious Gambler's Alley and Hairtrigger Block, filled with gambling houses. Mike McDonald's Store was at Clark and Monroe.

Toward the south end—from Adams to Twelfth Street and west from Wabash Avenue to the south bank of the Chicago River—was the old Levee and Little Cheyenne, named after Cheyenne, Wyoming, which was considered a very wicked place. (Cheyenne returned the compliment by calling their own vice district "Chicago.") Here were thirty-seven brothels—including the infamous "dipping houses": narrow closets in which victims were mugged by whores and pimps—forty-six saloons, many pawnshops, peep shows and streets filled with thieves and pickpockets. Some houses charged the customer only twenty-five cents; others, elaborate and expensive, were run by famous madams like Carrie Watson and Vina Fields, a large black woman who, like many saloonkeepers, fed the destitute during the Panic of 1893.

This vice area expanded and became more populous in 1893 when international attention was focused on Chicago as the home

111

of the Columbian Exposition. A new levee formed south of the Levee proper, between 18th and 22nd streets. This quarter-mile stretch was known as the Tenderloin, and Custom House Place ran from Harrison to Twelfth Street. The newly arrived Custom House gang included Frank Wing, Roy Jones, Ed Weiss and George Little, who was the manager for Jack Johnson, the black heavyweight champion. During the period of expansion, the factions of the old and the new Levees were at peace with each other; the 22nd Street regulars welcomed the newcomers.

The whole First Ward was run by two Democratic politicians, "Bathhouse John" Coughlin and Michael "Hinky Dink" Kenna; their reign lasted for more than forty years. Through agents like Dennis "The Duke" Cooney, tribute was paid each month to politicians by the Levee operators while the police looked the other way. Cooney ran the Rex Cafe at 2138 S State Street and paid off the police of the South Clark Street and Cottage Grove Avenue stations. He was Kenna's bagman, and in a later era he was to serve Al Capone in the same capacity.

Coughlin was born in 1869 in a tough Irish district called Connelly's Patch, west of the Loop, between Adams and Monroe streets. His first job, when he left school at fifteen, was as a scrubber in a Clark Street bathhouse. He moved from there to the famous, elegant bathhouse at the Palmer House, where he scrubbed the backs of politicians and powerful businessmen, as well as jockeys and gamblers. In 1882, through these connections and with his own savings, Bathhouse John was able to open his own bathhouse on East Madison Street and then a second one in the basement of the Brevoort Hotel. He met Oyster Joe Mackin, the Democratic boss, who brought him into the First Ward Democratic Club. From there Coughlin moved steadily upward, becoming first a precinct captain and then an alderman.

"Hinky Dink" Kenna, another product of Connelly's Patch, was a saloonkeeper and precinct captain. Together he and Coughlin controlled the First Ward, organizing events like the Democratic Marching Band and First Ward balls, buying votes for fifty cents apiece, extorting protection money from brothelkeepers and gamblers and taking bribes from tycoons like Charles Tyson Yerkes, who controlled the city's street railways.

Bathhouse John and Hinky Dink worked smoothly as a team, although they were very different from each other, both physically and in personality. Kenna was a dour, silent little man; Coughlin was large, bluff, hearty, given to writing atrocious poetry and wearing flamboyant clothing made for him by his special LaSalle Street tailor, Meyer Newfield.

The First Ward was certainly a colorful place. So thought the Englishman William Stead, former editor of the *Pall Mall Gazette*, founder of the *Review of Reviews*, dedicated reformer and fighter against white slavery,[8] who came to Chicago in late 1893 to investigate sin and corruption. He visited Custom House Place and wandered by chance into Hank North's saloon on Clark Street, between Harrison and Polk. North was an ex-minstrel who helped the destitute with free lunches in his bar. Stead, who was stout, bearded and well-dressed, attracted the attention of this group, who were discouraged from mobbing the visitor when North sprayed them with seltzer water, saying, "Back off, boys! This is Mr Stead from England!"

Stead visited the entire city—the brothels and saloons in the Levee, and the houses of the wealthy near the lake. He spent time with a vagrant named Frank Brown, an ex-vaudeville performer known as "Brownie, King of the Bums." He went to the Harrison Street lockup, a prison with stone floors and one gutter for its only sanitation. There the insane were mixed with street walkers, bums, pickpockets and homeless children. And Stead put on workmen's clothing and worked for three days with snow-removal gangs. The only pay for this hard labor in freezing conditions was a free meal and a place to stay the night.

With the encouragement of prominent reform-minded Chicagoans like Mrs Palmer, Jane Addams, Lyman Gage, William Demarest Lloyd, and the president of the Woman's Club, Sarah Hackett Stevenson, Stead held two mass meetings in November, 1893, in the Central Music Hall. The things he said about vice and corruption shocked the city, and led directly to the creation of the

Chicago Civic Federation, which went on working diligently for civic reform long after Stead left the city.

In the spring of 1894, Stead produced the fruit of all his investigations: a book called *If Christ Came to Chicago*. In it he named names: only two out of sixty-eight aldermen were not on the take; most policemen were for sale, and the pillars of the community—Marshall Field, George Pullman, Carter Harrison and others—were tax cheats. Needless to say, Stead described the dreadful practices of the Levee. But he also sketched out a Utopian future for the city, which he admired in spite of everything. He foresaw a Chicago with a magnificent lakefront filled with parks and gardens; with a happy citizenry taking free transportation to libraries, museums, lecture halls, and enjoying the benefits of an eight-hour workday, a free college education and free medical treatment. Mrs Potter Palmer, he said, ignoring the fact that women did not have the vote, would make an ideal mayor.

The book sold extremely well. It was read not only in Chicago, but all over the world, sparking controversy—some decried the book's sensationalism and accused Stead of being motivated by dislike of the Republican Party—and a good deal of praise. Chicago newspapers could not realistically deny the truth of his allegations. The 400-page book sold 100,000 copies in its first printing and another 200,000 after that.

The Civic Federation was an important legacy of Stead's sojourn in Chicago. In 1896 Bathhouse and Hinky Dink decided to put the squeeze on Yerkes, who was trying to get frontage rights on Jackson Boulevard to bring his lines into the Loop as final links to his west side streetcar system. Coughlin and Kenna joined with three others—one ward boss and two businessmen—to incorporate the General Electric Railway Company, and got frontage consents for streetcar lines for the new company adjacent to Yerkes's lines. Coughlin then presented an ordinance to the city council which would give the new company control of all west-side transportation.

After various political manipulations and a fierce fight in the council, the ordinance passed. The newspapers sparked a public outcry, the mayor vetoed the ordinance, and it was passed over his veto.

This blatant power grab enraged the reform community. Meetings were held, and the Civic Federation and others decided first to form a new political party—the Municipal Reform Party—to put up honest candidates in the spring aldermanic elections. This proved to be too difficult, so the reformers, headed by Lyman Gage and others in the Civic Federation, formed the Municipal Voters League, headed by George E. Cole, a small thickset fiery person who owned a stationery-and-printing shop. The League declared all First Ward aldermanic candidates unfit to serve. Despite this, Bathhouse John, who traveled the ward on election day with his pockets stuffed with coins to dole out to voters, won once more. Nevertheless, outside the First and Nineteenth Wards, the League defeated twenty-three targeted politicians.

It was a signal victory for the League, demonstrating what determined citizens could accomplish when they made up their minds to act. This is not to say that corruption ceased and the First Ward was cleaned up; that did not happen. But the reformers became a presence; the League had muscle. The First Ward responded by making reform gestures: Bathhouse John sponsored an ordinance barring the sale of cigarettes within 200 yards of a school and requiring shops to buy a $100 license to sell cigarettes. This won Coughlin some praise from the League and eased some of the pressure on the aldermen.

Carter Harrison II became mayor in 1897. He was close to Coughlin, but he was to some extent a reformer, who attacked Yerkes. Because of the reform pressure, it was becoming more expensive to buy aldermen. By 1901 Yerkes was defeated and it became evident that the great boodle era was on the wane.

In July, 1903, Lincoln Steffens arrived in Chicago in connection with a series of reports he was writing for *McClure's* magazine on municipal governments. He had pronounced Pittsburgh "a city ashamed" and Minneapolis "downfallen," but he had kind words for Chicago:

Chicago should be celebrated among American cities for reform, not moral fits and political uprisings, not reform waves that wash the "best people" into office to make fools of themselves and subside, leaving the machine stronger than ever; none of these aristocratic disappointments of popular government but reform that reforms. Slow, sure, political, democratic reform, by the people for the people. That is what Chicago has. It has found a way! I don't know that is the way. All I am sure of is that Chicago has something to teach every city and town in the country, including Chicago.

Bathhouse John said, "I found him a square, honest man, who seems to know his business. What we talked about is a personal, not a public matter. I would be the last to besmirch the fair name of Chicago. But I will say that I took a liking to Mr Steffens." But it was George Cole of the Municipal Voters League who earned Steffens's special praise.

In 1897 Hinky Dink became an alderman. In that year he opened the Workingman's Exchange, a saloon which he was to operate for thirty years. He gave free lunches to the destitute: if they could afford five cents for a huge glass of beer, so much the better, but they ate with or without the nickel. "Politics is business," Kenna told the French writer Jules Huret, who was touring America in 1904. "This is where we make voters. They drink 12,000 glasses of beer a week in my place." Huret, noticing water trickling from a faucet, asked Kenna why no one turned it off. "The running water makes 'em thirsty," Hinky Dink said. "That makes better business." When Kenna's saloon was finally closed because of Prohibition, it was estimated that he had sold 175,000 barrels of beer over the years.

The First Ward voting lists contained 40,000 names. Early in the century, the Municipal Voters League worked for an ordinance that would expand the ward south to 31st Street and add 22,000 names to the voting list. The First Ward aldermen successfully fought this measure; they did not want to risk losing control of the list. In 1903, Louis J. Behan, an attorney, was hired by vigilance committees of the First and Second Wards to secure indictments against keepers of disorderly houses. Carter Harrison II had promised on his re-election that year to clean up Custom House Place. Securing an indictment was one thing; winning a conviction quite another. In May, 1903, twenty-four resort keepers were brought before Judge Mack and twenty-three were dismissed. But the State's Attorney thought that he could convict the twenty-fourth man, Ike Bloom, proprietor of the notorious Freiberg's Dance Hall, who had violated the one o'clock closing law on five different occasions in that year. The state had nine witnesses who had agreed to testify against him.

Bloom invited the witnesses to his dance hall, bought them dinner and told them what to say. In court they all suffered memory lapses. The judge had to instruct the jury to return a not-guilty verdict.

In July, 1903, a grand jury returned indictments against property owners and landlords of the second Levee, but nothing came of them. One juror was asked whether conditions in the district remained that way because the police did not know what was going on. He put his hand behind him with upraised palm. "Although we don't say so," he said, "I think it's like this. No, I don't lay that sort of thing up against the patrolmen. They would do their duty if they were permitted to do so." All this caused a high level of frustration among the reformers. Louis Behan quit the vigilance committees because of a disagreement with a private detective on their payroll. The way of life of the wealthy Prairie Avenue neighborhood—bounded by 16th Street, Calumet, Indiana and Michigan avenues—was disrupted by the expansion of this second Levee which began during the Columbian Exposition. The pleasant little houses which had lined Armour Avenue, Dearborn and 19th streets were enlarged for nefarious purposes. Real estate agents and landlords welcomed the vice lords, and the way of life of the original residents was permanently disrupted.

The police were supposed to arrest all prostitutes who ventured past the Wabash Avenue elevated tracks into Prairie Avenue. As the Levee grew, between 1902 and 1912, it became increasingly apparent that the police were not cooperating with the vigilance committees organized by the residents. These committees could therefore do little and the internal bickering and disagreements reflected their impotence. Eventually the residents gave up and moved away.

This is not to say that nothing was done to curb vice. Carter Harrison II was told in 1903 that there were reports of respectable girls being lured to immorality in the vice dens along Plymouth Court. Two years later in 1905 State's Attorney John J. Healy pushed most of the brothels and winerooms farther south. A city ordinance defined a wineroom as "an interior shut off from the general public by doors, screens, curtains, portières or other devices." The code forbade dining and drinking by persons numbering fewer than four in a room connected to a bar. Saloon keepers got around this by placing potted palms in the doorways.

On March 1, 1905, the City Council curbed the activities of the dance hall operators by passing a strong measure banning liquor sales after one in the morning. Also outlawed were sales of alcohol in a public hall where men and women mingled, although this ordinance was rarely enforced. These dance halls were popular with new immigrants, and thus ripe for attack by the council. "These foreigners bring their native customs over here and inject them into our society," complained Alderman Dunn. "Everything here ought to be United States and in conformity with our customs and laws."

2

Each year thousands of girls, like Theodore Dreiser's Sister Carrie, stepped off the train at the Dearborn Street Station, coming to Chicago in search of the happiness they felt they could not find in their small Midwestern towns. They did not find the streets paved with gold, but with rough cobblestones, dusty in summer and hopelessly mired in winter. Many of them were forced to work in the sweatshops of the garment district: hell-holes without windows or ventilation, lit only by bare lightbulbs swinging overhead. One can imagine the misery engendered in the summer of 1901, for instance, when temperatures reached 118 F. in the Loop in July. There was no place to seek relief: some hospitals and public places used air convection over chunks of ice

118

which had been cut the previous winter from ice floes in the lake. But this was not the practice in factories and sweatshops.

More comfortable surroundings were afforded by the big department stores—Siegel-Cooper, Marshall Field's, the Fair Store, the Boston Store—which paid saleswomen six dollars a week. This sum was eroded by floorwalkers, who imposed fines on employees for minor infractions of the rules.

On State Street, between Van Buren and Polk, was Whiskey Row, a thriving vice district. There was the Senate, the Little White City (where Little Egypt danced in the window), the Grand Palace and Andy Craig's Tivoli. Craig, a convicted felon, was a bondsman at the Harrison lockup, the head of the infamous Pickpocket's Trust and a keeper of a disreputable house. In 1905 Chief John Collins cleaned up Whiskey Row and most of the low dives vanished. By 1907 the area was filled with a curious assortment of winerooms, penny parlors, dime museums, nickel cinemas and arcades.

Small boys hustled passersby for nickels so that they could go in and watch early movies which were nothing more than two-act sermons with titles like *Jealousy into Madness, Mary Dear* and *Retribution*. They were heavy-handed, violent and occasionally racy. The producers billed *Jealousy into Madness* as a "portrait of real life." A peasant's wife is kissed by a handsome stranger who enters her kitchen while her husband is busy elsewhere. She tells the impertinent visitor to mind his manners, but later steals out to meet him in the forest. The husband follows her and sees her kissing the stranger. The sight turns him raving mad and the couple commit him to a local asylum where he is locked in the basement and attacked by rats. The wife and the lover come to visit and jeer at him. He manages to escape, comes home, surprises the guilty pair, strangles his wife, kills the lover and shoots a policeman who tries to subdue him, after which he commits suicide.

Reformers called for the suppression of these films, but the real danger to society lay not in the films themselves but in the kind of audience they attracted. Pimps—called "cadets"—frequented the nickelodeons, and stood outside them and the winerooms,

119

recruiting girls for work in the Levee. When a constable walked by, the cadet would tip his hat and often warn denizens of illegal houses by pressing a doorbell cleverly concealed behind an awning or an electric sign. The denizens would leave the premises through a maze of secret panels and tunnels. It was not easy, in any case, for honest policemen to distinguish between legitimate cafes and illegal winerooms. Occasionally, Levee vicemongers stole into the heart of the downtown business district and operated under the noses of the law.

George Silver was one of those who made the pilgrimage downtown from 22nd Street. In 1903 he opened a Levee showplace called the Maxim, and spent $20,000 furbishing it. He did not secure a liquor license, boasting about his "pull" with Mayor Harrison to Captain William O'Brien; things were squared "by the boys downtown," Silver said. The next day O'Brien got a call from the City Collector saying that Silver was getting a license and should be left alone. Silver printed announcements for the Maxim, calling it "the mayor's place." This was more than having clout; this was flaunting it. Three days later the mayor revoked the license, saying that Silver had violated the midnight closing ordinance and was advertising "in a disgusting fashion," with paintings of undraped females outside on his signs.

"My pull is all right," Silver said. "It's them folks in the City Hall that don't understand it. This is a bad, bad business." But not even Kenna or Coughlin was willing to help him. Silver's big mouth had gotten him into trouble. "I can't stand for this fellow any longer," Hinky Dink said. "He isn't satisfied with running a straight business like the rest of us, and he must suffer for his nonsense."

Silver turned to the courts and found a friend in old Judge Gary, who restored his license. "I take it that it is the custom for employees after their nocturnal labors to drink a glass of beer before going to bed," Gary said. "That is sometimes the practice in private families." Silver promised that he would behave in the future, but he could not seem to control himself and the notorious Tenderloin could not stomach him. He was probably the only Levee dive keeper to be run out of the district.

He then opened the Rialto at Clark and Randolph streets, in the heart of the Loop. Local businessmen did not object, and Carter Harrison was no longer mayor: Fred Busse, a genial Republican who had been a postmaster and who liked to frequent saloons, had taken his place. Silver put in a polished mahogany bar facing Clark Street, and above it hung stiffly posed photographs of actors, prize fighters, jockeys and the same sirens who had helped to close his Dearborn Street dive.

The *Chicago Tribune* for August 18, 1907, described the Rialto as "a bar and wineroom in comparison with which many of the saloons and winerooms of the Levee district would have no cause to blush." From the lower level, sounds of laughter filtered up mixed with rousing songs and ragtime music. Business was good. Women of varied ages moved from table to table, socializing with men only as long as they bought drinks. As the one o'clock closing time approached, Silver announced to people who were not regulars to drink up and depart. Those he could trust, he moved into a secluded area of the wineroom; the marquee lights were dimmed to avoid the notice of the police. Inside, intimate little coteries sipped champagne, told ribald stories and generally enjoyed Silver's hospitality. It was a typical wineroom. And it was the place where the cadet took his new women for drinks and music.

Frightful tales of white slavery filled the press. It was said that the pimp would find an innocent new arrival from the country, and promise her devotion, a good time and even marriage, leading her on until she was lured into a "breaking-in house" where she was repeatedly raped and then imprisoned under guard, and even given cocaine and morphine. Some women passively accepted the life without drugs.

These horrible stories frightened women, some to death. On November 25, 1912, Maude Van Dusen, a 35-year-old schoolteacher from Falls City, Nebraska, leapt twenty floors from the top of the McCormick Building on Michigan Avenue, clutching a Bible. She carried also a 35,000-word typed statement in which she said her sister had been lured into prostitution and she was positive the same forces intended to seize her. She begged Mayor Harrison and Chief McWeeney to do something.

Wild stories and paranoia apart, white slavers did ply their trade in Chicago. There was the story of Caterina Bressi, a 16-year-old Italian girl, who was lured from her home in the vineyards outside Naples by Santina Pizzi, a well-dressed elegant lady from Chicago, who told Caterina's parents, a simple peasant couple, that a wonderful life awaited their daughter in America. Santina Pizzi bought Caterina a $100 third-class steerage passage on the White Star Line. At the dock the girl was met by two toughs who took her on the train to Chicago and delivered her to 407 S Clark Street, the house run by Baptista Pizzi, Santina's husband. Here she was raped by several men, her clothes were taken away and she was given expensive finery to wear and told that these were worth $600 and she had to work to pay for them. When she tried to escape, her face was slashed. The house doctor could not stop the bleeding, so she was taken to county hospital where the two toughs stood guard over her. In a few weeks she was released, but with scars on her face, and still a prisoner in the brothel.

Somewhat later, Pizzi's house was raided by the Vice Commission which had been set up by Mayor Busse on March 5, 1910, with Dean Sumner and U.S. District Attorney Edwin Sims as chairman and secretary respectively. Caterina was arrested. She was afraid to tell her story to the authorities, but it was discovered nevertheless and her fare back to Naples was paid by the Federal Government. On June 3, 1910, Pizzi was found guilty of pandering and sent to prison.

Another white slaver who was arrested was Maurice Van Bever, whose wife Julia worked with him. This couple had several houses and saloons and lived a luxurious life, often driving along the lakefront in a brougham complete with footman. On October 13, 1909, Van Bever was arrested by Federal agents in the Loop outside the Chamber of Commerce building. He was taken to the Desplaines Street station, where he posted a $2,000 bond, and explained that he had never been arrested before. "I have always lived up to the order of the police department in having all the girls registered at the station," he said.

But at Van Bever's trial the facts about his white slave operations came to light. Michael Hart, a bartender at Van Bever's

Paris resort at 2102 Armour Avenue, and his wife Mollie, testified that Hart had been sent by Julia Van Bever to procure a 19-year-old St Louis girl named Sarah Joseph whom Julia had seen somewhere and admired. "See that Jew girl and make sure she comes back with you," Maurice Van Bever had said, and promised Hart a new suit of clothes if he procured her.

It was the practice, Hart said, for Hart and another Van Bever bartender named Dick Tyler, to go to St Louis to pick up girls. When they got one, they would take her to a quiet hotel in East St Louis, where she would be told golden lies about the excellent employment opportunities in Chicago. If she agreed to go there, she would be taken to another small town to board a Chicago-bound train and get off in Englewood, where Julia Van Bever would meet her and drive her to a downtown hotel to be picked up by a resortkeeper. These elaborate precautions were taken because the police were watching downtown train stations for cadets soliciting single women. The Vice Commission had made a real dent in the traffic.

"A man can't hold a job in the south side Levee unless he is willing to go out and get girls," Hart testified. "It is the practice of those who manage to get any girls—and owing to the reformers that is becoming more and more difficult every day—to get off the train with the girls at some suburb of Chicago and either place them in a hotel or take a cab and drive them into the city at once."

Mollie Hart picked up Sarah Joseph at the train station and on the way to the Paris, the brothel, told her what she should say if the police asked her any questions. Sarah testified that she said she wanted to go home, but she was ignored, of course. When they arrived at the Paris, Van Bever told her that she was so good-looking that she would do very well for herself. She told him that she wanted to leave, but Van Bever replied that she would like it once she got used to it. When she insisted on leaving, he said he would get her some clothes and then she could go. But later, she testified, he told her she couldn't go until she paid him for the clothes.

She testified that Van Bever had told her to tell the police that she was twenty-one, although she was only nineteen, and that she

123

had been "in a place like that before," although she had not. She had not known what kind of place it was when she first went there, and when she realized it the first night, she asked immediately to go home, but she could not, she said, because she had no money.

"But men gave you money," the prosecutor said. "Didn't you get any money for selling drinks?"

"No," she said, "I didn't see any. I got checks."

Van Bever and his wife were sentenced to one year in the Bridewell and fined $1,000. David Garfinkle, a 29-year-old connection in St Louis, was given six months for aiding and abetting the illicit traffic, which included, in addition to Sarah Joseph, a girl named Maude Grace. "We have thoroughly cleaned up our docket along this line," prosecutor Clifford Roe beamed. "In this Van Bever conviction, we have put an end to a regularly organized traffic in girls between St Louis and Chicago."

In November, 1910, shortly before they were to depart for an extended European holiday, the Van Bevers were arrested again, this time for bringing another St Louis girl, Pearl Sypher, to the Paris resort.

Then there was Leona Garrity. In early June of 1907, she was arrested on a police tip that she had lured a 15-year-old girl, Belle Winters, to her houses at 75 and 83 N Peoria Street. When Garrity was arraigned on a pandering charge, it developed that she was married to Lemuel Schlotter, a wealthy jewelry merchant who resided on Green Bay Road in north suburban Glencoe, where her neighbors were less than enchanted to discover the kind of woman they had harbored in their midst.

There had been international conferences on the problem of the white slave trade beginning in 1899, but "white slavery" was a term virtually unknown to mainstream America before 1907. Federal laws protected immigrant girls from dockside hoodlums, but little was done to stop girls being transported across state lines. Wiley J. Phillips, chairman of the White Slave Traffic Committee, reported that 278 girls under the age of fifteen were rescued from Levee dens during a two-month period in 1907. Chicago was the Midwestern corridor of this illegal traffic.

Strong response to this situation—with pressure from people like the Rev M.P. Boynton of the Midnight Mission—resulted in the passage of the Mann Act, written by Republican Congressman James Robert Mann, who had been a Chicago alderman. Known as the White Slave Act, it provided heavy penalties for the transportation, for immoral purposes, of women from one state to another. President Taft signed the bill into law on June 26, 1910, after protracted discussion about whether Congress had the authority to regulate interstate commerce of persons, apart from commodities. Its constitutionality was upheld.

Far more powerful in the Levee than the Van Bevers was Big Jim Colosimo.

He had been born in Italy, emigrated to Chicago in the late 'eighties and worked as a laborer and as a street cleaner for the Chicago Department of Sanitation, where he caught the eye of labor racketeer "Dago" Mike Corrozzo, whom he helped to organize the street sweepers into a formidable political organization. Kenna and Coughlin appreciated his dedication to democracy and made him a precinct captain. But Colosimo really came into his own when, in 1902, he married a dumpy madam named Victoria Moresco, who owned a disorderly house on Armour Avenue, and went into the brothel business. Together, Victoria and Jim expanded: they opened a bagnio at Armour Avenue and 21st Street called the Victoria. Big Jim began to wear expensive clothes and displayed a fondness for diamonds. As he prospered, he worried about his health and brought in a young hoodlum named Johnny Torrio from New York to see to the peace in the Levee. By that time, Colosimo was the politicians' official bagman, picking up tribute from the brothelkeepers and extracting a fee before passing it on.

In 1910, he opened a restaurant and cabaret on Wabash Avenue. Colosimo's became a premier Chicago night spot: on a given night one might find Clarence Darrow, George Ade and Barrett O'Hara rubbing elbows with hoodlums and brothelkeepers like "Loving Putty" Julius Annixter and "Monkey Face" Charley Genker, and Mont Tennes, the gambling king. There were also opera singers: Enrico Caruso, Amelita Galli-Curci; Jim and Victoria were devotees of Italian opera. Certainly Jim had arrived; he also attracted the attention of the Black Hand. When Frank Razzina, a member of a secret society known as the Comorra, was sent to jail in 1907, he made the sign of death when someone mentioned Colosimo's name. That was one reason why Colosimo imported Johnny Torrio.

Suggestive songs, a street lit by gaslight, and young boys hawking newspapers and selling chewing gum from a street corner—such was the south-side Levee in 1910, and the House of all Nations, the Little Green House, Bed Bug Row, the Bucket of Blood, the Everleigh Club, Freiberg's Dance Hall and Ed Weiss's Capitol were the principal attractions. When Isaac Gitelson, better known in the district as Ike Bloom, converted his German *Weinstube* into a dance hall and wineroom in 1895, it became the command post of the Levee, the one place considered "untouchable" by the cops. From the back room of Freiberg's, orders were issued by Coughlin and Kenna, who operated through Sol Friedman, Ike Bloom's brother-in-law. Friedman handled the whiskey, taxicab and clothing concessions in the Levee, while the divekeepers were required to buy their insurance from Coughlin's own firm. Payoffs were made in the private office of Freiberg's, and each service carried a precise fee. To stop an indictment for pandering, it would cost $1,000. But the district was segregated from the central city, and there was some attempt at regulation.

Two plainclothes detectives were assigned to the Levee to "book" the names and addresses of the girls who lived there. The information was kept in a file at the 22nd Street station. Underaged girls were coached on how to answer the police questions by the keeper of the house. When the new prospect arrived at the bagnio (interviews were always conducted on the premises), she would invariably say that she was from out of town, had always led an immoral life, and was of the legal age. The booking system worked nicely for the resortkeeper. When a girl was found to be underaged and an arrest was made, the divekeeper would say that the booking agents allowed her to stay. (Birth certificates and photographs were not required by the police, so the abuses of this system and its graft potential were obvious.)

Within the Levee, there were extremes of good and bad taste. The California was a dollar-a-girl resort, built with sliding walls and a waiting room attended by a rotund black woman who urged the men on by saying, "Pick a baby, boys! Don't get glued to your seats!" The house was run by "Blubber" Bob Gray and his wife Therese McCafey. Blubber Bob's considerable girth got in the way when he tried to escape Federal agents on August 27, 1909. Five women of Belgian, Canadian and French extraction were arrested along with Gray, who was found protruding from the rear window, hopelessly stuck.

In the Casino at 21st and Dearborn, the wineroom was adjoined by private rooms, tended by a woman wearing a ring of keys at her waist. She admitted only those men who paid the "cover charge" to those rooms. In the wineroom at the Casino, as in similar establishments, white-vested waiters dashed about, calling orders to the barkeeps: "Two pints at four!" Pasty-faced professional escorts sat against the walls with their women, who were available for a price. The waiters greeted a new patron when he entered, saying, "Well, what do I see? What do I see?" and signalling two girls to come up and escort him to a table. The girls sat down with their new friend while the waiter slipped a "percentage check" on the table: each girl got ten cents on the dollar for each drink. Lively background music was supplied by a young black singer accompanied by a player piano.

Every house on the Levee employed a "professor." Sometimes he worked as the roper or the head cashier, but most of the time he was the piano man or balladeer, called a "coon shouter." These young black men received ten dollars a week, plus a percentage of the drink money. Their songs were suggestive, a fusion of Caribbean music and popular ballads. It was ragtime, the first popular music form of the twentieth century. It had begun in the late 1800s—St Louis was an early center for ragtime musicians— and ragtime sheet music was published all over the country after pianist Ben Harney introduced the style into New York in 1897.

The player-piano rolls were cheaply produced, and Scott Joplin, Tom Turpin and the great Jelly Roll Morton became known as ragtime virtuosos. The piano was the essential instrument. Ragtime's peak of popularity came about 1910; after that it began to decay and eventually its syncopated, multiple rhythms merged into jazz. On warm summer nights, the strains of Joplin's "Maple Leaf Rag" and "Guest of Honor" drifted from the back alleys through the streets of the Levee.

It was estimated that seven million bottles of beer were consumed in Chicago in 1910. Booze was the staple for everything; it was bought by the resortkeepers for 4 1/2 cents a pint and sold for between twenty-five cents and one dollar a bottle. Some customers received their beer laced with morphine, a drug difficult to detect in an autopsy.

More drug addicts roamed Chicago streets in 1900 than at any time in the city's history. Four Levee druggists sold four pounds of morphine and six ounces of cocaine each month; another sold 500 tablets a week of morphine sulphate. Drugs kept many girls in the life. They were called "air walkers," reflecting a dazed state brought on by the use of encaine, an insidious cocaine imitation.

Syphilis was an obvious hazard of the trade; the houses relied on their own doctors to administer confidential cures to the girls. One doctor charged as much as $400 for his cure, usually a vile red mouthwash laced with alcohol and morphine. It may have relieved some outward symptoms. And then there were the patent medicines, with names like Hood's Sarsparilla and the One and Only Wizard Oil. In these years before the passage of the Pure Food and Drug Act, these medications were unregulated, of course, and advertisements for cures for all forms of social disease appeared in the most respectable newspapers. Advertisements for V.D. cures were tacked to the bathroom walls of Levee houses. And some drug peddlers tried to remedy their own messes. An 1895 ad in the *Chicago Tribune* suggested that Dr Carlos Bruisard of 439 Race Street in Cincinnati, could provide a sure cure for the morphine habit in return for a small fee.

When the papers reported the sad tale of a girl's plunge into prostitution or her sad drug-related death, the public reaction was that she had paid the price for a serious character flaw. But when these stories concerned the deaths of the scions of wealth, idle sons of prominent families, the result was sometimes an attempt at reform of social conditions that contributed to such shame and disgrace. Or sometimes there was a coverup.

In 1905, Marshall Field, Jr., put a bullet in his head as he sat alone in the study of the Field Prairie Avenue mansion one morning. The *Tribune* reported that he had been cleaning his gun and was the victim of an unfortunate accident. There were whispers that young Field had spent the previous evening at the Everleigh Club, that he had been involved in gun play and had been carried back to the mansion from the Levee. This rumor reinforced the clamor of the reformers to shut down the Levee, and it was certainly remembered on January 10, 1910, when the 26-year-old heir to the Rock Island Railroad fortune was found dead at Vic Shaw's bagnio at 2012 S Dearborn Street.

Young Nathaniel Ford Moore had become a golf pro at the age of twenty. In 1905 he spent $20,000 on an after-theatre party at Rector's restaurant in New York. The favors were diamond cufflinks for the gentlemen and strings of pearls for the ladies. Twenty-dollar gold pieces, frozen on ice by the chefs, were dropped down the backs of chorus girls who sat at the table. Moore's wife threatened to leave him, and he promised to try working. "Loafing," he said, "makes one very tired, you know." He did go to work for his father, James Hobart Moore, who was so delighted that he gave Nathaniel $100,000 on his twenty-first birthday. But this arrangement did not last. The boy left work to hire a train with J. Ogden Armour's son and travel at breakneck speed across the California wilderness to arrive in time for a formal dinner party in Santa Barbara.

On the day of his death, Moore left the Everleigh Club in the wee hours and went to Vic Shaw's house, where he was found dead at five the next afternoon. Lieutenant Kelleher and Captain Cudmore of the 22nd Street district were called, along with

Moore's doctor. Although Moore's death was declared to be the result of heart disease by both his own doctor and a coroner's jury, the public perception was that he, like young Marshall Field, had been murdered in the Levee. It was not of course widely known that Moore was a morphine addict. The fact that both men had been in the Everleigh Club on the evening of their deaths was thought to be more than a coincidence. The heat was on and the days of the Everleigh Club and all the others were numbered.

3

The reformers were particularly upset by the First Ward Ball. This was a tradition that had begun in the late 1880s when saloon owners and brothelkeepers, policemen and politicians, crooks, pimps and hoodlums, had gathered in Freiberg's Hall on East 22nd Street to pay tribute to Lame Jimmy, a crippled pianist and fiddler who worked for the madam Carrie Watson. Every year, usually in the second week of December, this lively group toasted Jimmy in champagne and a good time was had by all. The party was not orchestrated by Coughlin and Kenna.

This happy situation came to an abrupt end when, at the 1895 ball, a drunken Harrison Street detective shot a fellow officer in an apparent dispute over a small amount of money. The resulting public outcry doomed the Lame Jimmy celebrations. But it occurred to Coughlin and Kenna that they could possibly do better without Jimmy and without Freiberg's, where only about 300 people had turned up, at a dollar a head. They could take the ball over, move it to a much larger, more impressive venue, and charge a lot more money. Further, they knew that in addition to forced attendance by the wealthy denizens of the ward, there would be other kinds of contributions: liquor, for instance, at low prices.

Consequently the next ball was held in the Seventh Regiment Armory, and the Levee responded handsomely. Boxes were set up for the important madams, saloon owners and wine vendors, who could decorate them to their hearts' content. Everybody bought tickets and blocks of tickets. Even the waiters paid five dollars apiece to be allowed to serve at this lavish event. And then there were the wild costumes, although nobody outdid Bathhouse John himself, who came attired in green and purple, set off by yellow pumps, pink gloves and a silk top hat. The whole thing was a rousing success. Hinky Dink said it was "a lalapalooza" and the profit came to $25,000.

The balls were held for more than a decade. They were moved from the Armory to the third Coliseum on Wabash Avenue and everyone, from the smallest crib operator, was required to attend. The social committee, which began planning in the ball in the autumn, was a Who's Who of Chicago vice. There were Pat O'Malley, a gambler who was an early ally of Mont Tennes in the gambler's war; Ferdinand Buxbaum, owner of the Marlborough Hotel where Levee girls took their customers; the convicted pickpocket Andy Craig, who lured Loop salesgirls to a disorderly life in his Tivoli; John Dineen, a State Street saloonkeeper; George Little, a small brothelkeeper; Ike Bloom, called "The King of the Brothels," who operated Freiberg's with his brother-in-law Sol Friedman, also a member, and Big Jim Colosimo.

The rental fee for the Coliseum was a thousand dollars. That was arranged through Alderman Charles Gunther who headed the board of directors of the hall and who had opened the place to convention business in 1900.[9] Tickets were sold in the Levee and in every gambling den on the north, south and west sides. The private boxes circling the main floor were sold for five dollars. The standard admission was one dollar, but Coughlin and Kenna gave out free passes to swell the crowd, although every man who came in had to pay a fifty cent hatcheck fee.

For the 1907 ball, Sol Friedman was in charge of the booze concession. He told the waiters' union that their members could be employed only if they paid: five dollars for the privilege of serving the boxes which dropped to one dollar to serve customers in the basement. Friedman responded to protests by saying he needed the "price of a good set of clothes."

Actually the ward organization needed cash for the upcoming elections in the spring of 1908.

The 1907 ball was a masquerade. Many celebrants were masked, and the 22nd Street doves appeared in full force as Indian maidens, geisha girls and queens of the Nile. Coughlin, appearing in his usual array of rainbow colors, was accompanied by Tim Sullivan, the boss of New York's Tammany Hall, two congressmen and the mayor of Kewanee, Illinois. At midnight came the Grand March, which Coughlin led, with the Everleigh sisters on either side of him. The orchestra played the dreadful song Bathhouse had written—"Dear Midnight of Love," the third stanza of which ran:

> Your promise, love, redeem; Your gentle words do thrill;
> Live as the rippling stream, Always, your friend I will.
> Now I must bid adieu. So cruel; why did we meet?
> List! love, what shall we do? Goodbye, when shall we greet?

Apparently the reformers were not outraged by these lyrics, but only by the ball itself. Arthur Burrage Farwell, the president of the Chicago Law and Order League, made a strong complaint to Mayor Busse, in which he pointed out that some 20,000 people had drunk as much as 10,000 quarts of champagne, women had been attacked, guest lay in various states of inebriation in the aisles, there had been fights all over the floor of the hall in which furniture, including a thirty-five-foot bar, had been smashed to bits, and a madam had stabbed her fiancé with a hatpin. The *Tribune* commented that if the Coliseum had been destroyed that night, there would not have been "a second story worker, a dip or plugugly, porch climber, dope fiend or scarlet woman" left alive in Chicago. The head of the Secret Service guarding President McKinley had remarked that London's Thieves Ball was a Sunday School picnic compared to the 1907 First Ward Ball. Farwell and a gaggle of city leaders and churchmen demanded that Busse refuse to issue a liquor license for the 1908 ball. But the mayor demurred. He thought they were exaggerating.

There were a few glitches before the ball was held on Monday night, December 14. On the 7th, the *Tribune* announced that it would print the name of every "respectable person" who attended the ball, in the hope that businessmen and "the better grade of politician" would keep away and "come pretty close to making the affair a failure from a financial standpoint." This shook up Hinky Dink, who increased the 1907 quotas on brothelkeepers and Levee merchants in order to make up for a possible loss in attendance by wealthy slummers. Then on December 13, a bomb was thrown at the rear of the Coliseum, demolishing a shack used for storage, and which housed a vagabond known as Pietrowsky the Junkman. No one was hurt, although a few windows were shattered in neighboring streets. The First Ward politicians blamed the reformers, while Farwell said it was the work of a First Ward element. It was the twenty-seventh bomb hurled in six months and may have had something to do with the gamblers' war. Inspector Wheeler of the Harrison Street detail stationed 100 policemen on the Wabash Avenue side of the Coliseum.

Bathhouse John visited the City Council before the ball; everyone was flabbergasted to see that he had eschewed his rainbow colors in favor of conservative black attire. He then went to the Coliseum where thousands of people were jamming the streets about the building, clamoring to be let in. The police could not control the struggling mob; trolleys were stalled all down Wabash and State Streets. Coughlin made his way inside and then he and Kenna ordered the doors open. As might be expected, no one could control the wild entry that resulted: tables, chairs, and plants were knocked over, the boxes were damaged, women fainted in the crush, and were passed hand to hand overhead toward the exits. To stop the invasion, the police locked the doors, although this was against the fire regulations. Fights broke out on the floor where the smoke was so thick that no one could see across the hall. Glasses were smashed, food was snatched from the trays of immobilized waiters. Things got so bad that a large contingent tried to leave, and were balked by the locked doors; in the meantime, the crowd outside was still trying to get in. The *Tribune* later reported that hats, scarves, jewelry and furs were scattered on the paving stones.

Finally the mob inside burst out through a side door. Coughlin rushed out with his guards to try to calm the celebrants, and walked into Lyman Atwell, a photographer for the *Record-Herald* who, with cartoonist Wyncie King at his side, had set up his tripod and camera to catch the scandalous scene. When Atwell set off his flash, Coughlin yelled that it was a bomb: Atwell was knocked down and his equipment smashed.

By eleven o'clock things had quieted down, the band struck up "Dear Midnight of Love" and the Levee ladies entered their boxes. The *Record-Herald* reported that the night was "a riot of unbridled license," where girls cavorted in pink and blue tights and other costumes unfit to be seen in public. Walter Sumner, Dean of St Peter and Paul Cathedral, who was there to watch and report to the reformers, was shocked to see a Levee whore wearing a nun's habit. He refused a genial offer of champagne from an expansive Bathhouse John.

At midnight Coughlin and Kenna led the Grand March, while the band played "Hail, Hail, the Gang's All Here." It was a slow procession, twenty-five abreast of madams, prostitutes, gamblers, pimps, jockeys, transvestites, thieves and all the dregs of the city. After that, began serious drinking: Minna Everleigh and her sister spent about fifty dollars an hour on wine; the bottles, which were left on the tables to demonstrate how sales were going, piled up. What took place was described by Dean Sumner as "unbelievably appalling and nauseating." There were constant fighting, assaults by drunks on women who were for the most part willing, and wild dancing. When it finally ended, in the wee hours of the morning, Kenna pronounced it another "lallapalooza." But actually profits were down from the year before; there had been too many gate crashers, too much free liquor.

Eight people were arrested that night, but only one was convicted, for trying to enter the building without paying.

The Vice Commission demanded action from Mayor Busse to see that this sort of thing was stopped once and for all: ". . . Those who attended were for the most part immoral women and men who are engaged in social evil business, the sale of liquor and gambling. . . . It's the opinion of this Commission that this and any other similar affair should never be allowed again."

The urge for reform was underscored by a visit to the Levee of Gipsy Smith, an evangelist born Rodney Smith in 1860 near Epping Forest in England. He planned to invade the Levee with fire-and-brimstone preaching and began month-long meetings on October 3 at the Seventh Regimental Armory. His oratory was impassioned:

> You women are to blame. You are too afraid to risk your white reputations to help the woman that has fallen, but the demon that ruined her you will take into your homes, to your dinners, to meet your daughters. You will marry your daughter to a scoundrel if he can dress well and drive in an automobile.
>
> A man who visits the red light district by night has no right to associate with decent people in the daylight, even though he may sit on the throne of a millionaire.

On October 18, 1909, 2,000 people listened to Smith and then followed him and a Salvation Army band to 22nd Street. By the time they got there, the following had reached about 20,000. The band played "Nearer My God to Thee" and "Where is My Wandering Boy Tonight?" The streets were choked with the righteous and the curious, but the lights were out in the dives and resorts, and the pianos were silent. Shades were drawn, doors were closed. The saloons remained open; barkeeps reported record earnings. Parents brought their offspring to the district to hear the preacher. One lad told a reporter that he wanted "to see it all so he could tell the other fellows who weren't so lucky." Only one person was arrested: a black woman named Mary Chase fired three shots over the heads of the crowd. The procession continued on to 34th and Wentworth, where Smith held another revival meeting.

When the crowd faded away, the Levee doors swung open, the player pianos started up, and the busiest night in Levee history began. Lieutenant Enright of the 22nd Street detail reported that every resort was filled and people were being turned away. "Far be it from me to moralize," one woman said. "We're here to make money and certainly it's coming in fast. If Gipsy Smith would lead a few more parades down here, I would soon make enough money to retire and live on the interest of my wealth."

But despite the rush in business—Minna Everleigh commented that she was sorry to see "so many nice young men coming down here for the first time"—Gipsy Smith's revival also increased feelings against Levee vice. In November, when Bathhouse John announced the 1909 First Ward ball, the reformers raised a considerable outcry, and the result was that Mayor Busse refused to issue the ball a liquor license. Coughlin and Kenna were reduced to holding a concert in the Coliseum. It was a dreary affair; only 3,000 attended.

The reformers were not satisfied to see the end of the ball. They wanted an end to the Levee. The 4,000 members of the Women's Christian Temperance Union, the thousands of members of the Church Federation made up of 600 Chicago congregations, all demanded that Mayor Busse appoint a committee to report on the Levee. The mayor had no choice. On March 5, 1910, he selected thirty prominent people to make up a Vice Commission which would explore the connections between the police, resort owners, druggists, the beer halls and the methods of procurement. Dean Sumner was named chairman and U.S. District Attorney Edwin W. Sims was secretary. Among the clergymen, business and civic leaders who made up the commission were such prominent Chicagoans as Julius Rosenwald, head of Sears, Roebuck & Co, Dr W.A. Evans, the city health commissioner and Ellen Henrotin, the only woman on the panel, who represented the Federation of Women's Clubs.

By the time the Vice Commission rendered its 400-page report, Carter Harrison II was once more mayor of Chicago. The First Ward had great faith in Harrison; they thought he would support them. But the Vice Commission had done a devastating job. It had looked into every aspect of vice in the city and come up with convincing figures. There were over 1,000 brothels, 1,800 madams and pimps and 4,000 prostitutes in the Levee, bringing in an annual revenue of sixty million dollars, on which profits were fifteen million.

The Commission called for an end to protected vice; for the extermination of the Levee; for the setting up of police morals squads and morals courts for prostitutes, and expressed dismay that working girls in factories and department stores made so little money that they were tempted into prostitution to keep body and soul together.

At around the same time, the Civil Service Commission began to hold hearings on the connections between the police and vice and gambling in the First Ward. The public was thoroughly aroused—Chicago, they were now aware, had a world-wide reputation as a protected den of iniquity. The era of the segregated vice district was rapidly coming to an end.

5

There had been attempts at reform by Fred A. Busse when he was elected mayor of Chicago in 1907. Busse, who had been born in Chicago in 1866, was a dependable Republican party man whose parents were German immigrants. His reputation was not soiled by any connections with graft: he had been town clerk, court bailiff and deputy sheriff, had served two terms in the Illinois House in 1894 and 1896 and then one term as state senator, was elected state treasurer in 1902 and finally, before he became mayor, was appointed postmaster of Chicago by Theodore Roosevelt. Busse cleaned out the police force when he became mayor: Chief John Collins was replaced by George Shippy, who transferred Captain Patrick Harding and his entire 22nd Street force, to the Attrill Street station. Harding was replaced by Edward McCann of the Englewood station, a robust Irishman, the father of nine and a picture of respectability, who wore a handlebar moustache and a small gold cross on his vest.

On May 22, 1907, McCann made a speech to the district patrolmen. "This is the beginning of a new era," he announced. "I have worked many hours in picking out the men I wanted for duty here. And I will say right here, from now on any person in the red-light district who claims to pay graft to any member of the department will be summoned to name who that officer was. Presents to patrolmen will avail them nothing, and it will go hard with the patrolmen or resortkeeper when I get evidence of the passing of tribute."

Ten months later, on March 10, 1908, McCann was made inspector and transferred to the Desplaines Street station. Conditions along Madison, Halsted, Carpenter and Curtis streets were only slightly better than they were in the Levee: this Desplaines district was the domain of Mike "de Pike" Heitler, Charley "Monkey Face" Genker and the Frank brothers, Louis and Julius. On his arrival, McCann informed the Franks that if the resortkeepers wanted to stay in business, they had better come up with some of the tribute that he had warned the 22nd Street cops not to accept.

Everyone was eager to accommodate the inspector. On the second of each month, each resortkeeper entered the Franks' saloon on the corner of Halsted and Madison with a $20 bill pinned to a note on which was written the name of the resort, so there would be no mistake. Louis Frank delivered the money—sometimes in a satchel—directly to McCann's house. This arrangement, which was not considered unusual by the resortkeepers, lasted until McCann discovered that some of his clients were not telling him the truth about the numbers of inmates in their houses. More in sorrow than in anger, he informed Frank that the deal was off.

"Here's their money," he said. "Give it back to them. This isn't dealing squarely with me and they'll have to deal squarely with me or not at all." The price of protection went up from $450 to $550 a month. This was too steep for some west side entrepreneurs: Morrie Schatz, a divekeeper at 108 Peoria Street, went to State's Attorney John Wayman, who began an investigation. Soon the newspapers carried full details of McCann's boodle scheme, and the stable of thoroughbreds in which he had invested his illicit gains. McCann was convicted on September 24, 1909. But he did not lose all his friends: Dean Sumner stood by him all the way; many reformers said they believed that he had been railroaded by Wayman, who had political ambitions. Finally, on

May 5, 1911, shortly before his pension eligibility was due to expire, McCann was pardoned by Governor Edward F. Dunne at the request of Theodore Roosevelt.

The McCann scandal cost Chief Shippy his job. He had supposedly "cleaned out" 22nd Street, but then he had quietly brought back many of the old hands. He was succeeded by LeRoy Steward, who appointed Captain William Cudmore to 22nd Street with instructions to ban liquor sales from the resorts. But Cudmore was not up to the job; when Steward learned that bartenders were slipping out the back doors of resorts and upstairs to fetch booze, a second great Levee shakeup took place on August 25, 1910, and John Halpin was brought in, to be replaced in his turn by Patrick Harding, who had originally been replaced in 1907. The more things changed, the more, it seemed, they remained the same. In 1912 Harding and two of his lieutenants were exiled to Desplaines Street after it was discovered that Harding had been concealing a special private bookkeeping system. He was replaced by Michael "White Alley" Ryan, a twenty-two-year veteran who had passed all the civil service exams, and who was probably the worst of a bad lot, because he was Mike Kenna's hand-picked lackey. When he moved into the station on February 1, 1912, Ryan hung a portrait of Ike Bloom, "The King of the Brothels," above his desk.

6

In 1911, in Chicago's first direct mayoral primary, Carter Harrison II won a narrow victory, aided by Coughlin and Kenna, who had enjoyed Harrison's first terms from 1897 to 1905. Harrison was an honest politician, but he had a live-and-let-live attitude toward many of the targets of the reformers, as his father had had before him. He was opposed to prohibition because Chicago's immigrant population were opposed to it, and he believed in segregated vice districts, because he was convinced that vice could not be eradicated, but should be contained.

However, things had changed in Chicago by 1911. As we have seen, Mayor Busse's Vice Commission had caused a tremendous uproar, and Harrison understood that he had to respond to public demand that the Levee be curbed. He began by closing the bookmakers and then ordered the removal of all loose women from Michigan Avenue, and the closing of call houses and cheap hotels on the avenue from 12th to 35th streets.

Then when he saw a brochure issued by Minna and Ada Everleigh to advertise their Everleigh Club, he used the occasion to clamp down on them. The brochure was restrained in the extreme, illustrated with photographs of the Club interior sans titillating inhabitants. The text said that the Club had long been famous for its decor, including luxurious furniture, elegant paintings and statues. It boasted steam heat in the winter, and electric fans in the summer, and it was generally magnificent.

Apparently unimpressed, on October 24, 1911, Harrison issued an order to Police Chief John McWeeney: "Close the Everleigh Club." This came as a shock to everybody in the First Ward and to a lot of people outside it. The Club had been an ornament of the ward since it had opened its doors on February 2, 1900. The sisters, Minna and Ada Lester, had arrived in Chicago from Omaha where they had operated a successful bordello during the Trans-Mississippi Exposition. They leased the Club building—a three-story, fifty-room mansion at 2131 S Dearborn Street—from Christopher Columbus Crabb, who had built it with Lizzie Allen in 1890, at a cost of $125,000. Crabb had inherited the building upon Lizzie Allen's death, and he rented it to the Lesters, who took the name Everleigh from their grandmother's habit of signing letters "Everly yours."

The Everleighs made substantial improvements in the property. They built a library to house rare books, and filled the house with rich rugs, oil paintings, valuable statuary and furniture—not the least was a gold piano which purportedly cost $15,000. The Everleighs were fond of gold: their building had twenty gold-plated spittoons at $650 each, golden silk curtains and drapes. gold-rimmed china and glassware, gilded bathtubs in the immense bathrooms, and a Gold Room with gilt furniture. There were twelve parlors, one with copper walls panelled in brass, cut-glass chandeliers and the rugs lay on floors inlaid with rare woods in mosaic patterns.

The Everleigh girls wore elegant gowns and were given elocution and etiquette lessons. "We only serve the best people," Minna said.[10] And their services were not cheap. It cost ten dollars just to enter the winerooms, and fifty dollars was a routine charge for an evening with the ladies. Dinner cost fifty dollars a plate, including wine, which was fifteen dollars a bottle in the bedrooms.

Thus the closing of the Club came as a blow to the Levee. The sisters tried to reach Harrison, but he did not respond, and neither did Chief McWeeney. Minna and Ada held one last celebration, with champagne and music; at one in the morning squads of police arrived. It was truly over, and the Everleigh sisters departed Chicago forever.

Harrison did nothing dramatic after that, although the reformers, led by the Committee of Fifteen and Arthur Burrage Farwell, kept up the pressure. This increased when Virginia Brooks, a young, fierce anti-vice crusader, brought her campaign to Chicago from Hammond, Indiana, where her followers had threatened to chop up illegal houses with axes. She led a demonstration, 5,000 strong, through the Chicago downtown, to the sound of "Onward, Christian Soldiers!" At her rally in Orchestra Hall, she attacked Mayor Harrison, Chief McWeeney and the State's Attorney, John E. Wayman, for dragging their feet in actions against the Levee.

Wayman immediately leapt into action, deliberately eclipsing the mayor. Wayman, born in West Virginia, was an educated man, who read Greek and had studied criminology. In 1908 he had run for state's attorney, defeating John Healy in the primary and surviving two recounts. He was an active state's attorney, advocating changes in the parole system and sending labor slugger Mossie Enright to the penitentiary. At the same time, he did not alienate the First Ward completely: in a 1912 poll he was Bathhouse John's choice for handsomest man in Chicago.

Bathhouse John's admiration for Wayman was sorely tried when the state's attorney got warrants, and sent his own detective force out on constant raids. He promised that every place in town would be closed by the time he left office. He had not been renominated in the last Republican primary, so he was a lame duck and had nothing to lose. The raids began on October 4, 1912, and continued without letup for a week, night and day. Wayman set up a "Levee court," which was open from nine in the morning to ten in the evening in the Criminal Courts building. While informants testified, McWeeney's men patrolled Whiskey Row, arresting unescorted women and shutting saloons that violated the one in the morning closing law. Wayman's men even searched county records to discover owners of Levee property: they found many names of deceased people and bogus holding companies. The respected Chicago Title and Trust Company was named as trustee of an Armour Avenue resort, but the company threatened a libel suit and Wayman announced a retraction. This did not damage Wayman's reputation at this point: special prayers were said for him in the churches by those reformers who had attacked him for dereliction of duty a week before.

The Levee fought back by urging the girls who had lost their cribs to go up and down Michigan Avenue and respectable streets in Hyde Park, ringing doorbells and asking for shelter, while wearing scandalous amounts of paint and garish clothing. Needless to say, these girls did not receive sympathetic responses, although doors were opened to them at the Florence Crittenden Anchorage, 2615 S Indiana, and the Lifeboat Home on Cottage Grove Avenue. Few women entered those doors. The purpose of this exercise was to demonstrate to the community the value of a segregated vice district, on the reasonable assumption that nobody wanted these obvious strumpets wandering all over their neighborhoods.

Mayor Harrison had at first kept aloof from Wayman's actions; he did not allow the police to take part, and he asked for a referendum on segregated vice. But when it became evident that it was political suicide to stay out of the crusade, he sent out the police to padlock house after house. Their inhabitants fled, often out of town. The *Tribune* announced triumphantly that the Levee had been smashed to pieces, and was gone. This was certainly a premature announcement.

7

In 1914 Governor Edward F. Dunne, who had been mayor of Chicago, signed a bill giving women the vote. For the first time a formidable candidate ran against Bathhouse John Coughlin in the First Ward: she was Marion Drake, a former stenographer and court reporter who had succeeded in passing the bar. She was also the first president of the Cook County Suffrage Alliance, and she found plenty of women and other reformers eager to help her campaign against The Bath. It was only through frantic ballot-stuffing that Coughlin succeeded in defeating her. The Levee celebrated.

Gradually the dives and resorts, the winerooms, bookie joints and hotels began to reopen. Johnny Torrio ran the Saratoga for Big Jim while Colosimo himself spent his time at his plush new cafe on Wabash Avenue, courting a 19-year-old choir singer named Dale Winter. Torrio had his own place at 2118 S Federal Street, and he had a dependable gang of pluguglies to support him and help protect Colosimo's enterprises. There were Torrio's cousin, Roxy Vanilla, originally Rocco Vanelli, imported from Montana; the pimp and bagman "Chicken" Harry Gullet; the Sicilians Mike Merlo and Joey de Andrea; Mac Fitzpatrick, alias W.E. Frazier; Jew Kid Grabiner and Billy Leathers.

To make the lives of this crew—and the other Levee denizens—complete, Mike Kenna arranged that Michael F. "White Alley" Ryan be appointed commander at 22nd Street. Ryan was totally beholden to Kenna and slavishly followed his instructions, ignoring any reform-minded orders from McWeeney. With this hearty support, the Levee started to revive. When James Franche, known as "Ed Duffy" or "Duffy the Goat," shot Isaac Henagow in Roy Jones's saloon at 2037 S Wabash Avenue, in a dispute over woman suffrage, Captain Ryan attempted to save Jones's license, which had only recently been restored by Mayor Harrison.

Jones had instructed his employees to tell the police that the shooting had not taken place in the saloon, and when Ryan appeared, he told the incredulous reporters that he agreed. "I don't believe that Henagow was shot while seated in the cafe," he said. "It would have been impossible for him to walk after the bullet struck him, and it is foolish to think that he came down the stairs unaided. The shooting could have happened in the city's best places. I believe the man was shot while out on the street." However, a stray bullet was found embedded in the wall of the dive, so it was undeniable that Henagow had been shot in the saloon.[11]

Mayor Harrison did not replace Ryan because he did not want to alienate Kenna and Coughlin completely. But he was in a difficult position.

He appointed Captain James Gleason as chief of police, a man with a flawless reputation, and in response to pressure from the Committee of Fifteen, set up a special Morals Squad to resume raids on the red light district. The squad was led by William C. Dannenberg, a former Federal agent who had been instrumental in destroying the Van Bever white-slave ring and sending Van Bever and his wife Julia to prison, and Major Metellius C. Funkhouser of the Illinois National Guard, who was also named second deputy of police. These two men were cordially hated in the Levee, and White Alley Ryan was outraged by their appointment. "This district has never been clean and it never will be," he announced. "We don't want no Dannenbergs around here. He uses stool pigeons and I won't stand for it."

They did indeed use stool pigeons. When the mayor revoked Roy Jones's saloon license, Jones got drunk and told a stool pigeon that Big Jim Colosimo and Maurice Van Bever were planning to murder Dannenberg and Funkhouser. This led Chief Gleason to issue an order that Colosimo's and all the others must be closed down. Ryan ignored the order. "This whole nasty affair can be placed at the door of politics," he said. "Nearly every great wave of so-called 'reform' in the police department runs back to politics." Whatever the reason, the Morals men in 1914 started a determined cleanup. Two hundred Levee bagnios were closed down.

"They're running us into a hole," Johnny Torrio moaned. "I'm gettin' tired of payin' dough to get a chance to run, and then havin' these guys bustin' me and my friends every day or two. I'm tired of havin' my women yell to me about gettin' no dough. We got to take a couple of 'em into an alley and kick 'em up some ... so's the others will wise up to the fact that they're not wanted around here."

Colosimo decided to think this over. He called a dinner meeting of his toughs, and included detectives Ed Murphy and Johnny Howe. Maurice Van Bever was there too. It was decided that the Morals men should be bought off, and accordingly Chicken Harry Gullet approached Dannenberg and offered him a $2,000 monthly stipend to undercut Funkhouser and leave the stews alone. Dannenberg immediately arrested Chicken Harry for proferring a bribe.

After that, Colosimo tried a smear campaign, allegedly paying several newspaper cartoonists to lampoon Funkhouser. When this failed, Colosimo tried to have Funkhouser declared bankrupt. It was a bizarre plot involving a legal claim held against the major by his partner. Colosimo's people bought up the claim and pressed for immediate settlement.

But the raids went on. The district had to pay $20,000 fines as Dannenberg closed over 2,000 brothels and arrested the owners and the women. Wild rumors spread through the city that Torrio was bringing in gangs of hit men, who were hiding in the underground labyrinths connecting the houses on 22nd Street. There was tension in the air anyway: war was imminent in Europe.

The event that finally doomed the Levee took place on July 16, 1914. Dannenberg left city hall with a squad of men. He was being closely watched: Detectives Michael McFadden and John Cook of the 22nd Street station had circulated photographs of the Morals men in the Levee so that they could be instantly recognized, and all their movements were quickly reported to the underworld. When word went out that Dannenberg was coming, the women were spirited away through the connecting tunnels, but Dannenberg succeeded in reaching The Turf, a three-story bagnio at 28 W 22nd Street while it was still open for business. He arrested two men and a woman on the second floor and left Joseph Merrill and Fred Amort, two new members of his squad, at The Turf to wait for a patrol wagon. A hostile crowd began to gather. After the prisoners were taken away by the wagon, Amort and Merrill set off on foot toward Michigan Avenue. The mob of pimps and hoodlums began to follow them, shouting threats, and trailed by Johnny Torrio's big red touring car; Roxy Vanilla and Mac Fitzpatrick rode with Torrio. The mob was angry and restless. "There goes Dannenberg's stoolie!" someone shouted. People began to throw rocks and bricks. A brick hit a woman in the crowd. The Morals men stopped in front of the Swan poolroom and drew their guns.

At that point the story becomes somewhat confused. Two detective sergeants, Stanley J. Birns and John C. Sloop, came up-on the scene, saw the Morals men with guns drawn, mistook them for hoodlums and shot at them. There was an exchange of gun-fire—not only between the two sets of lawmen, but apparently also from Roxy Vanilla and his men, who had exited the red touring car. The result was that Sgt Birns lay dead in the street, Sgt Sloop was seriously wounded and Merrill and Amort, the two Dannenberg men, were both shot in the legs. There were other wounded in the crowd—among these was Roxy Vanilla, who was taken into the red car by Torrio and Fitzpatrick and driven off to St Anthony de Padua Hospital, unimpeded by Detective Ed O'Grady of the 22nd Street station, who was present when they left.

This public massacre caught the horrified attention of the en-tire city. There were immediate attempts to fix the blame. White Alley Ryan pointed the finger at the Morals men, calling them "green cops, looking for someone to pick on them. They saw the plainclothes men coming, got scared and cut loose." But the bul-lets extracted from Sgt Birns and some of the wounded turned out to be dum-dum bullets, not the .38 calibre used by the police. Some witnesses had pointed the finger at Roxy Vanilla's big red car.

The newspapers pointed the finger at Hinky Dink and Bathhouse John, and at Kenna's man Ryan, who had sent squads of police into the Levee after the debacle, but who had not been able to find anyone responsible for it. Maclay Hoyne, who had succeeded John C. Wayman as state's attorney, began a grand jury investigation into political corruption and vice, seeking to indict Colosimo, Torrio and Van Bever. Colosimo was arrested, but released when none of the toughs would testify against him, even with a grant of immunity. The Civil Service Commission, at Chief Gleason's request, began an inquiry into dealings at the 22nd Street station. Everyone knew that Ryan was frustrating Dannenberg by forestalling his raids with raids of his own, the purpose of which was to warn suspects to disappear.

Ryan was transferred to the west side, to the West Lake station in the Austin district, and replaced by Captain Max Nootbar, who had studied at Heidelberg University, served in the German army and had an impeccable record.

The Levee was now on its last legs, so to speak. Captain Nootbar began to close dives and then told Ike Bloom that he would have to close Freiberg's Dance Hall at the legal hour of one in the morning. When Bloom tried to offer Nootbar a deal, the captain kicked him down the stairs of the 22nd Street station; he had already ripped Bloom's picture from the wall of his office where Ryan had put it.

While Ike Bloom was pursuing what was to be a fruitless attempt to get an injunction against police raids, the businessmen of the Austin district protested to the mayor about Ryan's character. Ryan resigned from the department, saying that he had been victimized for following orders. Bloom lost his plea and agreed to close at one in the morning. He was losing money, he said. But he dreaded a worse fate than one o'clock closing. He told Nootbar that his dance hall was a respectable place. The waiters put cards on the tables every evening, which read:

FREE INSTRUCTION IN MODERN DANCE TO OUR GUESTS.
Hand this card to the head waiter and he will send you one of our competent instructors.

Respectfully,
Freiberg's Dance Academy

Nootbar's men came to the hall to observe the proceedings and reported that the "instructors" were known prostitutes.

Affidavits were filed saying that whiskey highballs, beer and wine were served in the hall long after one in the morning. It was the end of the line for Freiberg's. At three minutes before one o'clock on July 26, Bloom told his patrons the place was closing. The band played "Home, Sweet Home." "That's the first time *that* tune has been played before daybreak," someone said, just before the lights went out. On August 14, Mayor Harrison officially closed both Freiberg's and Colosimo's.

Then the Chicago *Examiner* ran a statement Minna Everleigh had made to Chief Justice Harry Olson of the Municipal Court after her club had been closed down. Colosimo's people had threatened her life if she talked to the papers, but Justice Olson had decided to release her revelations. She said that she had paid Hinky Dink and The Bath for all "privileges"—whiskey, taxicab, groceries, clothing and insurance. She had paid the aldermen over $100,000 in cash over twelve years, and guessed that the 22nd Street Levee had paid out at least fifteen million dollars in graft during its lifetime. Sol Friedman collected the "privilege" money, and George Little was a bagman, as were two detectives from the Harrison Street station. Saloonkeeper Andy Craig and Kenna's lawyer Aaron Andrews took care of stopping indictments: $1,000 for pandering, $2,000 for harboring a girl and $500 for grand larceny. In addition, the brothelkeepers paid on a weekly basis for protection from undue competition.

This was disastrous publicity, coming on top of everything else. Carter Harrison, interviewed on vacation in Huron Mountain, Michigan, threw down the gauntlet to Kenna and Coughlin. "I have reached the conclusion, finally, that my idea of the vice question has been wrong. . . . I have no hesitancy in subscribing now to the general indictment of the segregation plan. Segregation means protected vice, and you can't have protected vice without running the big risk of seeing your law enforcement officials corrupted."

Kenna and Coughlin were splitting with Harrison anyway over the issue of County Judge John E. Owens, who had infuriated the aldermen by purging the First Ward voting lists of the names of dead and nonexistent voters. Harrison made it clear that

Coughlin and Kenna had to support Owens or they were through. This story played on the front page of the *Tribune*, next to news about the impending war in Europe. Owens was a friend of Harrison's, but Kenna and Coughlin refused to support him. At this point Roger Sullivan, a local politician who had been involved in graft and in an unsavory transfer of a gas franchise, asked for Kenna's and Coughlin's help in a run for the U.S. Senate. This made matters even worse, because Harrison loathed Sullivan. Harrison declared for Congressman Lawrence Stringer for the Senate, but Kenna and Coughlin openly defied the mayor by coming out for Sullivan. Hinky Dink testified openly in front of the grand jury that the vicemongers were his friends. "These conditions was in the First Ward before you and I were born," he said, "and they'll be there after we're dead."

Bathhouse John demanded indignantly to know why everybody always harped about the Levee, when the First Ward also included the great business area north of Van Buren Street. He and Hinky Dink went all out for Sullivan in the primary, and for Judge Thomas F. Scully to run in the primary against Owens. The result was that Scully won handily, and Sullivan defeated Stringer. Sullivan was eventually defeated in the general election by Republican Lawrence Y. Sherman, but Mayor Harrison had received a fatal political blow. In that same 1915 primary, he was defeated by Robert A. Sweitzer, a Sullivan loyalist who, being Catholic and Irish-German, was able to cut into Harrison's usually loyal immigrant base.

Sweitzer in turn was defeated in the mayoral election by William Hale Thompson, a Republican, who announced on election night, "The crooks had better move out of Chicago before I am inaugurated!"

8

Spirits in the Levee rose when Thompson transferred Max Nootbar out of 22nd Street and replaced Chief James Gleason with his
own man Charles C. Healey. Thompson snubbed the Committee
of Fifteen and the Morals Squad as well, cutting their power. But
Bathhouse John and Hinky Dink were not to be invited to share
in this administration, which began on May 15, 1915. In October
the mayor ordered Sunday closing of saloons and refused to discuss the regulation with the First Ward aldermen. But Ike Bloom's
license was restored on December 25, under a dummy company
called Hop Ling. By January 28, Colosimo was back in business.
In March, 1916, Thompson saw to it that funding for the Morals
Squad was quietly ended.

The Levee was alive, in a tattered and insecure condition, but
still alive. The brothels were transformed into cabarets: Freiberg's
was now called Old Vienna; later the name was to be changed to
Midnight Frolics. Colosimo remodeled and enlarged his saloon
and did a thriving business with people from all levels of moneyed
society. The old winerooms were replaced with new cheap cafes,
and the one-night hotels and call flats opened again. At the same
time, since Thompson was so unpredictable, and times had really
changed, many of the vice lords began to look to the suburbs
where they could be safe and comfortable. They liked Burnham,
Illinois, a town with a population of one thousand, located eighteen miles to the south of Chicago. The mayor was Johnny Patton,
who had spent his formative years working in a saloon. Jim Colosimo and Johnny Torrio bought the Arrowhead Inn in Burnham
for $15,000 in October, 1917, establishing the first "road house."
Jew Kid Grabiner ran Torrio's Speedway Inn there. Several of
Colosimo's hoodlums opened cheap saloons, gambling dens and
cribs in Burnham. Others migrated to Stickney and to Cicero.

It was now Big Jim Colosimo who controlled the Levee. Kenna and Coughlin had been bypassed: Colosimo did not need
them. He had his own voting bloc among Italian immigrants; he
ran social and athletic clubs and had his own army of thugs. He

was covered with diamonds, had vulgar expensive houses and dispensed greenbacks to everyone. His connections ran throughout the city government and into state government. Coughlin and Kenna accepted the situation. Coughlin was doing quite well with his insurance business, which squeezed businessmen for any city permits and licenses they might need. Hinky Dink maintained a political presence, helped Big Jim when he could, and ran his own saloons and breweries.

The face of the city was changing. The south end of the First Ward and the Second Ward were now filled with blacks, who had come up from the South attracted by high war wages, and who habitually voted Republican. Now race as well as ethnic loyalties became a political factor. Maclay Hoyne ran for re-election as state's attorney in 1916, and, before the election in November, raided City Hall looking for campaign issues. He found one in the form of letters written to Thompson's Police Chief Charles C. Healey by police captain William P. O'Brien about conditions at the Elite, a "black-and-tan" resort on 3030 S State Street and recommending a crackdown on Sam Hare's Schiller Cafe at 320 E 31st Street, part of a black belt along Cottage Grove Avenue and 31st Street.

The Second Ward was the domain of Oscar DePriest, the city's first black alderman, and State Senator George Harding, a real estate tycoon. Both Captain Healey and Alderman DePriest were indicted—Healey in late October and DePriest two months later. O'Brien had been suspended by Healey and provided evidence for Hoyne. At these trials, which were defended by Clarence Darrow, Hoyne painted the black Second Ward as a nest of political pollution and vice, a popular image, and attempted to tie Thompson to it, since DePriest was a strong Thompson ally. Thompson dismissed the charges by Hoyne and O'Brien as "brainstorms," but the state had phone-tap evidence and a "little black book." In January, 1917, Lieutenant White of the Lake Street station revealed the existence of a notebook listing transient hotels, cabarets, call houses and gambling dens that "could not be raided" because they were the "chief's places," and the resorts that "could be raided" because payments were not being made to Mike de Pike Heitler and Billy Skidmore, a bail bondsman and gambling fixer, who shared the payoffs with the chief.

Despite all this damning evidence, Hoyne lost the cases to Darrow. DePriest and Healey were acquitted. Thompson had been damaged—everybody read about the trials in the Chicago *Tribune*, where they were reported by Ring Lardner—and he replaced Healey with Herman Schuettler, a Haymarket veteran with a good reputation. Thompson was not so badly hurt that he would fail in the 1919 mayoral election against the Democrat Robert Sweitzer; he was helped by the independent candidacy of Maclay Hoyne.

Great changes were taking place in the Levee, apart from police dealings with reform. In 1920 the Volstead Act went into effect; it had been passed over Woodrow Wilson's veto. Prohibition became the law of the land. Hinky Dink Kenna's Workingman's Exchange was turned into a sandwich and cigar shop. Another blow was the death of Big Jim Colosimo, who had fallen in love with a singer named Dale Winter whom he had met in 1915 when she was nineteen years old. She had been introduced to Colosimo by Arturo Fabri, the bandleader at the Livingston Hotel in Grand Rapids, where she lived.

Big Jim gave Dale Winter star treatment: voice lessons from expensive professionals. She was both beautiful and talented; Flo Ziegfeld offered her a contract, but she turned him down because she was apparently really in love with Colosimo, who divorced Victoria, his devoted partner in the brothel business, on March 31, 1920, settling $50,000 on her. Two weeks later Victoria married Antonio Villano, twenty years younger than she, and on April 17 Colosimo and Dale were married in Crown Point, Indiana.

On May 11, 1920, Colosimo left his mansion to meet someone—no one is sure who, although he received a phone call from Johnny Torrio before he left—at his cafe. He walked through the lobby past a cloakroom and phone booth, and across the dining room to his office, where he consulted with his secretary and his chef. Then he walked back out to the lobby, and a few moments later two shots rang out. The secretary, Frank Camilla, rushed out to the lobby and found his boss lying dead with a bullet behind his right ear. A second bullet was found buried in the wall of the lobby.

No one was ever found guilty of Colosimo's murder. The chief suspects were Johnny Torrio and his lieutenant Alphonse Capone, newly imported from New York. They both had alibis. There was some talk about Victoria taking revenge on the man who had dumped her, but the police believed it was a gang killing. Johnny Torrio and his followers saw real money to be made from Prohibition in the area of bootleg liquor and Big Jim had apparently been dragging his heels on that, preferring to stay with the old-fashioned vice he was comfortable with.

The funeral was impressive; it was gangland's first great send off. Bathhouse John was inconsolable; he and Hinky Dink headed the funeral procession, followed by 1,000 members of the First Ward Democratic Club. Among the pallbearers and other honorary guests were ten aldermen and three judges, two congressmen, several opera singers, politicians and businessmen. The procession wound its way, with such shining lights as George Silver, Ike Bloom, Committeeman Diamond Joe Esposito of the bloody Nineteenth Ward, Mike Merlo and the terrible Genna brothers trailing behind. It was a nice mixture of old-line vice and the young bloods who were to become famous in the twenties. The $2,500 casket was laid into the ground in Oakwoods Cemetery; Archbishop George Mundelein refused to allow Colosimo to be buried in consecrated ground in Mount Carmel because he was a diplovorced man. After a prayer by a Presbyterian clergyman, Bathhouse John recited Hail Marys and the Catholic prayer for the dead. The Bath was devastated by this death, and it marked the passing of the old order.

But the Levee had been dead for some time. As early as 1916, a *Tribune* reporter named Henry M. Hyde had visited the area and found only neglected and abandoned buildings. "Tonight the district is dark and silent," he wrote. "There are no lights of any color. It is like landing in some remote and ruined city damaged by the plague." In many of the once elegant parlors, which had rented for two-to-three hundred a month, the floors were littered with broken glass and crumbled plaster an inch deep. All the lead pipes, marble cornices and indoor plumbing had been stripped away long ago. Outside a handsome three-story brick building that had not yet been ravaged by scavengers, a sign hung from the window: "For Rent Furnished. To Respectable People Only!" Hyde continued, "The old red light district is certainly closed. It took several murders . . . by gunmen employed by the overlords of vice to close it. Anyone who wants to know what the abomination of desolation means is invited to go down and look at it."

In 1923, a redistricting act created fifty wards in Chicago, with only one alderman for each ward. Kenna stepped aside for Coughlin, who now concentrated on his stable of race horses and his sartorial splendor. His days of power were over; it was Al Capone now who controlled the underworld and killed at will. Gradually The Bath's money drained away, as did his health and most of his friends, through death. His beloved wife Mary had died in November, 1919, after thirty-five years of marriage. He became a figure of fun when he proposed an ordinance decreeing separate trolley cars for women and another regulating the length of women's skirts. He died on November 10, 1938, at the Lexington Hotel, which had been Al Capone's headquarters. His funeral procession down 18th Street attracted thousands. There were ten cars bearing flowers, and the First Ward Marching Club wore black badges.

Kenna took Coughlin's place as alderman. He lived in a suite at the Auditorium Hotel and was a solid citizen, worth about two million dollars. He died at age eighty-nine on October 9, 1946, and was awarded the expected flamboyant funeral.

John Wayman suffered a nervous breakdown after an unsuccessful bid for governor in 1913. He died of gunshot wounds, either by accident or suicide, when he was alone in his study at 6832 S Constance. Before he died, he said, "I am sorry, old man, if I caused you any trouble. I didn't mean to do it. I guess I had a little sand in my gearbox when I did this thing."

William Dannenberg set up his own private detective agency. In September, 1923, he was back in the Levee, working to disprove an allegation by New York publisher W.E.D. Stokes that Stokes's estranged wife Helen had been a prostitute in the Everleigh Club in 1911 under the name of Helen Norwood. Stokes, attempting to discredit his wife in the course of his divorce suit, produced what he alleged was a photograph of Helen holding her illegitimate child inside the club. Stokes also averred that his wife had connections to various unsavory Levee characters who worked at the Pekin and the Beaux Arts Club. Dannenberg was able to locate Anna Johnson, the Everleighs' housekeeper, who testified that Stokes had tried to bribe her to corroborate this story, which was not true. Dannenberg found a trunkful of false affidavits, uncovering a gigantic attempted frame-up.

Although he had received numerous death threats in the course of his career, Dannenberg died peacefully in his bed on August 10, 1955.

Ike Bloom operated his cabaret until 1924. He was stopped by Federal agents from running a speakeasy, Deadville, in the Loop. He spent all his money on medical treatment and died after a double leg amputation, on December 15, 1930. On that same day a report appeared in the Chicago papers that Victoria, Big Jim's ex-wife, was seeking a divorce from her husband Antonio Villano, who she said had threatened to kill her and her seventeen brothers and sisters.

The Levee is now gone. Its southern tip has become Chinatown. You can walk along 22nd Street and retrace Inspector Birns's route, but there is nothing left of the rowdy past. The Everleigh Club was a hotel housing black transients before it was demolished in 1933. There remained the façade of the Chicago Coliseum, which was built from the remains of the Confederate Libby prison in Richmond, Virgina: in 1889, Charles F. Gunther and three other Chicago investors devised a scheme to dismantle the Libby and move it to Chicago where it was reconstructed as a Civil War museum. In 1899 Gunther converted the building to the Coliseum, a 15,000-seat stadium, which was dedicated by President McKinley on August 26, 1900. The ancient edifice closed its doors for the last time in 1971 and fell into a state of disrepair. All that remained of it was the outer wall, standing forlornly on Wabash Avenue, until it was demolished in 1994.

VII

INTERLUDE: LOVE AND BETRAYAL IN THE CITY

In 1907 it was certainly a man's world. Growing numbers of women were finding employment in Chicago's bustling factories and offices, but it was marriage that was considered the ideal state for women, and chastity was the path women were expected to take to this goal. The alternative could be deadly. There were two sensational suicides in the city—or rather one suicide and one attempted suicide—within a day of each other. The first apparently had nothing to do with social stress, but was caused by depression over a lingering illness.

On July 17, Anna Normoyle leapt to her death from the fifteenth floor of the Masonic Temple, at five in the afternoon, when the spacious rotunda was filled with Loop workers on their way home. She made so forceful an impact that there were cracks in the marble floor. The event caused a near riot: screams, shouts, fainting women and horrified men.

The next day Anna Scott, a thirty-year-old housewife, distraught over an impending divorce on grounds of adultery, walked into Washington Park wearing a diamond tiara and an expensive white dress, and drank carbolic acid. Her husband was divorcing her because he had found out that she had met a strange man at three in the morning on Madison Street, a fortnight earlier. Mrs Scott survived.

In March of that year Frances Riccollet committed suicide, firing a bullet into her head at a rooming house on Western Avenue. Her story was not an unusual one. She was born in Sault Ste

Marie, Michigan, of French-Canadian parents; no one gave the date of her birth. When her parents died, she had to make her own way in life, getting a job as a domestic in Kenosha, Wisconsin, where she met Nicholas P. Neilson, a prosperous saloonkeeper. For two years, while Frances kept her job, the two carried on an affair and Neilson kept promising to marry her. The pair went to Chicago together on February 11, 1907, and lived in the rooming house at 483 S Western Avenue (now 1000 Western) for several days before Neilson ostensibly went to St Paul to interview for a job. After a few weeks Frances received a postcard from him, postmarked Seattle, in which he said: "I am gone from Chicago forever—Nick."

At three that afternoon the landlord heard two shots come from the upstairs bedroom. He rushed up and found the girl, barely alive. She was taken to St Elizabeth's Hospital, where she died. She had left a trunkful of letters from Neilson, and two notes—one to the coroner and one to her sisters in Sault Ste Marie.

To the coroner: Not knowing that my folks can take care of my body, I ask you to lay me away the best you can. I have no money, only $12.50. My health has been poor, and I have waited in the hope that P.N. [*sic*] Neilson, 16 Main Street, Kenosha, who has trapped me for two years would marry me. He has made me many promises and now to know that he has left me has killed me. I see in the card just sent me he is going east. I am completely helpless and in tears and completely broken down.

Frances

To my sisters: It is with a broken heart that I write these few lines that I have fallen away. I cannot longer resist the temptation to end it all. In tears I am left alone, forgotten and forsaken. I see no other way but to kill myself, as I am tired of knocking about the world homeless. I am set back in my future happiness and I do not care for anything. I am now dying in sin; don't despair. Pardon me for taking my life, but my troubles are hard to endure. I have been dying by inches a long time. Goodbye to all my sisters and brothers.

Your sister, Frances

The body was held at the morgue the required nine days. The sisters made no attempt to claim it, so the body was given to the dental school of Northwestern University.

In October of 1907, Maria Sexton, a 23-year-old worker at the Chicago Box Factory, who lived in a miserable little flat at 950 N Robey Street—now Damen Avenue—paid a call on Joseph Gillespie at his house on Augusta Street. She went to make a final plea to him to marry her, since she was pregnant with his child. When Gillespie refused, she went home to write two letters, and then returned to Augusta Street with the letters, a Bible and a small pistol. She shot herself in an alley near No 57, where Gillespie lived, and lay there in the rain until five in the morning, when she was discovered by a paper boy named Joseph Zevertnick.

It was still dark, but a flash of lightning illuminated the body in the alley; Joseph ran to the West Chicago Avenue station and the police returned with him, carrying lanterns. They found the girl clutching the Bible in her left hand and the revolver in her right. Her handbag contained a few coins, her flat key and a cheap comb. The letter to Gillespie was tucked into her shirtwaist.

> Dear little boy: I know you feel bad, but you have a comfortable home and relatives and friends to help you pass the dreary hours of your life; a good position and you earn enough money for any man to be satisfied with. You have no worry for the outcome of the future.
>
> What have I? The cold shoulder from every one, no home and the little place I now call home I'll have to part with, for I can't stay here any longer. Clothes to be bought for myself and the baby. Then to a hospital to work for my board, and God himself only knows what treatment I will get there.
>
> And yet you can desert the girl you love or once loved. Joe Darling, you know I was as true to you as any girl could be. I told you the truth before you ever took me to your home. Why did you not leave me then?
>
> It is not one that you are harming, but two. Oh, may God forgive you shall be my prayer night and day.
>
> Joe please, for God's sake return to me again for it is killing me. I can't stand it if you don't return sweetheart, and you will regret it the longest and last day you live.

Darling, please return to me and be my loving little Joe. I will never again do anything to offend you as long as I live. My heart is broken and my life is a wreck.

After her signature, she appended these lines:

Ah truly those are the saddest words of tongue and pen—It
   might have been! It might have been!
Everybody is loved by someone. Everybody knows that to be
   true.
Some have a father and mother dear, and brother and sister
   too—
All this I remember since I was a babe so small.
I have seemed to be the only one nobody loves.

At the inquest the next day, Gillespie said, "At one time I was engaged to marry Miss Sexton. But I found out some things which caused me to change my mind." Deputy Coroner Andrews commented on the man's remarkable indifference under questioning and his cold response to the girl's tragic end. But he had committed no crime, and he walked out of the inquest to resume his life.

In early March of 1907 the Salvation Army opened a facility at 399 S State Street. General William Booth himself visited it and praised Mary Stillman and Alexander MacMillan for saving thirty-five friendless souls from suicide. "Before you preach to them," said Mary Stillman, "fill their stomachs." But no amount of food could have saved the lives of Frances Riccollet and Mary Sexton.

VIII

BOMBS, GAMBLERS AND NEWSPAPER WARS

In 1900 there were varied interests vying for control of gambling in Chicago. There was Mike McDonald's combine, run by Frank McWhorter, Harry Holland, safeblower Paddy Guerin, Dan Brown and John Ryan. The most influential was a syndicate run by John Condon, Charles "Social" Smith, Harry Perry, Bud White and Tom McGinnis. Big Jim O'Leary stood sometimes with the latter syndicate, and sometimes alone. He was the son of Patrick and Catherine O'Leary, whose cow had been accused of starting the Chicago Fire by kicking over a lantern in the barn near their house at 137 (now 558) W DeKoven Street.

In 1904, in response to an outbreak of reform fever in Chicago, O'Leary opened a huge handbook in DuPage County. The enormous building was protected by two sets of spiked fences and patrolled by packs of watchdogs. The Santa Fe Railway ran three Gamblers Special trains with eight to ten cars every day, charging the gamblers twenty-five cents apiece, to O'Leary's fortress, and Western Union supplied wire service. *The Chicago Daily Journal* undertook a crusade against the place with such ferocity that the governor and the attorney general stepped in and persuaded both the railway and Western Union to cease their dealings with O'Leary, who then closed the place down. He and his seventeen employees were indicted on a long list of charges, all of which were dismissed when O'Leary came up with payment of a $1,700 fine.

O'Leary had a two-story fortress in the city at 4183 S Halsted Street, across the street from the entrance to the stock-yards. This "Palace" was a maze of false partitions, tunnels, trap doors and doors reinforced with steel. During the "gambling war" which began in 1907, bombs were aimed at the Palace, but none of them did any damage to speak of. The place was raided regularly, but the gamblers escaped each time through skylights, false chimneys and hidden passageways, probably because O'Leary had been tipped off in advance; he had invested in police protection. Adding to the confusion was the fact that in addition to a saloon and gaming rooms, O'Leary ran legitimate businesses at the Halsted Street location: a Turkish bath, bowling alley and billiard room, a barber shop and a restaurant. His shady customers could mingle with the honest patrons of the other enterprises and elude arrest. He posted an alluring advertisement on his premises:

> Why go downtown? Everything in the city brought right here for your enjoyment and comfort. Do you want a Turkish bath? Here is the place. Shave? Come in. Bowling alleys? The best in the city. Restaurant? We serve anything that can be had from land or sea. A little wager on dice or the ponies? We might be persuaded to take your money.

It was never clear to the police which gamblers were working for O'Leary and which for the Smith-Perry-White-Condon organization. Loyalties frequently shifted. For instance, "Blind" John Condon opened the Roby Racetrack, outside Hammond, a mile across the Illinois-Indiana state line, with the financial backing of Mike McDonald and Jim O'Leary. Tom McGinnis of the Smith-Perry syndicate was an ally of O'Leary's, as well as the owner of a saloon at 311 S Clark Street and a link to Kenna and Coughlin, who had a share of everyone's pie. Retaliation against perceived treaty violations came in the form of raids by hired constables who had secured arrest warrants. The police welcomed the assistance of these "private cops" because when the syndicates were at war, the town generally closed down, and this reflected well on the chief of police.

By 1900 the "sport of kings" was never more popular, though it was coming increasingly under attack because of the syndicates which sold "book" at the track. In 1895, the Illinois General Assembly had enacted the first of two racing prohibitions. With the exception of a few harness races run at Ingalls Park in Joliet, the ban held until 1898. The economic loss to Illinois was incalculable; the big horse breeders took their stables out of the state until the legislature bowed to pressure from lobbyists and approved a schedule of racing dates for Washington Park, Hawthorne and the Harlem track in River Forest. No attempt was made to curtail the activities of the gangsters.

In 1901 the syndicates met in Evanston to agree on some common objectives and end the bickering. It was decided to abandon handbooking in Chicago during the winter and to confine gambling to one suburban poolroom. Several of the older poolrooms—off-track betting parlors—that had been constructed along the drainage canals in Evanston and Indiana were closed by mutual agreement. Handbooking was allowed during the summer racing seasons as long as nobody tried to gain an upper hand. In 1902 the first of several costly wars broke out when O'Leary violated the agreements by pushing his influence in the city proper and at the racetracks.

The poolrooms were operated by the gambling combines profiting from the legal races at Hawthorne, Washington Park and the Harlem Jockey Club. Racetrack owners did not of course like losing business to the poolrooms, which provided results from all the tracks as well as from faro and roulette. When the poolroom operators were not fighting each other, they fought against the tracks, sometimes violently.

On May 30, 1902, a fire was started at the Hawthorne track after the fourth race. Two men were seen standing near the base of the cupola. It was not unusual for people to stand on the roof to watch races, but this time there was a puff of smoke and flames burst out. The structure was made of wood and went up quickly; the paddock, considered by horsemen to be the finest in the west, was also destroyed. Hawthorne was rebuilt in just seven weeks, this time of concrete and steel. But no one ever knew who had burned it.

The other gamblers suspected that Jim O'Leary, who had an interest in Blind John Condon's Roby Track, might have had a hand in the arson. A year later someone set fire to a can of oil underneath the grandstand at Washington Park. Police Inspector Nicholas Hunt from the stockyards district, a loyal friend of O'Leary's, stood idly by while the flames were extinguished.

Frank McWhorter, Mike McDonald's man, said, in 1903, "The fight that is in progress is not an effort to force anyone to give up a portion of their business. It is a fight to force compliance with the terms of a contract that is going to be enforced. Two years ago all the bookmaking interests of Chicago entered into an iron-clad agreement extending over a period of nine years by which there was to be no handbooking or poolselling in Chicago what-soever."

Nobody seriously believed that the gamblers would stay out of the city. On August 30, 1903, the *Daily News* offered a realistic appraisal of the situation.

> The trust gamblers call out the police one day. The anti-trust gamblers call out the police another day. There is no attempt on either side to disguise the fact that it is a fight to determine which set of gamblers shall control the city, or that part of the city which may be controlled by the influences that do not always make for good. Our mayor [Harrison] is in Yellowstone; our chief of police [O'Neill] is composing melodies; all the rest of them are afraid to move lest they move the wrong way. And so the gamblers are compelled to settle the matter between themselves.

Armed with axes and shotguns, constables, headed by Dickie Dean, a paid agent of the Smith-Perry group, raided O'Leary's fortress on August 27. O'Leary appeared in court to post bond for his men, and said to the Smith-Perry people, "I can stand raids as long as you can. I am willing to follow my profession on the propo-sition and bet that I will be up when the gambler's trust is a back number."

The next day O'Leary's agents burst into Tom McGinnis's Clark Street resort to arrest a group of Chinese playing "bung-a-loo." While this was going on, Smith-Perry men raided Mont Tennes's place at 123 N Clark. Tennes, who controlled North side gambling, had refused to join the trust, and his independence was considered to be an acknowledgment of his partnership with O'Leary. This was not the case, however.

Mont Tennes had stood on the sidelines during the struggle among the other gamblers, waiting for an opening. He was christened Jacob after his father, but everyone called him Mont, a nickname his mother had given him. He was born in Chicago on January 16, 1874, the son of German immigrants; his career began around 1900 when he trimmed some suckers in a State Street crap game. He wandered into the illegal gathering with a few dollars and emerged with $3,800. Two days later he went back to the same game to bet higher stakes, this time on a prize fight, put down his entire wad and won $7,600. In 1898 he opened his own billiard hall and saloon at 287 N Center Street, where he met the scions of the old gambler combines, the safe blowers, confidence men and mustachioed whist players in tweed suits and derby hats, with their concealed tiny derringers and "sleeve holdouts"—pulley devices sewn into jackets to produce winning hands in the palms, when necessary.

In July, 1904, a special grand jury indicted sixty-four gamblers, including Mont Tennes and his brother Peter. At that time Tennes was backing hundreds of betting parlors and was working with a west side syndicate. He pled guilty to a charge of bookmaking and paid a $200 fine. This would not happen to Tennes again until 1922.

The drive to clean the bookies out of the Hawthorne Racetrack was spearheaded by Louis Seeberger, president of the Citizens' Association, who pressured the grand jury to order Sheriff Thomas Barrett to arrest known bookies on sight. Barrett consulted attorney Levi Mayer, who told him that a grand jury had as much authority to direct the sheriff as the man in the moon. So Barrett told the jury to mind its own business. It was obvious that he was shielding the powerful racetrack owners and this annoyed

Bud White, who said, "It looks to us like what is sauce for the goose is sauce for the gander." If this legal opinion were true, he thought that their poolrooms should be allowed to operate without interference.

O'Leary cautiously opened a room on Blue Island Avenue. The Citizen's Association appealed to Attorney Charles Deneen, who gave them the stock reply: he sympathized, but there was nothing he could do; the statutes clearly left it to the sheriff to police the racetracks. The Citizen's Association of neighboring Harlem tried to draft Barrett for their gambling squad—he was a citizen of the community and could not be exempt from service—but before that could be resolved, the indictments against the Hawthorne gamblers collapsed when the key witness, Detective Otto Schubert, disappeared. He had supposedly gone undercover to place bets with the track bookies.

In 1904 Mayor Carter Harrison II decided to put a stop to bookmaking at the tracks. "It is my intention to witness the sport of kings without the vice of kings," he said in June, on the eve of the final Derby Day. After securing a favorable opinion from the city corporation counsel, the mayor eliminated the betting ring at Washington Park. On the second day of the 1904 meet, fewer than 1,500 railbirds showed up at Washington Park. Without the lure of legalized betting, thoroughbred racing was a dead issue in Illinois. The Washington Park situation was repeated in the next few days at the Hawthorne and Harlem tracks. There was to be no thoroughbred racing in Illinois for the next eighteen years. There were other, out-of-town races to wager on, however, and the emerging technology provided the gambling bosses the means to offer wagering via the poolroom "wire."

When Edward Dunne was elected mayor in 1905, the gambling territories were still in dispute. Tennes expanded his interests by purchasing several saloons—one was The Turf at 499 N Lincoln Avenue—which were simply fronts for back-room gambling. The new mayor reappointed Police Chief Francis O'Neill on June 26, 1905—a first, because till then no police chief had survived a change in mayors. But it was short-lived. A month later O'Neill was replaced by John Collins, a veteran of the Haymarket trouble.[12]

166

He had stood in the third column of patrolmen when the bomb went off, but had not been injured. His appointment was applauded. The *Tribune* praised Collins's statement that "gambling in this town is a disgrace. We have handbooks, poker, craps, slot machines, and every gambling device known. Men are waylaid on their way home from work and solicited by barkers and touts. We can drive every damned one of them out of Chicago, and we'll try to do it."

A series of spectacular raids the next day convinced the reformers that Collins was a man of his word. "Chicago s got a live one now. It's off the map for you fellers," someone said, as gambling inmates from the Madison Street Calhoun Club were led into patrol wagons. Detectives armed with sledge hammers turned the betting tables into kindling, while poker chips were crunched underfoot. Five raids in the downtown district filled the Harrison Street station. Men identified as city hall employees were given bonds supplied by Andy Craig, the bondsman, pimp and convicted felon, who was waiting for them. While the bonds were being written, the gamblers were instructed to report back the next day. Craig shook his head sadly. "Just about sixty-five forfeitures and fines for me tomorrow," he said.

Telephones, wheels of fortune, and city directories were seized at thirteen more gambling parlors and were brought to city hall as evidence. Most of the paraphernalia was taken from Mont Tennes's three Clark Street establishments. The Gem Cigar Store at 123 N Clark was a favorite target of the raiders during every reform drive. It was said that the place was raided so many times that a bondsman was kept on the payroll full-time.

Collins was satisfied with his day's work. "I don't want to talk any more unless I have done something. I am determined to drive out every gambler in the city," he said.

Perhaps that is why he removed Herman Schuettler from the gambling detail and placed himself in charge. The Collins raids caused the gamblers a minor inconvenience: bail bondsmen had to be summoned, and gambling fines were paid, ranging from $1 for visiting a handbook to $100 for keeping a house. And that was it. They reopened just as quickly and continued to operate until the next wave of reform gripped the department. During this time, Tennes became the big fish among Loop gamblers.

Faro, roulette and the handbooks yielded up to fifty percent of their gross to the Tennes syndicate. Certain police officials were allowed to keep whatever winnings they accumulated. It was good public relations and smart politics. Because of this, no cop would dare arrest J.E. Ackerman, Tennes's business solicitor, who stood outside the poolroom at 14 Federal Street. Each day during the noon hour, Ackerman handed out business cards reading "Pool & Billiards."

"It's a fine place," he said. "Tennes, you know. Nice big rooms. Pleasant play, and the right sort of crowd." Inside, a group of thirty men huddled around a billiard table, shooting dice. The stakes were a quarter a throw. Around this time Tennes announced for the first time, but not the last, that he was "retiring." In fact, he operated a poolroom inside the Board of Trade, and another across from the Chicago Avenue police station.

2

About the same time that Mayor Dunne came into office—1905—the Smith-Perry camp, including Big Jim O'Leary, announced that the *City of Traverse,* a 36-year-old steamer purchased from the Hibernian Bank which had foreclosed on it, would set sail from the Illinois Central Slip at the 68th Street crib. The combine spent $40,000 to make the ship, which had cruised Lake Michigan, seaworthy, to redecorate the cabin and build a well-stocked bar where the infirmary had stood. Dr Lee DeForest, who pioneered wireless telegraphy, agreed to the installation of his invention on board, and thus initiated a score of legal battles with the city on the question of whether he was aiding and abetting an illegal enterprise. He eventually obtained an injunction against harassment, on the argument that what the ship owners did with his invention was not his concern. Bud White tested the transmissions forty miles out in the lake, and pronounced the ship ready for business. Sharp flashes of light and metallic clicks brought the race results over the wires to a single operator sitting in the cabin, who in turn telephoned the names of horses in code to the bookmaking stands in the lower deck.

The *City of Traverse* set off on June 29, 1905, with hundreds of sporting men on board. Bud White anchored the vessel twenty-two miles southeast of Chicago, ten miles north of the Indiana shore. Detectives Breternitz and Schubert from Herman Schuettler's gambling squad were on board, but they could do nothing legally. "Gentlemen," Bud White announced to his patrons, "we are now outside the jurisdiction of Illinois. Start gambling." Pasteboards bearing the names of horses running in the first race at Buffalo were posted while a string ensemble played ragtime. "And there are no U.S. laws prohibiting gambling," White said. "I think this here undertaking's going to be a big success." The ship returned at six in the evening, after all the betting slips had been tossed into the boiler, and the gamblers disembarked at the South Water Street pier.

State's Attorney John Healy, in response to questions, said that any action would have to be taken by the Chicago police. The ship was to run three full seasons, shutting down in August, 1907. The Illinois Central Railroad provided special race trains running to the dock. Twenty-one ex-constables who had been fired by the municipal court worked on the ship and the *Tribune* alleged that the Smith combine was paying $2,000 a week in protection money. Later, after the Sumner report had been issued, attorney Ben Hyman testified before the Civil Service Commission that he and three others had paid $1,700 a month to get Hinky Dink to allow them to run the ship out of Chicago.

On the Fourth of July holiday, 1906, the combine lost over $10,000 when the board flashed a horse named Beau Brummel, a seven-to-one longshot, as the winner. In fact this was a mistake: the winner was Attention. The board did not correct itself until after the Beau Brummel bettors had jammed the windows to redeem their stubs and by that time the real winners had destroyed their tickets or were so far back in line they could not cash in before the windows closed.

In that week Mont Tennes tried to get into the gambling-ship business himself. "Why, there is good money in it," he said, from the deck of his *John R. Sterling*. "I might as well run a boat just like those people." It was not, however, as easy as Tennes thought. He could not compete with the *City of Traverse* and he lost nearly $75,000 in the attempt. Ben Hyman was able to defuse efforts by the state's attorney's office to stop the combine's ship, and when Herman Schuettler built a wireless station on the Indiana shore to intercept and jam the boat's circuit, the Smith-Perry forces burnt the station down in the middle of the night.

In May, 1907, seventy-five gamblers were arrested at the South Water Street dock when the tugboat *Robert Burke* brought them in from the *City of Traverse*. The license of the gambling boat was revoked on July 10 and in September the Smith-Perry group sold it to the Graham & Morton line, where it ran excursions between Chicago and St Joseph, Michigan. Later the ship became a permanent fixture at the Benton Harbor dock.

3

On July 10 a bomb was thrown at Blind John Condon's house at 2623 S Michigan Avenue. Blind John, who had begun as a barber and had lost his sight in 1899, was one of the most powerful gambling bosses. He had been an early partner of Mike McDonald in The Store and had bought up racetracks in Indiana before taking over the Harlem Racetrack in 1898. Luckily for him, the bomb caused only slight damage to the front of his house; he was relaxing in the rear at the time. The bomb signalled a declaration of war, but it was never clear what the war was about.

George Shippy, who had replaced John Collins as chief of police, sent twenty policemen to scour the south side for clues after the Condon bombing. They came up with nothing. Shippy made a token raid on Pat O'Malley's establishment at 421 N Clark Street, seizing dope sheets, blackboards and the keeper of the house. "Arrests will be made as fast as I can find these places," Shippy announced.

On July 25, at nine in the evening, a steel-cased bomb landed in a paved alley directly behind Mont Tennes's house at 404 W

Belden Avenue. The only damage was some broken panes of glass and Tennes, who was taking a bath at the time, was not injured. He remarked to Sgt Kilgore of the Halsted detail, "It was just the work of some mischievous boys who set off a cannon cracker."

On August 12, a bomb went off at Jim O'Leary's place at 4183 S Halsted Street. O'Leary offered the explanation that a cap on his gas pipe had blown out.

After this, the bombs flew and there were more raids. Each deafening blast was followed, after an interval, by the arrival of three helmeted policemen hefting nightsticks and blowing whistles. On August 19 a bomb went off in Mont Tennes's front yard, causing little damage. The bomb was found to contain "safeblower's soup"—a combination of nitroglycerin and TNT used by the infamous Paddy Guerin, who had recently escaped from Devil's Island and who was well known to Pinkerton agents. Guerin operated a hand-book in the back of Paddy Grimes's saloon at 63rd and Cottage Grove Avenue. Attempts were made to find links in these actions with the gambling boat. "I know nothing about the *City of Traverse*," Mont Tennes replied to questions. "I was as surprised as anyone when the government put it out of business." Guerin was arrested, but the bombing continued.

On August 25, O'Malley's saloon at Clark and Kinzie was hit. "I don't mix with gamblers and I don't have no enemies," O'Malley said. Ex-Sheriff James Pease became a victim on September first, when a group of men, wearing straw boaters and driving in a touring car, apparently mistook his house for Bud White's, which was two blocks away on Magnolia Avenue. Pease said he thought it was a firecracker.

Chief Shippy appointed Herman Schuettler, who had survived numerous scandals and shakeups with his reputation intact, to head a special task force on the bombings. Schuettler said he had traced them to an inner circle of safe blowers and ex-*Traverse* employees. The motive, he said, was revenge. On September 7, Elihu Rosencranz and Ed Kelly, known dynamiters, were arrested. Several months earlier Kelly had been arrested and, while being taken to a Desplaines Street cell, had slipped a pistol out of a policeman's holster and escaped, backing out of the station. This second arrest, on circumstantial evidence, lasted only as long as it took defense attorney Charles Erbstein to arrive at the jail.

Schuettler was imaginative and conscientious. His men disguised themselves as railway conductors, teamsters, peddlers, cattlemen in bearskin gloves and telephone linemen, climbing poles to watch the games in progress. Once, legend tells us, they traced a game in progress to a locked bank vault. When the gamblers refused to come out, Schuettler sprinkled red pepper under the door; the gamblers emerged coughing and choking.[15] When the bookies discovered that Schuettler's men were placing bets undercover at the handbooks, they devised a code for transmitting race results to the parlors. The code was cracked by the gambling squad in a matter of weeks.

Schuettler raided Mont Tennes's clearing house at 823 N Larrabee Street a dozen times: each time gamblers were discovered playing checkers or holding prayer meetings in an empty room. Once, several squad members scaled a telephone pole next to the clearing house, broke through the window, smashed the switchboard and confiscated several valuable oil paintings hanging on the walls. When gamblers' wives read about these raids, some of them telephoned Schuettler's wife to plead for an end to the games that drained away their husbands' money.

Over the years, Tennes disguised his activities with a variety of fronts: his Western Cash Register company at 123 N Clark Street was the best cover. In the back was a gamblers' annex and a "ladies betting salon." When a ninth bomb was hurled at the Western Cash Register office, the cops theorized that Tennes might be the target of a protection racket for gamblers. "Why would anyone want to be put on the payroll of a little cash register store?" Tennes asked innocently.

There was a grand jury inquiry into all these shenanigans. One hundred subpoenas were served on gambling bosses, but none of them would talk. A bomb was thrown at the Madison Street saloon of former alderman Johnny Rogers, one of those subpoenaed, possibly as a warning. Horace Argo, a Tennes confidant, was cited for contempt for refusing to answer during a strong interrogation by State's Attorney John Healey, who asked Argo at one point whether he knew that "certain poolrooms and gambling games are permitted to operate in Chicago with police protection?" Argo's response was, "No comment."

"Do you realize," Healy asked, "that you are likely to go to jail for this?"

"It's all part of the game," Argo said philosophically.

There were no grand jury indictments. Argo was sentenced to six months and fined $500, but he won on appeal and never spent a night in jail. Several more bombs were thrown that winter, and then the "war" ended.

In 1911, Tim Murphy, a disgruntled ex-associate of Tennes's, told the newspapers that in 1907 a crime syndicate was exacting protection money from gamblers in Chicago, placing nightly phone calls in which they identified themselves as "Smith and Jones." Tennes himself was alleged to have paid $1,500 a week after the second attempt on his home. There was in fact some Black Hand activity in Chicago in 1907, which lends credence to Murphy's story. In any case the great bomb war fizzled out with no fatalities and no indictments, in mid-1908, when Tennes made peace with O'Leary and the others and was on his way to control of racetrack gambling.

4

Racetrack results had been transmitted to bookies by telegraph during the 1890s by the Ditmus Company of New York. In 1899 Western Union offered high percentages to racetrack officials for exclusive rights, which, when it became public knowledge, caused a scandal. Respected millionaires Chauncey DePew, J. Pierpont Morgan and John Jacob Astor IV were officers of the Western Union corporation. In 1904, F. Norton Goddard of the New York City Club launched a civic crusade to smash the cozy relationship of Western Union with the underworld and at the urging of stockholder Helen Gould, the company withdrew from the field.

The gap was filled by the Metropolitan News Company of St

Louis—its income from this was estimated at a million a year—and by a Cincinnati telegraph operator named John Payne, who eventually serviced fourteen states and Canada. Mont Tennes subscribed to Payne's service, receiving race returns in the Forest Park train station at a switchboard that consisted of a trunk line with about forty-five wires distributing the information in code to several hundred Tennes handbooks and poolrooms. At the poolroom the switchboard operator handed the race results—from tracks like Latonia, Saratoga and Gravesend—to a caller with a megaphone. The bookies paid Tennes twenty-five to fifty dollars a day for this information, and Tennes paid routine protection to the police. All income derived from this operation went into a ledger labeled the "Caldwell Account." The Chicago Telephone Company would not divulge the names of these rooms even to grand juries.

Tim Murphy—who was later to tell the papers about the gamblers' war of 1907—went into competition with Payne, but found it so difficult that in November of 1909 he went to Chicago and made a deal to sell out to Mont Tennes, who eventually took over ninety percent of the business, and then set out to eradicate competition from John A. Payne.

One month after he made his deal with Murphy, Tennes's agents bombed Jake Webber's poolroom in Columbus, Ohio, when Webber refused to stop dealing with Payne. There were further bombings in Hanover, Indiana, and St Louis, and Payne employees in Chicago were harassed. In May, 1910, H.I. Brown challenged the Tennes men to "do their worst" to his Jacksonville, Florida, racetrack. They burned it down three times.

John Payne's spacious house at Crystal Lake, Kentucky, was also destroyed. On May 1, 1910, Payne met Tennes secretly in Hammond, Indiana, and sold out for $300 a day and a five percent interest in the business. Mont Tennes renamed it the General News Bureau and went national, blazing a trail of bombs and extortion across the country. Bookmakers in the following cities paid monthly tribute to Tennes's bureau:

New York	$3,000	San Francisco	$1,800
Detroit	400	St Louis	1,000
Louisville	750	Albany	1,000
West Baden	400	Pittsburgh	700
Buffalo	963	Oklahoma City	105
Cleveland	300	Salt Lake City	125
Baltimore	125	San Antonio	62
Toledo	100	Terre Haute	25
Norfolk	800	Muncie	193
New Orleans	100	Cincinnati	415
Indianapolis	400		

Tennes competed in Canada with the Metropolitan News Company in open defiance of the Miller Law which prohibited this kind of activity, and burned a racetrack there.

In December, 1911, Big Jim O'Leary announced his retirement from gambling. Since he made these announcements every few years, the effect on the community was minimal. But this time he tried to sell his Halsted Street property to the county for $60,000 to be used as a hospital. "Reform is here to stay," he said, "and Chicago is no place for a gentleman." The county, however, balked at the price, so Big Jim stayed on in the gambling business. But he had had some business failures and he was not the power he had been. The territory was more or less divided into three fiefdoms: Barney Grogan controlled the west side, Hinky Dink the area south from Madison Street to the river and James Aloysius "Hot Stove" Quinn the river north to Wilson Avenue. Schuettler continued his raids, but the gamblers were always tipped off in advance.

In April of 1911, Carter Harrison II was re-elected mayor after an absence of seven years. Tennes donated $20,000 to Harrison's campaign, hoping that he might have softened his stance against gambling. This was certainly a vain hope, since the Sumner Vice Commission report was issued just after the election and there was a strong demand for reform. Henry Brolaski, who called himself a "reformed gambler" and lectured on that vice to women's clubs, civic federations and religious groups, testified that Hinky Dink had ended the gamblers' wars in 1908 by mediating with Mont Tennes, Big Jim O'Leary and Tim Murphy, and had made $40,000 out of it.

By 1914 Hinky Dink and The Bath had almost given up on Mayor Harrison, but they still had enough clout with him to have Chief James Gleason replace tough Herman Schuettler as head of the gambling detail, with William Schubert, a portly veteran who had failed the police department physicals. Schubert raided black policy rings and some gamblers who had worked against Harrison's election, but he did not touch Tennes's places, where baseball pools were now being run in addition to racetrack betting. If there was a raid, Tennes's lawyers always demanded a jury trial and the case was transferred to a north side court and eventually dropped.

The poolrooms and lotteries ran unmolested for the most part until, on August 30, 1916, during the Thompson administration, the *Daily News* asked, "Does Tennes control the police?" a question that may have been prompted by the fact that Tennes had just become chief concessionaire at the Hawthorne Racetrack by paying $10,000 to the Jockey Club, whose members included William Wrigley, Jr., Jim Colosimo and Captain Morgan Collins of the first precinct.

Judge Kenesaw Mountain Landis, a highly respected U.S. District judge, who had been on the Federal bench since 1905, held a formal inquiry into Tennes's business dealings. Judge Landis had won wide acclaim in 1907 by imposing a $29,240,000 fine on Standard Oil of Indiana in a rebate case. Although this decision was reversed on appeal, the judge was much admired for his courage. He was to serve as Commissioner of baseball from 1921 to 1944, erasing the terrible stain on the sport left by the White Sox scandal.

On October 1, 1916, Judge Landis subpoenaed Mont Tennes; his brother Willie; Horace Argo; a gambler named Eph Harding; John Morelock, manager of General News; Bernard Sully and F.W. Tracey of the Chicago Telephone Tunnel Company. Tennes hired Clarence Darrow to represent him.

Horace Argo was the first witness. His occupation, he said, was running a company that marketed the "Argo Eye Remedy." He and Mont Tennes, he said, owned 37 1/2 percent and Tennes's brother owned twenty-five percent of that company.

176

"Are you doing well?" Landis asked.

There was a pause. "There's a lot of competition," Argo said.

Willie Tennes refused to testify, but Mont Tennes took the stand. He said his principal occupation was real estate, with offices in the Straus Building. The judge suggested that the gambler did not need Clarence Darrow in the courtroom, but Tennes demurred. "I don't understand the law," he said. "I'd rather have him stay."

The judge, tongue in cheek, handed Tennes a racing sheet. "Do you know what kind of real estate journal this is?" he asked.

"I'd rather not answer that," Tennes said. "I'd incriminate myself."

Before Judge Landis closed down the inquiry on October 4, he gave Tennes some advice about paying Clarence Darrow. "Don't give Mr Darrow money covered with dirt and slime, with the blood that has come from a lot of young fellows about the town who are made criminals," he said. "Better give Mr Darrow money from your eye remedy funds."

In the summer of 1919, some weeks before the White Sox threw the World Series, Mont Tennes was gambling in Saratoga, New York. It was reported that he mentioned to his old friend and one-time owner of the Chicago Cubs, Charles Weeghman, that he had had a tip that the Sox might lose. He himself, according to Weeghman, said that he, "liked baseball but wouldn't get in on a crooked deal." Weeghman said that in spite of the tip, Tennes bet $30,000 on the Sox. Tennes told the press that he was willing to tell the grand jury investigating the scandal in 1920 "all I know about baseball and betting on baseball games, but I can't tell them nothing about fixed games. I never told Charlie Weeghman about fixed games. Weeghman's intentions are good, I'm sure, but he was misunderstood. Whether Weeghman and I met at Saratoga, I can't say. I remember meeting him at the racetrack last summer. I bet on the Sox, I lost my bet and I made no cry of fraud."

It was said that before the opening game Tennes had told Charles Comiskey, the owner of the White Sox, that the players had been bribed and Comiskey did nothing about it.

In 1920 Police Chief Michael Hughes went after the gamblers using the Illinois Criminal Code rather than the municipal code, which had weaker penalties. With Mayor William Hale Thompson and Chief Hughes calling the shots, the cost of protection went up. When the horse Paul Jones won the Kentucky Derby as a long shot, favored politicians had been given inside information, courtesy of the General News Bureau, then located at 431 S Dearborn Street.

On March 27, 1922, Tennes was tried on the petty charge of conspiring to operate horse-race-betting handbooks. It was the second time Tennes had been indicted. Since Clarence Darrow was not available, Tennes hired Maclay Hoyne who, as state's attorney, had just been defeated by the Republican Robert Crowe. The case was *nolle prosequi*; the prosecution was unable to prove the conspiracy. Crowe had announced a war on vice, much to Hoyne's annoyance.

In 1923 Mayor William Dever took office, and there was a real crackdown. Over a few months, Police Chief Morgan Collins closed 200 Loop handbooks, forcing Tennes into the suburbs. By the end of the year Chicago gambling had been effectively shut down and Tennes announced his retirement.

By 1925 most of Tennes's rivals were retired or dead. Prohibition had created a new and much more dangerous gangster class, since violation of the Volstead Act was a Federal offense. In 1920 Judge Landis shut down O'Leary's Palace after O'Leary explained that "a mysterious stranger" had left the liquor found in the place by Federal agents. O'Leary said he himself sold only milk, and the stranger had poured the liquor from his own bottle into the milk he had bought from O'Leary, drunk it and departed, leaving the liquor behind, and at that point the agents had come in before O'Leary had a chance to return the liquor to its owner. In 1921 another raid uncovered more whiskey, and O'Leary was also fined for violating gambling laws. His career was over. He ran a brokerage business on Halsted Street until he died at home on January 22, 1925, at the age of 56.

Tennes was no longer the big shot he had been. In 1924 his losses were reported to be $500,000 because of competition from the Empire News Service in New York, which was controlled by the crime syndicate. For a time, Tennes sold his racing information to both Al Capone on the south side and Joey Aiello and Bugs Moran on the north side. But Capone decided that there was no point in paying for things that could be gotten for nothing. Several Tennes handbooks were bombed and Jimmy Mondi, Capone's gambling spokesman, demanded twenty-five percent of Tennes's earnings for "protection." Thinking it over, in 1927 Mont Tennes decided to sell a fifty percent interest to Moses Annenberg, and two years later he sold off the remaining fifty percent.

5

The Annenberg brothers, Moses and Max, grew up in the Patch, a tough Irish neighborhood at 48th and Halsted streets. They were tough themselves, as befitted the sons of German-Jewish immigrants in a hostile environment.

William Randolph Hearst started his Chicago *Evening American* in 1900. In 1902, *American* publisher "Long Green" Andy Lawrence hired the Annenberg boys to boost newsstand sales by whatever means they chose in competition with the *Tribune* and the *Inter-Ocean*. The *American* was a scandal sheet that departed from the traditional "tombstone" newspaper format by employing five-inch headlines—"Beautiful Young Woman Victim of Poison Plot"—and sensational photographs. The Annenbergs recruited a gang of toughs that included Red and Dan Connors, Maurice "Mossie" Enright, Joe Kane, Walter Stevens, Tom Looney and James Ragen, sponsor of the south side "social athletic" club known as Ragen's Colts. These men intimidated newsstand dealers into accepting larger quantities of the Hearst paper—a practice known as "bootjacking."

In the same year that Lawrence hired the Annenbergs, Hearst introduced a morning paper, the *Examiner,* and a circulation war began in earnest. Robert McCormick and his cousin Joseph Patterson, owners of the *Tribune,* gave editor James Keeley a one-million-dollar budget to take the battle to the streets. Keeley had been favorably impressed with the Annenbergs' work for Hearst:

at one point Max and sixty delivery drivers and newsboys had picketed Marshall Field's department store, chanting, "Field's closed! Field's closed!" and wielding clubs and chains. The day after this, the store reinstated an advertisement in the *American* which they had cancelled. The *Tribune* offered Max Annenberg $20,000 to increase its circulation, and Max happily deserted Hearst, who sued him for breach of contract but accomplished nothing. Max took his gang of hoodlums with him. Lawrence responded by hiring his own collection of thugs, among them Dion O'Banion, the future bootlegger; Frank McErlane, who was later to work as a killer for Al Capone, and the four Gentleman brothers, Peter, Mike, Gus and William, and issued guns and blackjacks to them all.

By the time the last shot in the circulation war had been fired in 1913, twenty-seven newsdealers had been gunned down by the armies of Hearst and the McCormicks. There are no figures on the number of newsboys beaten almost to death.

The Briggs House was a popular Loop watering hole for low lifes of various stripes. On the afternoon of March 23, 1911, Vincent Altman, an ex-cop who had recently been hired by the *American*, stood at the bar chatting with Mossie Enright of the *Tribune*. Suddenly Enright put his hand on Altman's right shoulder, jerked him downward and fired two shots into his abdomen. In May, Enright shot William "Dutch" Gentleman in Pat O'Malley's saloon where Gentleman had come looking for him. Enright pumped six slugs into Gentleman, explaining his action with the immortal words, "I had to get him before he got me."

Enright was sentenced to life in prison for these murders, despite Charles Erbstein's efforts on his behalf. Mrs Enright fainted and Enright attacked Erbstein in a rage, calling him a liar and a four-flusher. But Enright was pardoned by Governor Dunne and went on to launch a reign of terror in labor disputes that resulted in many deaths. Finally on February 3, 1920, he was killed in a drive-by shooting in front of his house at 1110 Garfield Boulevard, where he was trying to start his car. The killer was Sunny Jim Cosmano, a Sicilian Black Hander, who was later deported.

Peter Gentleman was shot by Marty Guilfoyle on September 1, 1919, when Gentleman burst into Guilfoyle's poolroom at 2220 S Wabash, annoyed at having lost some money to Guilfoyle, and heaved a brick through the cigar case. Guilfoyle, who was playing poker at the time, stood up and fired five shots into Gentleman's back. Detective Mooney commented, "As hard as it may be to say, I confess I'm glad he's gone."

This was the world of the Annenbergs, the beginning of the gangster era in Chicago. Moe made a fortune in Wisconsin, buying up newspaper distributorships. In 1922 he bought the *Racing Form* from its founder, a former *Tribune* sports editor named Frank Bruenell, delivering $400,000 wrapped in newspapers to Bruenell in New York. Annenberg then turned his attention to Mont Tennes's General News Bureau and in 1927 bought half of the hundred shares of the Bureau stock. In 1929, forty shares were sold for $500,000 to Jack Lynch, the operator of a large handbook in the rear of a barbershop at 3114 W Madison Street. The rest were bought by Tennes's nephew, also named Mont, and Lionel and Edward Lenz. Somewhat later young Mont was stabbed almost to death by his 19-year-old bride of five months. He barely survived.

Getting involved with any of these people was risky business. With Capone on the scene, murder was supplanting warning bombs as the competitive weapon of choice. There was Alfred "Jake" Lingle, a *Tribune* crime reporter who was shot in the back of the head in the Illinois Central Station underpass at Randolph near Michigan in June, 1930. Lingle, who earned $65 a week, had explained his summer home, his suite at the Stevens Hotel and his expensive car by saying that he had inherited $50,000 from his father. Colonel Robert McCormick of the *Tribune* and his rival newspapers assumed that Lingle had been murdered to stop the papers from printing gangster exposés. Rewards were offered for information on the killer or killers and much was said about Lingle being a martyr to the cause of a free press.

It evolved, however, that Lingle had inherited $500, not $50,000, and had lost the $500 in the crash of 1929. He died wearing a diamond-studded belt given him by Al Capone, and he had various savings and brokerage accounts and was a heavy gambler. He was a go-between for the police and the underworld and one of his brokerage accounts was in partnership with Police Chief William Russell. The considerable scandal that arose from these revelations shook the *Tribune* to its foundations and the Colonel published an embarrassed editorial pointing out that there were "other weak men" besides Alfred Lingle in positions of responsibility on other newspapers, and in business.

Kidnapping was also a weapon of choice. On August 20, 1921, Jack Lynch, Annenberg's minority partner in General News, was forced off the road outside Lake Geneva, Wisconsin, dragged from his car by three men and taken to a nearby cottage. They demanded $125,000 for his safe return from Marty Guilfoyle, the gambler who had shot Pete Gentleman. He expressed regret, but said he could not raise the money. The next call went to Lynch's wife Anna who said she could come up with only $50,000. Finally, Al Capone paid $50,000 and Lynch was returned with two broken ribs and a damaged ego. This scare prompted the old-line gamblers to form a protective association to guard against kidnappings, which were all too prevalent.

Meanwhile Annenberg had put hoodlum James Ragen in charge of General News. It was located at 431 S Dearborn Street, nicknamed "Annenberg Alley." Annenberg had begun a trade war with the Empire News Service and the Greater New York News Service owned by racketeers Frank Ericson and Waxey Gordon, respectively. In December, 1934, Jack Lynch and the Lenz brothers, holders of General News stock, sued Annenberg and Ragen for an accounting of profits dating back to 1929, claiming they were owed about a quarter of a million dollars. Annenberg's lawyer Weymouth Kirkland offered an ingenious defense: Lynch, he said, had not come into court with clean hands. Kirkland cited a 1725 English decision denying highwaymen the right to recovery of illegal profits. Despite appeals, the case was thrown out of court.

Annenberg had frozen his partners out of profits by establishing the Nationwide News Service on August 27, 1934, to compete directly with General News. The first year, General News reported profits of $1.4 million, while Nationwide had losses of $3,788. A year later the picture was reversed: General News lost $45,634 while Nationwide reported a $1.1 million profit.

In May, 1937, Annenberg was sued for unfair competition by the Chicago *Turf Bulletin Record.* He also had some income-tax problems. On November 15, 1939, he sold Nationwide to James Ragen, who renamed it Continental Press. Annenberg eventually went to jail for income tax evasion. He was by that time a newspaper czar, holding among other things, the bitterly anti-New Deal *Philadelphia Inquirer.* Annenberg's decidedly shady past did not prevent his son Walter from buying respectability and eventuallly becoming ambassador to England.

Mont Tennes died in bed in August, 1941, after a heart attack. He had gone legitimate, involving himself in some big land deals in the Egewater community and taking over management of the Shafer Roller Bearing Company. He bequeathed $10,000 a year to the establishment of a "character home" for wayward boys, to be called Camp Honor.

James Ragen was not so fortunate. In his later life he did not drink, smoke or gamble, and he tended to avoid the new breed of thugs like Jake "Greasy Thumb" Guzik and Tony Accardo, who tried to buy half of his 600 Continental shares. Ragen did court politicians, including Dan Serritella, a state senator who had been a partner of Ragen's in General News. On June 24, 1946, Ragen was driving south on State Street. At Pershing Road, a truck loaded with orange crates pulled up next to his sedan, the car in front of him stopped abruptly, and shotgun blasts tore into Ragen from the tarpaulin-covered truck. He lingered for almost two months and said before he died that he had given the state's attorney, William Touhy, an affidavit claiming that Guzik, Accardo and Murray "The Camel" Humphreys were plotting to take over his news service.

That may have been the reason for the shooting. But there was also the fact that Ragen had set up the *Green Scratch Sheet* in direct competition with Dan Serritella's *Blue Scratch Sheet.*

In any case, no affidavit was ever found.

The times had changed, certainly not for the better, and the days of the colorful gamblers and saloonkeepers were over. It was in a sense the reformers—the prohibitionists who had had their way despite the warnings from thoughtful politicians like Woodrow Wilson—who had helped to create the deadly scourge of organized crime. Perhaps O'Leary was prescient when he said "Reform is here to stay and Chicago is no place for a gentleman."

IX

1919: The Summer of Lost Innocence

1

May 26 was a pleasant spring day—a day, a reporter noted, when "anxieties and troubles" were over and "a time of rejoicing" could begin. A parade was being held down Michigan Avenue to honor the 33rd Prairie Division, heroes of the Meuse-Argonne battles, newly returned from France. Governor Frank Lowden stood, flanked by General Leonard Wood and Major George Bell, in the official reviewing stand.

Across the avenue was another reviewing stand, set up on the last-minute orders of Mayor William Hale Thompson, hardly a friend to the governor, although both were Republicans. Thompson, with an eye to the large German constituency of Chicago, had opposed both America's help for the Allies, and her entry into the war. As late as September, 1917, Thompson had welcomed a largely socialist anti-war group which wanted to organize a meeting in the city. Governor Lowden had instructed Chief Schuettler to disperse the meeting, which he did. Thompson had allowed the group to organize a second meeting which was held; Lowden dispatched the militia to Chicago by train to prevent it, but the rally was over before they arrived.

Thousands of people lined the parade route from 12th Street north to Randolph along the avenue, west to State Street and south to Adams. Girls carried baskets of flowers, strewing the marchers' path with poppies and roses. A flivver designated for Company L of the 132nd Machine Gun Division displayed a sign reading, "No More Beer? No War Stories"—a reference to a wartime prohibition law which was scheduled to go into effect on July first. Overhead, a biplane circled the Loop. Just eleven days earlier, the Navy Seaplane NC-4 had made it to the Azores from St Johns, Newfoundland, a landmark flight.

To the sound of the Illinois state anthem, the Prairie Division marched smartly past the governor's reviewing stand, led by Colonel Abel Davis, veteran of the Spanish-American War, the Mexican battles and now the European conflict. Davis was returning to his job at Chicago Title & Trust and to what he hoped would be a political career. He ordered his men to salute the governor "Eyes right"—and then noticed the second reviewing stand on the other side of the street. The mayor had had a large sign with his name on it placed across the platform shortly before the parade began—it was an election year—but someone had convinced him to take it down in the interests of good taste. Davis ordered the men: "Eyes left" in a salute to the mayor.

People were in a good mood that day, despite the fact that many young men had not and would not come home, and there had been many changes because of the war. Prices were up, and labor, including teachers and policemen, was restive. Thousands of blacks had poured into the city since 1915; indeed, the black Second Ward had helped to elect Thompson. The Woman Suffrage constitutional amendment was being debated in the Illinois legislature, and there was the imminent implementation of the Federal prohibition law.

And although peace was supposedly being established in Europe, enough was going on there to upset ethnic groups in Chicago. Lithuanians and Jews were both angry at Poles: the Lithuanian National Congress was meeting in Chicago in June, and would accuse the Polish army of oppressing Lithuania. Twenty-five thousand people marched in the Loop in May to protest Polish pogroms, which the Polish-language newspaper had dismissed as rumors even though the *Jewish Courier* ran eyewitness accounts. Jews took to the streets in the Jewish district of Lawndale to defend themselves against a rumored Polish invasion. Poles took to the streets in July, rioting because of a rumor that a Jewish grocer had murdered a Polish child.

The Irish, too, were upset. In early June, at the same time that the Lawndale residents had gathered, eight thousand strong, to fight off the Polish invasion, the Irish filled the Auditorium for an independence rally, attended by Mayor Thompson and the president of DePaul University, which awarded an honorary degree to Eamon De Valera, the Irish patriot. De Valera spoke at Cubs Park in July to 25,000 people, including Thompson, who introduced him to the city council as "president of the Irish Republic," and former mayor and governor Edward F. Dunne, who had traveled to Versailles to lobby the American peace delegation on Irish independence from Britain.

2

Hinky Dink Kenna had some serious "evaluatin'" to do: the whole world was changing before his eyes. The Sunday school reformers like Arthur Burrage Farwell, with their narrow ideas of what was good for society, were about to have their day. So the Dink went off to Hot Springs, Arkansas, on May 17, for a long holiday. One afternoon he was spotted sneaking out of a side door of the hotel wearing a false beard and golfing togs. He was about to try his hand at golf and he did not want the boys at Pat O'Malley's saloon to get wind of it. But they did get wind of it. "The country's goin' dry on July first, and Hinky Dink is playing golf," moaned Baldy Sowers. "What's this world coming to?"

That was a good question. All sorts of social mores were changing. Couples were dancing cheek to cheek at the South Shore Country Club, outraging older members. Offenders were handed cards on salvers by page boys, requesting their presence in room 101, where it was explained to them that they had violated the rules of proper conduct and were risking the suspension of club privileges. On Decoration Day, 1919, notices were posted outlawing cheek-to-cheek dancing and smoking in the club's public rooms.

On Decoration Day that summer, the White Sox, the finest group of players ever assembled by owner Charles Comiskey and his manager, William "Kid" Gleason, were playing the Cleveland Indians at Comiskey Park in Chicago. Among the Sox's best players were outfielders "Shoeless Joe" Jackson and Oscar "Happy" Felsch, shortstop Charles "Swede" Risberg; first baseman Arnold "Chick" Gandil; infielder Fred McMullin; third baseman George "Buck" Weaver, and the star pitchers Eddie Cicotte and Claude "Lefty" Williams. The team had won the 1917 World Series and now in 1919 they had won twenty-three of thirty games and were leading the American League. However, they were not a happy group: they were among the lowest-paid players in baseball and had been agitating for more money for several seasons, but this year, Comiskey to paid them bonuses in cheap champagne.

They were a tense team and on this Decoration Day Chick Gandil became annoyed with the Indians' Tris Speaker in the eighth inning when Speaker chopped a grounder to Gandil at first and hot-dogged it by sliding into first, spikes flying. Gandil's shins were cut and at the end of the inning, when Speaker came out of the dugout to take his place at center field, the two men got into a fight, rolling in the dust for a full three minutes before seven cops were able to separate them.

The fans were upset and began to throw pop bottles at the Indians. Kid Gleason had to go out to left field, accompanied by a police officer, to ask the fans to stop before somebody got hurt and the game was forfeited. They settled down and the Sox won. The next day both players were temporarily suspended by Bancroft B. "Ban" Johnson, president and co-founder of the American League.

Gandil was heading for much bigger trouble than this. He and the seven other players—Gandil, Risberg and Cicotte were said to be the ringleaders—agreed to throw the 1919 World Series for $20,000 put up by a group of gamblers headed by New Yorker Arnold Rothstein. Supposedly the men never got the full amount they were promised, but they conspired to throw the Series to the Cincinnati Reds. The Sox lost the first game in Cincinnati nine to one on October first and then they lost the second. Players not in the fix won the third game for the Sox at Comiskey Park, but the Reds won the next two there. After that the Sox won twice, but on October 9 the Reds won the last game and became the champions.

There were many suspicions, but nothing happened until September, 1920, when a gambler named Billy Maharg told the Philadelphia *North American* about the fix. The eight men, who were eventually dubbed the Black Sox by sports writers, were suspended by Comiskey, indicted, tried and acquitted on August 2, 1921, by a friendly jury. Cicotte, Jackson and Williams had confessed, but their confessions had mysteriously disappeared. The jury was out for only two hours, forty-seven minutes.

As a result of this scandal, in 1920 Judge Kennesaw Mountain Landis was appointed the first Commissioner of professional baseball by the owners of the Major League teams. He banned the eight players from the game for life.

In May of 1919 Henry Ford, the inventor of the Model T car that revolutionized transportation, sued the *Chicago Tribune* for libel in Mount Clemens, Michigan, a small town outside Detroit. Ford claimed that his reputation had been damaged by an editorial that had appeared in the paper on June 23, 1916, in which writer Clifford Raymond had called him an anarchist. Ford had strong opinions about foreign policy and about war. When President Woodrow Wilson called up 150,000 National Guardsmen to seek retribution against Pancho Villa for his raids into Columbia, New Mexico, Ford was incensed. He instituted a company policy which withheld wages and benefits from Ford employees who were called up for service in Mexico. The editorial did, indeed, call Ford an anarchist:

FORD IS AN ANARCHIST
Inquiry at the Henry Ford offices in Detroit discloses the fact that employees of Ford who are members of, or recruits in the National Guard will lose their places. No provision will be made for anyone dependent on them. Their wages will stop, their families may get along in any fashion possible, and when and if they apply for their jobs again, they will be on the same footing as any other applicants. This is the rule for Ford

employees everywhere. . . . If Ford allows this rule of his shops to stand, he will reveal himself not as merely an ignorant idealist, but as an anarchistic enemy of the nation which protects him in his wealth.

What, Raymond asked, would Ford do if Villa's band attacked his Detroit factory?

Colonel Robert McCormick, the *Tribune*'s owner, was a staunch patriot who had, with his cousin Joseph Medill Patterson, ridden with General Pershing in his futile pursuit of Pancho Villa.

This was not the first time that Ford had tried to involve himself in foreign affairs. In December, 1915, he had sponsored a "peace ship," the *Oscar II,* to sail to Europe in an attempt to put an end to the World War; he thought a delegation of leading citizens would succeed where politicians had failed. The expedition proved to be a fiasco. But Ford had a strong faith in his own attitudes and a healthy contempt for professors and book learning. "Now I say history is bunk," he said, "bunk—double bunk. Why, it isn't even true. They wrote what they wanted us to believe, glorifying some conqueror or leader or something like that."

The judge in this million-dollar libel case was James G. Tucker of the Circuit Court of Macomb County, Michigan, where Ford had changed venues after first filing in Chicago. Jury selection was completed on May 16, 1919. Ford, determined to take his fight with the *Tribune* to the American people, set up his own news service across the street from the courthouse with telephone and telegraph lines, sending 15,000 dispatches to interested newspapers. Ford's staff stuck colored pins into a map of the country, marking cities with newspapers that were friendly or unfriendly to their man. Ford instructed them to "send out the uncolored truth."

The trial went on for fourteen weeks. Ford's lawyer, Alfred Lucking, accused the *Tribune* of being pro-German and of seeking to profit from a war with Mexico. The McCormick family held stock in International Harvester, which bought $14 million a year of sisal fiber from Mexico, and in Standard Oil, which purchased one-fifth of all its crude oil from Mexico.

The *Tribune* lawyer, Elliot Stevenson, called Colonel Henry Reilly, commander of the 149th Field Artillery, as a character witness. Colonel Reilly testified to the bravery in battle of both Robert McCormick and Joseph Patterson, while Stevenson pointed out that Henry Ford had secured a draft exemption for his son Edsel. The judge threw out the issue of patriotism as irrelevant. It was difficult to prove Ford unpatriotic, since his company was a leading producer for the U.S. of ambulances, airplanes, munitions and tanks during the war. Ford's lawyer Theodore Delavigne told the court, "Henry Ford, curse him as you will, is the Lincoln of today. A Lincoln with hands clean of blood."

On July 14, Elliot Stevenson questioned Henry Ford on the stand after reading him a paragraph Ford had supposedly written, that said in part, "The men of the world . . . are beginning to take these preachers of war at their true worth and to see in all of them . . . only ballyhoos of their own wares of death." Stevenson asked Ford if he knew what "ballyhoo" meant. Ford, wearing a light grey suit, looked nervous and uncomfortable, fidgeting and wringing his hands.

"No," he said, "I don't believe I do."

"What did you understand the people who read it were going to understand it meant?"

"Ballyhoo was a blackguard," Ford said.

"What?"

"Ballyhoo is possibly a blackguard. I don't know what it really means."

Stevenson asked him whether he knew what treason was. Ford responded that "treason is unlawful, I know that."

He was asked whether he had ever heard of Benedict Arnold. He said he had heard the name.

"Who was he?" Stevenson asked.

"I have forgotten just who he was," Ford said. "He was a writer, I think."

"What subjects do you recall he wrote on?"

Ford said he didn't remember.

"Did you ever read anything he wrote?"

"Possibly I have," Ford said. "I don't know."

"Would you be surprised to be informed that Benedict Arnold was a general in the American army who was a traitor and betrayed his country?"

"I don't know much about him," Ford said.

Ford's attorney attempted to turn his client's ignorance into an advantage. "Mr Ford is willing to confess anything against himself," he said.

The central question was whether Ford had been defamed by having been called an anarchist. Experts were called by both sides to testify to what anarchism meant. The case was given to the jury on August 14, and they were out for ten hours. They found in favor of the plaintiff, but awarded only six cents for damages. The *Tribune* people were relieved, and Ford's attorney said that money damages were "entirely subordinate" and were not sought by his client, who had been "vindicated."

Ford was not finished with philosophical questions, however. He founded the *Dearborn Independent*, in which he expressed virulently anti-Semitic views. "The International Jew: The World's Problem," was the title of a representative article.

In 1941 Colonel McCormick apologized to Ford and the two agreed that the whole thing had been a mistake.

On June 10, Illinois became the first state in the Union to ratify the Nineteenth Amendment, the Woman Suffrage amendment.

The dreaded July first date of wartime prohibition approached: it meant loss of revenue and jobs, to say nothing of the favorite recreation of thousands of people. On June 7 the Sherman Hotel announced a raise in room rates from fifty cents a night to one dollar, to make up for losses. The manager of the hotel dining room promised to make recipes, shakers and non-alcoholic ingredients available to patrons who wanted to create their own concoctions.

As the deadline drew closer, wholesale prices of whiskey dropped, and surplus whiskey began to pile up in Chicago government warehouses. A gallon of hooch sold for just six cents, but the tax on it was a stiff $6.40. This act, which banned the manufacture or sale of all beverages containing more than one half of one percent alcohol, was decreed to remain in effect until the end of the war and until demobilization was over. In a May referendum Chicagoans had overwhelmingly voted against prohibition. But there had been no official declaration that the war had ended. "Chicago may be dry for two months, but not any longer," Alderman Anton Cermak declared. "It will be a sort of recess." One saloon posted a sign: "We'll reopen after July 2." And then after July 2, a second sign: "Eat, drink and be merry, for tomorrow we dry up."

Shortly before midnight, cars raced pell-mell down Madison Street, drunken revelers punched holes in their straw boaters and an orator at Washington and Wells streets demanded, "Where's your liberty? The foundation of our liberties is being knocked from under us—" At that point the wooden crate he was standing on was kicked out from under him. The police arrived in the nick of time.

The next morning State Street was a gloomy trail filled with broken bottles. Groups of the bereaved gathered at Hinky Dink's Workingman's Exchange, mourning the passing of "the world's biggest schooner" which had sold for a nickel. "Naw, we ain't got no real beer, just this sissy near beer," one of the white-aproned bartenders said; he and others would soon be looking for work at the U.S. Employment Service at 116 N Dearborn Street. These men were offered jobs in Kansas doing field work during the harvest season for sixy cents an hour.

Most bars did not close; they simply changed their bill of fare. The LaSalle Hotel bar offered a "buttermilk frappe" and others introduced "loganberry highballs," phosphates and ice cream sundaes. As if things weren't bad enough, a small harvest of natural ice during the winter had caused a critical ice shortage in Chicago that summer. During a typical heatwave 75,000 gallons of ice cream were consumed, and it took sixty to seventy-five pounds of ice to freeze one gallon of ice cream. "The night of June thirtieth won't be a comparison with the night they shut off the ice cream," sneered Carnation Dan O'Leary. "I can see them right now sitting on high stools at drugstores, bawling and fighting for that one more little sundae."

On July sixth, for the first time in many years, Chicago saloons were open for business on a Sunday, serving ice cream and all sorts of non-alcoholic beverages.

3

In June two Englishmen, John Alcock and Arthur Brown, flew a Vickers Vimy biplane from St Johns, Newfoundland, to Clifton, Ireland, eight years before Lindbergh's trans-Atlantic solo, and won the London *Daily Mail*'s $50,000 prize for the first non-stop trans-Atlantic flight. They flew 1,960 miles in sixteen hours and twelve minutes. The plane crashed into a sandbog, but the pilots emerged in good humor. "Our flight has shown that the Atlantic flight is practicable," John Alcock said. "But I think it should be done not with airplane or seaplane, but with flying boat."

Aviation history on a smaller scale had been made in Chicago on May 15 when Trent Fry, after several earlier attempts, finally inaugurated the Chicago-to-New-York airmail service. The mail was flown to Cleveland and then sent the rest of the way by train. On June 17, the first airmail plane arrived from St Louis carrying a letter from Mayor Henry Kiel to Chicago's Mayor Thompson. Loop spectators were given an air show when Omar Locklear, the copilot, climbed a rope ladder let down by another biplane flying above him.

Chicagoans had witnessed air shows since August 12, 1911, when the Chicago Aero Club sponsored the International Aviation Meet above Grant Park, with prize money supplied by Harold McCormick. During that show, William Badger attempted a 300-foot dive and crashed after failing to pull out of it twenty feet above the park. Despite this, and over many objections, the show went on. The next day an estimated crowd of 400,000 filled Michigan Avenue, some people renting hotel rooms facing the avenue. A far worse air tragedy was to take place on July 21, 1919.

It was a hot, muggy Monday. Fourteen thousand people were in Comiskey Park to watch the White Sox capture their third in a row from the New York Yankees, who were in second place. The World Series was on everyone's mind. At ten minutes of five in

194

the afternoon, a jet of flame spurted from the belly of a 153-foot balloon called the *Wing Foot*, which had been circling lazily above the Loop. The game stopped as everyone watched in frozen horror. The great dirigible quivered, buckled and then plunged 1,200 feet toward LaSalle Street. Five men parachuted out; one chute was consumed by fire. That parachutist, a mechanic named Carl Weaver, crashed through the skylight of the Illinois Trust and Savings Bank at Jackson and LaSalle streets , and was followed in seconds by the great bulk of the *Wing Foot.*

The bank had been closed to customers for an hour and clerks were balancing their cash drawers, getting ready to leave. There was little warning. Rose A. Meyer was sorting mail when she saw a sudden flash of light overhead. "It did not startle us," she said. Everyone thought it was a picture being taken for a house magazine. Then Weaver fell through the skylight, followed by two fifty-foot LaRhone engines, their gasoline tanks exploding instantly on impact. Glass fragments fell from the broken skylight; the fuel splashed on the clerks and ignited them at once. Eleven people were killed instantly, six of them burned beyond recognition.

The marble rotunda was surrounded by wire-enclosed teller cages. Streams of blood ran across the marble floor; blood was splashed against the walls. People were trapped in the rotunda, many ablaze. Most of them were women—stenographers and telegraph operators. There were only two exits from the bank. Many clerks jumped to the street from second-story windows. Those fortunate male employees who had not been severely injured carried women to the exits and manned the emergency fire hoses along the walls.

Firemen appeared on the scene within two minutes, responding to a 1-11 fire station alarm. There was little anyone could do. Thousands of spectators lined the streets outside the bank, watching ambulances speeding off to the Iroquois Hospital at Market and Madison streets. It was not a well-equipped hospital, and many of the doctors had left for the day.

John N. Mitchell, the bank president, was on a train heading for his suburban home when he learned about the disaster. Four hours after the flames were quenched, Mitchell was back in the bank, supervising the clean-up and reconstruction. Six policemen were on hand to guard the hundred million dollars untouched in the vault. Incredibly, a number of injured employees returned to the bank to help in the cleanup and salvage operations. One, C.E. Smithman, had been burned and lost most of his hair.

The bereaved families were informed of their loss. Carl Otto's wife was sitting on the front porch, rocking her baby; a newspaper reporter broke the news to her. Her husband had been crushed to death under the wreckage of the motors. This was his first day back on the job after several weeks of illness. His wife had thought he was not strong enough to go back to work and had begged him to stay home. But he went back.

In spite of everything, the bank opened for business fifteen hours after the last victim had been carried out by soldiers called in to assist the rescue efforts. Mitchell ran an ad in the morning papers announcing that the bank would transact business that day, Tuesday, July 22, "and thereafter as usual." Several employees had been injured and killed, he said, but "the teller's cages and other facilities were not affected."

The *Wing Foot* was owned and operated by the Goodyear Company of Akron, Ohio, which had spent more than half a million constructing a hangar and airfield for the blimp at Wing Foot Lake, outside Akron, and which wanted to sell the balloon to Adams Aerial Transportation of New York. This was intended to be a test flight which would demonstrate the potential for commercial dirigible business. The flight was almost cancelled because mechanics had discovered that the fuel mixture was faulty. But hasty repairs were made. The balloon took off from a hangar at the White City amusement park at 63rd and South Park on the south side, because the army and navy were using the Wing Foot Lake facility for pilot tests.

Captain Jack Boettner, a commercial pilot and veteran of forty-two dirigible flights, had landed his balloon at Grant Park on the 21st after a routine flight. At noon he had taken off again for a short trip over Diversey Avenue and then back again over the Loop. On board were White City publicist Earl Davenport, Milton Norton, and mechanics Harry Wacker and Carl Weaver.

Boettner acted quickly and saved himself, but Davenport and Weaver hesitated too long. Weaver fell through the skylight, as we have seen, Davenport crashed onto the bank roof and Wacker broke his back. Thirteen people died in the accident.

There was an investigation, but no one could say for sure what had happened. Boettner testified that he had been flying at 1,200 feet and that possibly static electricty had caused the accident. Later he suggested that the LaRhone motors may have been at fault; perhaps a rush of air from the propellers had fanned exhaust fumes against the bag. William C. Young of the Goodyear Company said that he himself had not considered the blimp safe without further testing and he had discouraged the flight. White City owner Herbert Byfield did not know what had happened, either. The blimp had simply been assembled at his hangar, in which Goodyear had built "the first two airships used by Uncle Sam for the war."

The victims' families received about $1,000 from the bank's insurance company, and Goodyear agreed to settle all claims arbitrated by a committee of three: Henry Horner, who was to become governor of Illinois, John H. Wigmore of Northwestern Law School and John Mitchell, the bank president.

The night of the accident, at an emergency meeting of the city council, Anton Cermak introduced a measure to ban flying over the city, saying, "This accident shows we must stop flying over this city sooner or later and we had better do it sooner." Alderman Guy Guernsey of the Seventh Ward disputed this. "Some regulation is necessary," he said, "but don't forget that aviation is here to stay. I think flying over Chicago should not be prohibited, and I am an interested party, inasmuch as had it not been for this council meeting, I would have been in that blimp that fell today."

The council eventually passed a watered-down resolution, which called for the public works commissioner to review petitions for flights over the Loop. But this panic soon died away. The White City hangar eventually became a roller rink. The Goodyear Company went on during the twenties with their plans to market dirigibles, signing contracts with the U.S. Government and with the German Zeppelin Company. The U.S. bowed out of the deal in the '30s after the first two ships, the *Akron* and the *Macon*, were destroyed in storms. The deathknell for these balloons came in 1937 when the *Hindenburg* burst into flames over Lakehurst, New Jersey.

There was another tragedy that July. Janet Wilkinson, six years old, the younger daughter of Scottish immigrants who owned a grocery store, vanished on the near north side. That morning, she had been allowed to go with two friends to a playground on Chicago Avenue near the lake. At noon she left her friends at Rush and Superior to walk home for lunch to the family apartment at 114 E Superior Street. That was the last time she was seen.

Hours after she was reported missing, a massive hunt began. The lake off Chicago Avenue was dragged. Much of that area was a soggy marsh, not to be transformed for another year, and tall reeds growing along the shore were cut back in the search for the girl. Then Marjorie Burke, one of the two friends who had been with Janet, told the police that after she left them, they saw Janet stop to talk to a man named Thomas Richard Fitzgerald whom they all knew because he lived on the second floor of the Wilkinsons' apartment building. Fitzgerald, 38, a slight taciturn man who wore gold spectacles, was married and worked as a night watchman at the Virginia Hotel. He was arrested and taken to the basement of the Chicago Avenue police station, where he was interrogated for 104 hours by various policemen and a host of reporters who drifted in and out of the building. Walter Howey, the legendary editor of Hearst's *Herald-Examiner*, along with James Doherty and George Bryant of the *Tribune*, joined the police in the interrogation.

The suspect was deprived of sleep, threatened and even confronted by a detective disguised as a priest and a reporter disguised as a Wilkinson relative—all in attempts to force a confession. Finally at eight o'clock on a Sunday morning, Fitzgerald confessed to Lieutenant William Howe, who had been playing the role of good cop.

He said that he had seen Janet walking to the playground when he returned from his job at nine in the morning. He went to bed but woke at noon when Janet was coming home for lunch. He opened his apartment door and asked her if she would like some candy. She hesitated, and he seized her, brought her into the apartment, panicked when she struggled and screamed, and choked her into unconsciousness. He thought she was dead, although she was not. He took her to the basement and buried her alive under 120 tons of coal between the chimney and the furnace.

The body was uncovered; there were no signs of violence or sexual abuse. Janet's father told the police that Fitzgerald had earlier made an improper move toward Janet, but Mrs Wilkinson had talked her husband out of pursuing any action against him. It evolved that Fitzgerald had been in prison for grand larceny and had once before, several years earlier, been questioned about molesting a child.

An angry mob appeared at the Chicago Avenue station; the city was in an uproar. The city council held lengthy discussions about what the press called "the moron problem." What were the differences between idiots, imbeciles and degenerates, and between a "low grade" and "high grade" moron? When should these people be removed from society, at what age? The *Tribune*, in an editorial entitled "The Noose and the Moron," called for speedy justice. And justice was speedy. Fitzgerald went on trial for murder on September 22; the trial lasted one day, Fitzgerald was found guilty and sentenced the next day, and hanged on October 27 in the county jail.

It was not a pleasant summer. Worse was to come.

Chicagoans could always find relief from the heat on the Lake Michigan beaches. At Clarendon Beach a rope extended across the sand into the water, to separate the ladies' part of the beach from the men's, since bathing dress was slightly more revealing than street clothes. This was not good enough for Louise Osborne Rowe of the city welfare department, who began a campaign that July to outlaw the indecent exposure of female legs on the public beach. On the 13th of the month, she made a personal inspection of south side beaches, and was not pleased by what she found. "I feel they must be morally degrading," she said, "these suits which permit the exposure of female flesh." From 51st Street all the way to Wilson Avenue and on to Clarendon, the situation was the same. "Trunks," Miss Rowe said, "should extend to the knee. A dainty skirt should rebuke the too-interested male stare. Girls should keep their hair neatly done under a cap because if it flows about the neck it gives a *September Morn* look."

Louise Rowe filed her report with the city council. Alderman Edward Armitage of the 27th Ward did not accept her strictures. "Things have changed, boys," he said. "We are living in the twentieth century now." But Police Chief John J. Garrity, on receiving a tip that female ushers at the Ziegfeld Theatre on Michigan Avenue were wearing bathing suits to help publicize a showing of *Mack Sennett's Bathing Beauties*, went to see for himself. "You know," he said, "they just might catch cold wearing those things." He found preferable the kind of bathing dress worn in 1869.

4

On Sunday, July 27, 1919, five black teenagers decided to go swimming to escape from the heat. The boys, John Harris, brothers Charles and Lawrence Williams and Eugene Williams, no relation to the brothers, had a favorite swimming spot, where they kept a homemade raft. This was between the 25th Street (sometimes called 26th Street) beach, where blacks swam, and the 29th Street beach, which whites had made their own. As they brought their raft into the water, the five boys did not know that a nasty racial confrontation had just taken place at the 29th Street beach, where whites had thrown rocks at a group of black men and women who had tried to swim there. The blacks had left, to return shortly with reinforced numbers and rocks of their own, driving the whites away, temporarily. They returned and there was a real racial battle, with rock throwing and screamed insults on both sides.

The boys, swimming and diving from their raft, noticed a white man standing on the shore near 26th Street and hurling rocks at them. Since he was about seventy-five feet away, the boys thought his actions were harmless. But Eugene Williams, who was in the lake, was hit in the head by a rock and slipped under the water. The other boys, seeing blood, became panicky, while the rock-thrower, who might have been under the impression, as the boys had been, that he was playing a sort of game, evinced some panic of his own and ran toward the 29th Street beach. The boys went to the 25th Street beach and fetched the lifeguard. Half an hour later Eugene's body was recovered.

With a black policeman from the 25th Street beach, the boys went to 29th Street and pointed out the man who had thrown the rock to the white officer on duty, Daniel Callahan. The rock-thrower was later identified as George Stauber of 2904 Cottage Grove Avenue. Officer Callahan refused to arrest Stauber or to allow the black officer to arrest him. The two policemen got into an argument, and the boys ran back to get their clothes and rush home. They paused long enough to tell the people at 25th Street what had happened, and this led to a host of rumors, all of them alarming. Officer Callahan, who was later suspended by Chief Garrity, continued to refuse to arrest Stauber and instead arrested a black man for disorderly behavior.

While this was going on, the beach filled with whites and blacks: some blacks had heard that Callahan had helped to kill Eugene Williams; whites were told that a black man had stoned a white man to death. By the time the patrol wagon pulled up to take away the man Callahan had arrested, the crowd was going out of control, and throwing rocks and anything else they could find. Then a black man with a gun, James Crawford, fired into a group of policemen, wounding one. A black officer shot and killed Crawford. There was more gunfire. A race war had started which was to last for five days.

This was not unexpected. Beginning around 1916, there had been extremely heavy migration to Chicago from the rural South. The impetus was of course a better life, with the possibility of a good education and the absence of overt legalized racism and segregation. Northern industries actively recruited Southern blacks because they needed them: the war in Europe had virtually cut off the flow of immigrants and America's entry into that war had drained away male workers. Chicago was a logical destination for rural blacks: all the railroads were centered there, as well as the stockyards, steel mills and factories of all kinds. The Chicago *Defender*, a black newspaper circulated widely in the South, urged readers to move to Chicago; it carried classified advertisements for jobs and housing.

The result was culture shock on the part of the newcomers, some fearful resentment on the part of the established black residents of the city, and anger and hatred from whites, especially the Irish.

Feeding this hatred was the refusal of blacks, particularly in the stockyards, to join unions. This was not a new situation: black strikebreakers had been brought in by management in major strikes in Chicago in 1894 and as recently as 1905, when anger against black anti-union activity had led to race riots with acts of violence on both sides. In 1918 the stockyards workers had won an eight-hour day and other benefits. But even this, and the fact that servicemen would soon be coming home, war industries would shut down, and blacks would be fired first when the labor glut developed—first black women, then black men and then white women—even these things did not encourage most blacks to join unions.

One reason was that the newly arrived blacks did not trust the white unions, where racism was and always had been the order of the day. Ninety percent of the established black stockyards workers belonged to a union, but the Southern migrants had had no experience with labor-management difficulties; they tended to trust management, which supplied them with the money they lived on. They had no inborn resentments against the companies that hired them. And they were to some extent manipulated by management's contributing to charities like the YMCA, which held out a helping hand to poor migrant blacks. There were advantages to being non-union, and some black newspapers and leaders, including ministers, advised these new members of the community to avoid unions. In 1919 ninety percent of the white stockyards workers belonged to a union; only a quarter of the new black workers had joined one. They did not trust the unions and they did not trust their white co-workers.

And there was good reason for this lack of trust. Especially volatile were the white "social-athletic clubs" like Ragen's Colts, who beat up any black people who crossed Wentworth Avenue, the demarcation line between black and white neighborhoods. This was particularly bad because the stockyards, where many blacks worked as slaughterers and meat packers, was in a white area. Black parents were forced to send their children to often inferior schools in the black belt—an area between 12th and 57th streets and Wentworth and Cottage Grove avenues—or risk their being beaten up by young toughs belonging to these clubs, which operated with tacit police support. The newspapers reinforced black stereotypes; it was common to see the word "darkies" in the Chicago daily press.

As if all this were not bad enough, as the war ended the cost of living skyrocketed—prices of food and clothing; workers in those days did not fret about luxuries. Rents were very high in the black area because there were not enough homes and apartments for the swelling black population. Before the Chicago Fire, there had been no black areas of the city; black Chicago residents were domestics who settled near the large houses where they worked. But after the fire the population grew. By 1912 the black areas on the south and west sides were already saturated. By 1919 the housing shortage for blacks had reached catastrophic proportions, with some estimates of needed units running as high as fifty thousand. The population had nearly tripled, but the area had not expanded. Returning servicemen were looking for homes and apartments and, to make matters worse, there was no construction because of a lockout in the building trades. Landlords took advantage of the situation by raising rents, in some cases doubling them, while at the same time neglecting rental property. This, apart from increasing general unpleasantness, presented a health hazard.

In addition to disease, the overcrowded conditions led to crime. Vice was rampant in the district: it was filled with "black-and-tan" cabarets with names like The Pekin and Dreamland, and with brothels and pool halls, much like the old Levee. People were desperate to get out and they began to move into bordering white areas like Hyde Park, where in 1917 alarmed white residents formed the Hyde Park-Kenwood Property Owners Association, expressly for the purpose of keeping blacks out of the area. It would appear that they would go to any lengths to do this, using threats to keep real estate agents from selling to blacks and conspiring with employers to fire blacks who refused to move out of white areas. In 1917 some people resorted to bombs.

In July, 1917, four months before the Hyde Park-Kenwood Property Owners Association was formed, the first bomb was thrown into the S.P. Motley home on 53rd Street. The Motley family had been the first black family on the block, having bought the house in 1913. No one was hurt, although there was considerable damage to the house. Blacks were not intimidated; they continued to move into the neighborhood. But in 1918 the bombings began in earnest: from March of that year until June 27, 1919, twenty-five black homes and real estate offices were bombed. In May of 1919 the home of Richard B. Harrison, a prominent black actor, at 4807 S Grand Avenue, was hit twice by bombs. Mr Harrison was away at the time, helping to sell war bonds. His wife had had a warning several days earlier that her house, which the Harrisons had occupied only since March, was going to be a target. The police were called, but they shrugged off the information. After the bombing a police detail was sent to protect the house, but the next night the house was bombed again, this time from a vacant flat next door. Windows were shattered in the Harrison house, the roof was damaged and the front porch was destroyed. There was also retaliation against the white agent who had sold the house to the Harrisons: William B. Austin received hate mail and his north side home was hit by a bomb in June. A few weeks later the Harrisons moved out of their Grand Boulevard house.

Nobody was arrested in connection with any of these bombings. A black delegation was twice turned away from Mayor Thompson's office; he refused to see them. This was doubly galling to the black community because in the 1915 mayoral election Thompson had had solid support from the black Second Ward, and he could not have won without it. Elected with Thompson was

Oscar DePriest of the Second Ward, the first black alderman in the city council, who about ten years later was to be the first black in the U.S. Congress since the turn of the century. Consequently there was bitter disappointment in the black precincts with Thompson's refusal to act in the bombings and a militant spirit grew stronger there, encouraged by the black newspapers the *Defender* and the *Whip*. Blacks were wage earners, often courted by management, and many black men had now been in the army, trained in the use of firearms. Further, they had political strength. They were no longer willing to be passive in the face of physical attack and attempted humiliation.

Thus the incident at the lake shore on July 27 ignited a tinderbox. The weather was very hot. Mobs of white hoodlums beat blacks caught on the street; black hoodlums attacked white storeowners and deliverymen. Whites fired shots from automobiles; black snipers were posted on roofs. People were shot and stabbed and beaten to death. On the first night it was the Ragen Colts and other gangs which killed and wounded blacks. The next day Mayor Thompson was told by at least one police officer that he should call out the state militia. The mayor took the position that the police could handle the situation, if necessary by cordoning off the black belt. That afternoon black workers leaving the stockyards were viciously attacked and chased; some were stabbed and murdered even on streetcars stopped by mobs. Thousands of blacks milled in the streets in the area of 35th Street between State and Wabash. At least three white men working in the area were murdered. There was a bloody confrontation between an enraged black mob and one hundred policemen, some mounted. Meanwhile, shootings continued in the streets from whites in cars and black snipers. The exhausted police made futile attempts to disperse the mobs. Many policemen did not enthusiastically protect endangered blacks, and even attacked the wounded and arrested potential victims. Seventeen people were killed that Monday, and over 240 people injured, of which 172 were blacks.

The mayor called on Governor Lowden to mobilize the National Guard, which was billeted accordingly in Chicago armories, but the mayor did not deploy them for active service. There was bad blood between Mayor Thompson and the governor, even though both were Republicans, because Lowden had not given Thompson sufficient patronage, and because of Lowden's attempts to stop Thompson from holding pacifist meetings in 1917, and his support of Thompson's opponent in a 1918 senatorial primary.

Tuesday morning, public transportation closed down because of a traction workers' strike. Blacks did not report to the stockyards for work. The violence now spread to the Loop, where black men were beaten and shot and even robbed by young toughs, many of them servicemen. Mobs broke into the Palmer House and the Sherman Hotel looking for black maids and porters. Governor Lowden said he could not order the troops out of the armories until he received the word from the mayor. This despite the fact that he had unilaterally deployed the militia to stop Thompson's pacifist rally in 1917. Inflammatory rumors spread in both white and black areas and there were riots on the north side; and on the south side, where people huddled in their homes, the streets were dark; street lamps had been shot out.

By Wednesday, the third day, thirty-one people had been killed and hundreds wounded. Still the governor waited for the mayor, and the mayor refused to call out the guard. Maclay Hoyne, the state's attorney, added fuel to the fire by claiming that guns were being stockpiled at the black-and-tan cabarets, and that a white policeman had "gone about distributing revolvers and cartridges among vicious colored persons who would likely engage in rioting." The city council called a special meeting and asked Chief Garrity for 1,000 special patrolmen. Black leaders, although wary because of the militia's racist behavior in other riots, called on the mayor and the governor to release the National Guard now. Still the mayor and the governor refused to act. People in the black belt had run out of food; no deliveries could be made because unions had forbidden drivers to enter the area for fear of the mobs and snipers. Garbage was piling up, and the inhabitants had not received wages because they had not gone to work.

Finally on Wednesday night, July 30, Thompson capitulated and called out the National Guard. He had heard that there was a plot afoot to torch the entire black belt. That evening there had already been thirty-seven fires in five hours in that area, some set very close together, at least one set by the Ragen Colts, a mob of two hundred who had broken into one house after throwing bricks and shooting into it, smashed the furniture and burned it down. The police were on the verge of physical collapse. It was nearly ten that night when the soldiers entered the black belt. They had been instructed to draw no color line, and they went after the athletic club members with zeal. As an important help to them, it began to rain, and things cooled off in general, although black workers were attacked in the stockyards on Thursday, August first.

Six thousand guardsmen, representing seven reserve units, were stationed on State Street, south to 51st, up and down Cottage Grove, with guns mounted on sandbags. Separate blocks were quarantined and special details of motorcycle police and the horse patrol toured Halsted, State, and 35th streets and Ashland Avenue. First Police Deputy John Alcock, R.R. Ronayne of the militia and Charles Fitzmorris, the mayor's secretary, toured the riot area and reported to Thompson that things were under control, although their car had been fired on at 36th and Vincennes.

On Saturday, August 5, the hovels of Poles and Lithuanians living behind the stockyards were set on fire; more than 900 homes were destroyed. No one was ever arrested for this arson, although accusations flew thick and fast. Governor Lowden said that conspirators belonging to the Industrial Workers of the World had blackened their faces and set the fires, hoping blacks would be blamed. The governor chose to overlook the fact that many of the homeless immigrants belonged to the IWW. The victims themselves and the fire department blamed blacks, while black spokesmen pointed out that black people would not dare to go near that neighborhood; they had not gone there even to pick up paychecks which they desperately needed. A grand jury blamed the white social clubs, which had indeed been central to all this death and destruction.

On Thursday, August 7, 12,000 black workers reported to the stockyards, protected by 1,500 policemen, deputies, detectives and a regiment of the National Guard. On August 8, the militia were released from duty, and on the ninth they paraded through the Loop.

Fourteen whites and twenty-two blacks had been killed—a number that varies by one or two on each side—and more than 500 people had been injured. Seven blacks had been shot by the police. Maclay Hoyne presented seventeen cases to a grand jury for indictment—all black men. Although the judge, Robert B. Crowe, was asking that these "anarchists" should be hanged, the twenty-four white men on the jury angrily refused to indict unless Hoyne presented white people for indictment as well. Hoyne tried to use the riot for political advantage by blaming the Thompson administration for "catering" to "vicious elements of the Negro race." He was not alone in this attempt to rewrite history. Mayor Thompson took credit for "prompt action" and blamed the *Tribune* for encouraging lawlessness.

The grand jury recommended that a curb be put on the white social-athletic clubs. As early as July 12, 1919, the *Defender* had complained about them:

> Gangs of young hoodlums from the district west of Wentworth Avenue have been making it a practice of attacking our people under the cover of darkness, and so far have been able to elude the police. Most of these young men come from the so-called "athletic clubs" that are so numerous in the territory aforementioned. These clubs are nothing more than hangouts for gangs and young toughs The records of the police department show that much of the banditry now prevalent in this city is due to the activity of this class of men.

There were seventy-five Irish clubs in the city, of which the Ragen Colts were the best known; others were the Aylward Club, Gerdon's, Lorraine, the Our Flag Club and the infamous Dirty Dozen from Hyde Park, one of whose members was killed on a trolley by a black woman wielding a razor, whom he was attempting to rob. There were close to 100 Italian gangs from "Little Hell" on the north side and 148 Polish ones from "Pojay Town." Jewish gangs from the near west side fought both of these. The weapons were bricks, glass and stones, although occasionally someone got shot. Fredric Thrasher identified 1,313 organized gangs in Chicago during the 1920s, averaging six to ten members. But the Ragen Colts were the biggest and the meanest of the clubs; their motto was "Hit me and you hit two thousand." Their territory was back of the stockyards, south from 43rd Street to 63rd. Their clubhouse was a store front at 5528 S Halsted Street. They were the sons of Irish stockyards workers, and they had organized themselves in 1902 as the Morgan Athletic Club. But in 1908 Frank Ragen had taken them over. He was a Democratic Cook County commissioner who paid the rent on the clubhouse and supported the club in other ways in return for their help in beating up political opponents, tearing down campaign posters and intimidating voters in polling places. Ragen himself often went beyond debate: in 1914 he punched Joseph Mendel in the eye and clouted Commissioner Cooney over the head with a book. When he did speak, he usually confined himself to accusing his opponents of lying. Without Ragen, the Colts could not survive financially on membership dues. With Ragen, they were able to play football, rugby and baseball, boxing and wrestling matches, and hold picnics and dances.

When these club members grew up, they opened saloons or went to work for the city. Richard Daley was one who went from the presidency of the Hamburg Athletic Club to the mayoralty; the Hamburg district extended from 31st to 40th streets. Another gang member was Dion O'Banion, who fought the Italian gangs in Little Hell, killed freely and was killed himself by Capone in the '20s.

As a result of the riots, Mayor Thompson revoked the clubs' charters—these had been given to the clubs by a nebulous body called the South Side Clubs Association. Thompson had little to lose, since he was a Republican with heavy support from the black belt. But pressure was applied from Ragen's city hall connections, and the charters were soon restored.

Governor Lowden promised better housing for black Chicagoans, but nothing came of it.

Nothing was done to remedy this volatile situation as the city, and indeed the nation, lurched toward the 1920s, a decade that was to taint the name of Chicago for at least the rest of the century. National Prohibition went into effect on January 1, 1920, and brought with it a new kind of organized crime. Chicago had had a golden age of architecture and city planning with the work of Daniel Burnham, Henry Ives Cobb, John Root, Dankmar Adler, Martin Roche, William Holabird and Louis Sullivan. It had had a cultural golden age with writers like Theodore Dreiser, Frank Norris, Vachel Lindsay, Sherwood Anderson, Edgar Lee Masters, Ring Lardner, and with Harriet Monroe's *Poetry* magazine and Margaret Anderson's *Little Review*. It had produced commercial giants like Philip Armour, Potter Palmer and Marshall Field; these in turn had endowed the city with cultural landmarks, and had supported Jane Addams's settlement house and the impressive Columbian Exposition of 1893. But the city was to be thought of primarily as the home of criminals so vicious as to make the old vicemongers and politicians of the Levee seem almost quaintly charming.

The old order had ended. The streetcar—the days of which were numbered—was pulling away from the curb.

APPENDIX

Population of Chicago, 1871–1920*

They came from all corners of the globe—Italians, Poles, Swedes, Irish
Jews, Germans, Chinese—all in search of a better life. This chart reflects
the phenomenal growth of the city in that time.

Year	Population	Year	Population
1871	334,270	1897	1,490,937
1872	367,396	1898	1,557,164
1873	380,000	1899	1,626,333
1874	395,408	1900	1,698,575
1875	400,500	1901	1,747,236
1876	407,661	1902	1,795,897
1877	430,000	1903	1,834,558
1878	436,731	1904	1,893,219
1879	491,516	1905	1,941,880
1880	503,185	1906	1,990,541
1881	540,000	1907	2,039,202
1882	560,693	1908	2,087,862
1883	580,000	1909	2,136,525
1884	629,885	1910	2,196,238
1885	665,000	1911	2,249,363
1886	703,715	1912	2,301,946
1887	760,000	1913	2,354,529
1888	802,651	1914	2,410,806
1889	935,000	1915	2,464,189
1890	1,099,850	1916	2,517,172
1891	1,148,795	1917	1,569,755
1892	1,199,730	1918	2,622,338
1893	1,253,022	1919	2,675,921
1894	1,308,682	1920	2,766,815
1895	1,377,813		
1896	1,427,527		

*Source: *Daily News* Almanac, 1946

Bon-Ton Directory,
Giving the Names in Alphabetical Order
and Addresses and Hours of Reception
of the Most Prominent and
Fashionable Ladies Residing in
Chicago, 1879–1880
(An Excerpt and Partial Listing)

"Notes of invitation to a large party can be printed in any style you wish, but always worded in the third person. Invitations should be written or printed upon a whole sheet of small note paper, and should be issued at least a week before the time appointed for the party, so that if necessary, a suitable dress may be obtained. For a costume ball or masquerade, two weeks is the usual time allowed for preparation.

"The letters R.S.V.P. are sometimes put at the end of a note. They stand for the French phrase Respondez s'il vous plait: an answer if you please. It is better, however, when an answer is particularly desired, to say, an answer will oblige. It is courtesy to reply promptly to a note of invitation requesting an answer. If no reply is requested, and you send no regrets, it is understood that you accept the invitation.

"Send invitations to persons in your own city or neighborhood by your own messenger. It is regarded as a violation of etiquette to send them by mail."

Armour, Mrs P.D.   987 Prairie Avenue.
Friends always welcome.

Baker, Mrs O.P.   48 St Johns Place.
Friends received Tuesdays and Thursdays after October 1.

Barbe, Mrs Martin   1677 Wabash Avenue.
A most hearty welcome accorded friends at all hours, day and evening.

Bonfield, Mrs J. F.   1476 Wabash Avenue.

Comiskey, Mrs John   142 Lytle Street.
Friends most cordially received at all times.

Dent, Mrs Thomas   43 S. Sheldon Street.
A welcome always awaits my friends.

Dexter, Mrs Wirt   869 Prairie Avenue.

Field, Mrs Marshall   923 Prairie Avenue.
Fridays.

Leiter, Mrs L.Z.   60 Calumet Avenue.
At home after September.

Owsley, Mrs J.O.   245 Ashland Avenue.
No reception days.

Palmer, Mrs P.B.   844 W. Adams Street.
To friends always.

Pullman, Mrs George   879 Prairie Avenue.
At home Fridays.

Rumery, Mrs M.A.   11 S. Sheldon.
Our friends know that we are always glad to see them.

Spalding, Mrs Albert G.   212 Vincennes Avenue.

VanPelt, Mrs John   41 Honore Street.
Friends always welcome.

Cook County Government and
Law Enforcement, 1871–1920

Year	Mayor	Chief of Police	State's Attorney	Sheriff
1871	Joseph Medill	W.W. Kennedy	Charles Reed	Henry Cleaves
1872	Joseph Medill	Elmer Washburn	Charles Reed	Timothy Bradley
1873	Harvey D. Colvin	Washburn-Rehm	Charles Reed	Timothy Bradley
1874	Harvey D. Colvin	Jacob Rehm	Charles Reed	Francis Agnew
1875	Harvey D. Colvin	Rehm-Hickey	Charles Reed	Francis Agnew
1876	Monroe Heath	Michael Hickey	Luther L. Mills	Charles Kern
1877	Monroe Heath	Michael Hickey	Luther L. Mills	Charles Kern
1878	Monroe Heath	Hickey-Seavey	Luther L. Mills	John Hoffman
1879	Carter Harrison	Seavey-O'Donnell	Luther L. Mills	John Hoffman
1880	Carter Harrison	O'Donnell-McGarigle	Luther L. Mills	Orrin Mann
1881	Carter Harrison	William McGarigle	Luther L. Mills	Orrin Mann
1882	Carter Harrison	McGarigle-Doyle	Luther L. Mills	Mann-Hanchett
1883	Carter Harrison	Austin Doyle	Luther L. Mills	Seth Hanchett
1884	Carter Harrison	Austin Doyle	Julius Grinnell	Seth Hanchett
1885	Carter Harrison	Doyle-Ebersold	Julius Grinnell	Seth Hanchett
1886	Carter Harrison	Fredrick Ebersold	Julius Grinnell	Canute Matson
1887	John A. Roche	Fredrick Ebersold	Julius Grinnell	Canute Matson
1888	John A. Roche	Ebersold-Hubbard	Joel Longnecker	Canute Matson
1889	Dewitt Cregier	George Hubbard	Joel Longnecker	Canute Matson
1890	Dewitt Cregier	Fredrick Marsh	Joel Longnecker	James Gilbert
1891	Hempstead Washburn	Robert McLaughery	Joel Longnecker	James Gilbert
1892	Hempstead Washburn	Robert McLaughery	Jacob Kern	James Gilbert
1893	Carter Harrison	Michael Brennan	Jacob Kern	James Gilbert
1894	John Hopkins	Michael Brennan	Jacob Kern	James Pease
1895	George Swift	John Badenoch	Jacob Kern	James Pease
1896	George Swift	John Badenoch	Charles Deneen	James Pease
1897	Carter Harrison, Jr	Joseph Kipley	Charles Deneen	James Pease
1898	Carter Harrison, Jr	Joseph Kipley	Charles Deneen	Ernest Magerstadt
1899	Carter Harrison, Jr	Joseph Kipley	Charles Deneen	Ernest Magers adt
1900	Carter Harrison, Jr	Joseph Kipley	Charles Deneen	Ernest Magerscadt
1901	Carter Harrison, Jr	Francis O'Neill	Charles Deneen	Ernest Magerstadt
1902	Carter Harrison, Jr	Francis O'Neill	Charles Deneen	Thomas Barrett
1903	Carter Harrison, Jr	Francis O'Neill	Charles Deneen	Thomas Barrett
1904	Carter Harrison, Jr	Francis O'Neill	John Healey	Thomas Barrett
1905	Edward Dunne	O'Neill-Collins	John Healey	Thomas Barrett
1906	Edward Dunne	John M. Collins	John Healey	Pease-Strassheim
1907	Fred Busse	George Shippy	John Healey	Chris Strassheim
1908	Fred Busse	Shippey-Steward	John Wayman	Chris Strassheim
1909	Fred Busse	Leroy Steward	John Wayman	Chris Strassheim
1910	Fred Busse	Leroy Steward	John Wayman	Michael Zimmer
1911	Carter Harrison, Jr	John McWeeney	John Wayman	Michael Zimmer
1912	Carter Harrison, Jr	John McWeeney	Wayman-Hoyne	Michael Zimmer
1913	Carter Harrison, Jr	McWeeney-Gleason	Maclay Hoyne	Michael Zimmer
1914	Carter Harrison, Jr	James Gleason	Maclay Hoyne	John Traeger
1915	Wm. Hale Thompson	Charles Healey	Maclay Hoyne	John Traeger
1916	Wm. Hale Thompson	Charles Healey	Maclay Hoyne	John Traeger
1917	Wm. Hale Thompson	Healey-Schuettler	Maclay Hoyne	John Traeger
1918	Wm. Hale Thompson	John J. Garrity	Maclay Hoyne	Charles Peters
1919	Wm. Hale Thompson	John J. Garrity	Maclay Hoyne	Charles Peters
1920	Wm. Hale Thompson	Charles Fitzmorris	Hoyne-Crowe	Charles Peters

NOTES

Chapter II: Haymarket

For this chapter *The Haymarket Tragedy* by Paul Avrich is an indispensable source.

[1] Two days after Schaak was promoted to captain, Anna Kledzic was found clubbed to death in her house. Schaak, declaring the detective bureau incompetent (and reorganizing it), solved the crime himself. He found some burned letters in Anna Kledzic's stove from a man named Mulkowsky and tracked him down by dressing his—Mulkowsky's—sister in men's clothing and photographing her. The photograph was circulated in the Chicago Polish ghetto and Mulkowsky was soon caught. It evolved that he had just gotten to know Anna Kledzic and learned she kept some valuables in her home. Mulkowsky clubbed her to death while she was bending over a washtub, and stole a wedding ring and other jewelry and some vouchers. It took a jury just twenty minutes to convict him.

[2] Seliger admitted on the stand that he had been paid by Schaak for his testimony against Lingg. Seliger and his wife returned to Germany, their expenses paid by the Chicago police, and remained there permanently.

[3] Both Lucy and Albert Parsons insisted that Lucy's ancestry was Mexican and Indian, and that she had no African connections. However, there are discrepancies in her records and it is believed that she had in reality been born a slave in Texas, where Parsons met her. Her photograph supports her biographer's conclusion that she had at least one black parent.

[4] Nina Van Zandt Spies was devastated by the executions. She locked herself in her father's house and placed a photograph of Spies in the

front window. In 1891 she was married, but was divorced in 1907 by her husband, Stephen Malato, a lawyer suspected of ties to the Black Hand. After her parents died, she was reduced to penury, running a rooming house in the crowded tenement district along Halsted Street. She died on April 9, 1936, and was buried at Waldheim Cemetery, not far from the Haymarket monument. The funeral was well attended by old radicals and young ones as well.

5 Birmingham was eventually suspended from the force for consorting with criminals and trafficking in stolen goods. However, during the Columbian Exposition of 1893, he conducted tours to the Haymarket site, and gave his firsthand account of his role in the tragedy. He earned money this way, and many a drink from a fascinated fairgoer. He died destitute at county hospital on September 26, 1912.

The statue too—the only known monument dedicated to the police—was dogged by ill luck. Damaged by vandals in 1903, knocked over by a runaway streetcar in 1925, it was restored and moved first to Union Park and later to a special platform east of the Kennedy Expressway on Randolph Street. In March of 1968 during demonstrations against the Vietnam War, when the police were held in low esteem by protesters, it was covered with black paint. On October 6, 1969, it was blown up by the Weathermen faction of the Students for a Democratic Society. It was restored once more and then blown up once more in February of 1972. After that it was rebuilt and moved to the lobby of Chicago police headquarters. The base still stands near the Randolph Street entrance to the Kennedy Expressway.

Chapter IV: 1896: The Summer of Silver and Gold

For information on the Democratic Convention of 1896 and the Bryan campaign, see *Bryan: A Political Biography of William Jennings Bryan* by Louis W. Koenig.

6 The *Tribune* for May 17 commented on the future of the bicycle.

The vehicle of the future, say those who ought to know, are the horseless carriage and the bicycle. For luxury, speed, and scenic effects, the motorcar driven by electricity and built in any of the magnificent forms of which it is capable will be the proper thing, but as a poor man's vehicle, both of pleasure and business, the bike is going to have no rival.

But the handwriting was on the wall on July 15, 1903, when Ernest Pfennig, a dentist, bought the first Ford in Chicago for $850.

7 Thomas E. Watson was born in Georgia in 1856 and practiced criminal law there. He was devoted to the agrarian ideals of the Confederacy. In 1882–83 he served in the Georgia state legislature. From 1891 to 1893 he was in the U.S. Congress as a Farmers Alliance Democrat, and worked hard to achieve free rural delivery of the mail. He was a strong believer in reform politics and became a Populist because he rejected the Democratic Party, which he believed was a tool of big business. He was far more of a social radical than Bryan. By 1906 he had become identified with the Ku Klux Klan, urging disenfranchisement for the Negro in his newspaper *The Weekly Jeffersonian*. In 1915, after the lynching of Leo Frank, an innocent executive of a pencil company, Watson waged an anti-Semitic campaign in Georgia. He also made virulent attacks upon Catholicism, publishing a book in 1910 called *The Roman Catholic Hierarchy*, so vicious that he was indicted three times for having written it, although he was never convicted. This did not prevent Watson from being elected as a Democrat to the Senate in 1920, where he served until his death in 1922. When he died, he was eulogized by both Eugene Debs and the Klan, and both sent flowers for his funeral. He wrote biographies of Jefferson and Andrew Jackson.

Chapter VI: Low Life in the Levee

The definitive work on the Chicago red-light district is *Lords of the Levee* by Lloyd Wendt and Herman Kogan.

8 So determined an advocate for reform was Stead that in 1885 he had been briefly imprisoned in England for his attacks on Government policy toward white slavery. In his later years he became strongly interested in psychical research. He lost his life in the *Titanic* disaster.

9 It was Gunther who first came up with the idea of a State Street mall. In 1897 he suggested a downtown mall free of livery, horse-drawn carriages and trucks. This was actually implemented in 1979, although the mall idea has now been abandoned.

10 The genteel image of the Everleighs was dented somewhat in 1908 when Belle Schreiber, one of their girls, ran off and married Jack Johnson, the black heavyweight boxing champion. Johnson was banned from the Club, and eventually divorced Belle. But in August, 1912, he

met Lucille Cameron, a 19-year-old Minneapolis girl, in his saloon, the Cafe de Champion, at 41 W 31st Street. Soon the two were seen dancing until dawn in the south side cabarets. This situation did not go down well; Lucille's mother accused Johnson of violating the Mann Act, hate mail poured in from all over the country and he was hanged in effigy from a lamppost at the corner of State and Walton. When he was leaving court, an inkwell was hurled at him from the upper floor of an early skyscraper. Booker T. Washington said that Johnson had done "a grave injustice to his race." Despite all this, Johnson and Lucille were married on December 3, 1912, at a private ceremony on Wabash Avenue. He was convicted on the Mann Act charge, sentenced to a year in prison and fined $10,000, but fled to Canada and from there to Europe, where he defended his title in several fixed bouts. He finally surrendered to authorities in Los Angeles in 1920 and served his sentence.

[11] Franche was indicted for murder. He was defended by Charles Erbstein, a colorful criminal lawyer who had saved one hundred accused murderers from the gallows in the course of his 22-year career. Nevertheless, Franche was found guilty. The verdict was overturned on appeal because of a technicality. In Franche's second trial Erbstein convinced the jury that the shooting was an act of self-defense, and Franche was aquitted.

Chapter VIII: Bombs, Gamblers and Newspaper Wars

[12] Collins had caught the attention of Edward Dunne's father in 1889, after his work on the Cronin case. Dr Cronin, a wealthy physician, was involved in Irish nationalist politics. A secret organization known as the Clan-Na-Gaels murdered him for his opposing views. For years, the Clan-Na-Gaels exerted influence over prominent members of the police force. Collins was transferred to Simon O'Donnell's westside district by Joseph Kipley, a Clan-Na-Gaels sympathizer himself. (Even in 1900, O'Donnell's 12th Street district was the political graveyard for cops who fell from grace.) When Kipley was ousted as chief, Collins made a belated comeback.

[13] Red pepper figures in many Chicago anecdotes. It has been said that O'Leary put red pepper inside the doors to his palace, which was constantly being raided—and the police were overcome by it when they broke open the door with a hatchet.

Chapter IX: 1919: The Summer of Lost Innocence

For information on the White Sox baseball scandal, see Dr Harold Seymour, *Baseball in the Golden Age*. The definitive study of the 1919 race riot is *Race Riot: Chicago in the Red Summer of 1919* by William Tuttle.

BIBLIOGRAPHY

Archival Documents

At the Chicago Historical Society I have had access to the scrapbooks, containing contemporary newpaper clippings, of Charles Harpel (Vol VII, 1887–1903), of Herman Schleutter (Vols I and II) and of John D. Shea, a famous Chicago detective. I have also read the papers of Sheriff Canute Matson, which include letters from August Spies; the Edward Steele papers containing letters from Bonfield to Ward and from district commanders to Chief Ebersold before and during the Haymarket incident; and the John Kelly papers. The CHS also holds the First Precinct Arrest Book, January 2–June 30, 1885, the only detailed record of police activity in a city precinct, listing arrests, disposition of cases, suspensions, transfers and comments of supervisors.

I have consulted the Annual Report to the City Council by the General Superintendent of Police, 1886–1920, and The Anarchist Cases in the Supreme Court, Abstract of the Record, Vol II, 1887.

Unpublished dissertations that have been helpful: "Policing Labor Disputes in Chicago: A Case Study" by Howard Barton Myers, Chicago, 1929; "The Prarie Avenue Section of Chicago: The History and Examination of its Decline" by Robert Pruter, Roosevelt, 1976; and "The Natural History of Vice Areas in Chicago" by Walter Cade Reckless, Chicago, 1925.

Articles

Bushnell, George. "When Chicago Was Wheel Crazy." *Chicago History*. Vol. 4, no. 3 (Fall 1975), 167–75.

Clayton, John. "The Scourge of Sinners: Arthur Burrage Farwell." *Chicago History*. Vol. 3, no. 2 (Fall 1974), 68–77.

Duis, Perry, and Glen Holt. "Playing the Ponies on Lake Michigan." *Chicago Magazine* (Aug 1981), 108–12.

Fanning, Charles, and Ellen Skerritt. "James T. Farrell and Washington Park: The Novel as Social History." *Chicago History*. Vol. 8, no. 2 (Summer 1979), 80–91.

Goler, Robert M. "Black Sox." *Chicago History*. Vol. 17, nos. 3 & 4 (Fall & Winter 1988–89), 42–69.

Griffin, Richard. "Big Jim: Gambler Boss iv th' Yards." *Chicago History*. Vol. 5, no. 4 (Winter 1976–77), 213–22.

Kogan, Herman. "William Perkins Black: Haymarket Lawyer." *Chicago History*. Vol. 5, no. 2 (Summer 1976), 85–94.

Lindberg, Richard C. "The Evolution of an Evil Business." *Chicago History*. Vol. 22, no. 2 (July 1993), 38–53.

Nelson, Bruce C. "Anarchism: The Movement Behind the Martyrs." *Chicago History*. Vol. 15, no. 2 (Summer 1986), 4–19.

Russell, Charles Edward. "Chaos and Bomb Throwing in Chicago." *Hampton's Magazine* (Mar 1910), 307–20.

Steffens, Lincoln. "Chicago: Half Free and Fighting On." *McClure's Magazine* (Oct 21, 1903), 563–77.

"Vice Investigation Demanded by Churches." *The Survey* (Feb 12, 1910), 695–96.

Books

Adelman, William. *Haymarket Revisited*. The Illinois Labor Society, 1976.

Allen, Frederick. *Only Yesterday: An Informal History of the 1920s*. NY: Harper & Row, pb edition, 1964.

Asbury, Herbert. *The Gem of the Prarie: An Informal History of the Chicago Underworld*. NY: Alfred A. Knopf, 1940.

Ashbaugh, Carolyn. *Lucy Parsons: American Revolutionary*. Chgo: Charles Kerr, 1975.

Asinof, Eliot. *Eight Men Out: The Black Sox and the 1919 World Series*. NY: Holt, Rinehart & Winston, 1963.

Avrich, Paul. *The Haymarket Tragedy*. Princeton: Princeton Univ Press, 1984.

Bryan, William Jennings. *The First Battle*. Chgo: W.B. Conkey, 1896.

Casey, Robert J. *Chicago Medium Rare*. Chgo: Herald-American Publishers, 1949.

Clark, Herma. *The Elegant Eighties*. Chgo: A.C. McClurg & Co, 1941.

Coletta, Paola. *William Jennings Bryan: Political Evangelist, 1860–1908*. Lincoln, Neb: University of Nebraska Press, 1964.

Cook, Frederick. *Bygone Days in Chicago*. Chgo: A.C. McClurg & Co, 1910.

Cooney, John. *The Annenbergs: The Salvaging of a Tainted Dynasty*. NY: Simon & Schuster, 1982.

Corbitt, Robert L. *The Holmes Castle*. Chgo: Corbitt & Morrison, 1895.

David, Henry. *The History of the Haymarket Affair*. NY: Russell & Russell, 1937.

Dedmon, Emmett. *Fabulous Chicago: A Great City's History and People*. NY: Random House.

Dornfeld, A.A. *"Hello Sweetheart, Get Me Rewrite!": The Story of the City News Bureau of Chicago*. Chgo: Academy Chicago Publishers, 1988.

Dreiser, Theodore. *Newspaper Days*. NY: Horace Liveright, 1922.

Duis, Perry. *The Saloon: Public Drinking in Chicago: 1880–1920*. Champaign: Univ of Illinois Press, 1983.

Erbstein, Charles. *The Show Up: Stories Before the Bar*. Chgo: Pascal Govici, 1926.

Flinn, John, and John Wilkie. *The Chicago Police*. Chgo: Policemen's Benevolent Ass'n & W.B. Conkey, 1887.

Foner, Philip, ed. *Autobiographies of the Haymarket Martyrs*. Chgo: Charles Kerr, 1976.

Franke, David. *Torture Doctor*. NY: Hawthorne Press, 1975.

Geyer, Franklin. *The Holmes-Pitezel Case: History of the Greatest Crime of the Century*. Publisher's Union of Philadelphia, 1896.

Gies, Joseph. *The Colonel of Chicago: A Biography of the Chicago Tribune's Legendary Publisher, Colonel Robert McCormick*. NY: E.P. Dutton, 1979.

Ginger, Ray. *Altgeld's America: The Lincoln Ideal Versus the Changing Realities*. NY: Funk & Wagnalls, 1958.

Golden, Harry. *A Little Girl is Dead*. NY: Avon, pb, 1965.

Gosnell, Harold F. *Negro Politicians*. Chgo: Univ of Chicago Press, 1935.

Green, Paul M., and Melvin C. Holli. *The Mayor: The Chicago Political Tradition*. Carbondale & Edwardsville: Southern Illinois Univ Press, 1987.

Halper, Albert, ed. *The Chicago Crime Book*. NY: World, 1967.

Harrison, Carter. *Growing Up With Chicago*. NY: Bobbs-Merrill, 1944.

————. *The Stormy Years*. NY: Bobbs-Merrill, 1935.

Harrison, Mrs Carter. *Strange to Say: Recollections of Persons & Events in New Orleans & Chicago*. Chgo: A. Kroch & Sons, 1949.

History Of Chicago, Volume Three. Chgo: A.T. Andreas & Co., 1884.

Johnson, Claudius O. *Carter Harrison I: Political Leader.* Chgo: Univ of Chicago Press, 1928.

Kebabian, John S. *The Haymarket Affair.* NY: H.P. Kraus, 1970.

Kinsley, Philip. *The Chicago Tribune, Volume Three: 1880–1900.* Chgo: Tribune, 1946.

Kobler, John. *The Life and World of Al Capone.* NY: Putnam, 1971.

Koenig, Louis W. *Bryan: A Political Biography of William Jennings Bryan.* NY: Putnam, 1971.

Kogan, Herman. *Chicago Haymarket Riot: Anarchy on Trial.* Boston: D.C. Heath & Co., 1959.

Lait, Jack, and Lee Mortimer. *Chicago Confidential: The Lowdown On the Big Town.* NY: Crown, 1950.

Landesco, John. *Organized Crime: Part III of the Illinois Crime Survey.* Chgo: Univ of Chicago Press, 1929.

Lindberg, Richard C. *To Serve & Collect: Chicago Politics and Police Corruption From the Lager Beer Riot to the Summerdale Scandal.* Westport, Ct: Praeger, 1991.

Longstreet, Stephen. *Chicago: 1860–1919.* NY: David McKay, 1973.

Lowe, David. *Lost Chicago.* Boston: Houghton-Mifflin, 1975.

Lum, Dyer. *The Trial of the Haymarket Anarchists.* NY: Arno, 1969.

Mayer, Harold, and Richard Wade. *Chicago: Growth Of a Metropolis.* Chgo: Univ of Chicago Press, 1969.

McPhaul, John. *Deadlines and Monkeyshines.* NY: Prentice Hall, 1962.

————. *Johnny Torrio: First of the Ganglords.* New Rochelle, NY: Arlington House, 1970.

Murray, George. *The Madhouse On Madison Street.* Chgo: Follett, 1965.

Reckless, Walter Cade. *Vice in Chicago.* Chgo: Univ of Chicago Press, 1933.

Riggio, Thomas P., ed. *Theodore Dreiser: American Diaries: 1902–1926.* Phila: Univ of Pennsylvania Press, 1983.

Sasuly, Richard. *Bookies and Bettors: Two Hundred Years of Gambling.* NY: Holt, Rinehart & Winston, 1982.

Sawyers, June Skinner. *Chicago Portraits: Biographies of 250 Famous Chicagoans.* Chgo: Loyola Univ Press, 1991.

Schaak, Michael J. *Anarchy & Anarchists.* Chgo: F.J. Schulte & Co, 1889.

Seymour, Harold, Dr. *Baseball in the Golden Age.* NY: Oxford Univ Press, 1971.

Sharpe, May Churchill. *Chicago May: A Human Document by the Queen of Crooks.* NY: Gold Label Books, 1928.

Smith, Carl. *Urban Disorder and the Shape of Belief.* Chgo: Univ of Chicago Press, 1995.

Smith, Page. *The Rise of Industrial America: A People's History of the Post-Reconstruction Era*. NY: McGraw-Hill, 1984.

Stead, William. *If Christ Came to Chicago*. Chgo: Laird & Lee, 1894.

The Social Evil in Chicago. Chicago city document: Gunthrop & Warren, 1910.

Thrasher, Frederic. *The Gang*. Chgo: Univ of Chicago Press, 1927.

Tuttle, William. *Race Riot: Chicago in the Red Summer of 1919*. NY: Atheneum, 1978.

Washburn, Charles. *Come into My Parlor*. NY: National Library, 1934.

Weimann, Jeanne Madeline, and Anita Miller. *The Fair Women*. Chgo: Academy Chicago Publishers, 1981.

Wendt, Lloyd. *Chicago Tribune: The Rise of a Great American Newspaper*. Chgo: Rand McNally, 1979.

Wendt, Lloyd, and Herman Kogan. *Big Bill of Chicago*. NY: Bobbs-Merrill, 1953.

————. *Lords of the Levee: The Story of Bathhouse John and Hinky Dink*. NY: Bobbs-Merrill, 1943.

Wik, Reynold M. *Henry Ford and Grass Roots America*. Ann Arbor: Univ of Michigan Press, 1973.

Wilson, Samuel Paynter. *Chicago and its Cesspool of Infamy*. No publisher listed, January, 1909.

Winslow, Charles. *Historical Events of Chicago*. Chgo: Soderlund Printing, 1937.

————. *Biographical Sketches of Famous Chicagoans*. Chgo: Public Library Collection, 1948.

Yardley, Jonathan. *Ring: A Biography*. NY: Random House, 1977.

Newspapers (1880–1920)

Chicago American

Chicago Daily News

Chicago Defender

Chicago Herald & Examiner

Chicago Inter-Ocean

Chicago Journal

Chicago Post

Chicago Record-Herald

Chicago Times

Chicago Times-Herald

Chicago Tribune

New York Times

Index